Journalism and Free Speech

John Steel

Routledge
Taylor & Francis Group

LONDON AND NEW YORK

First published 2012
by Routledge
2 Park Square, Milton Park, Abingdon, Oxon OX14 4RN

Simultaneously published in the USA and Canada
by Routledge
711 Third Avenue, New York, NY 10017

Routledge is an imprint of the Taylor & Francis Group, an informa business

British Library Cataloguing in Publication Data
A catalogue record for this book is available from the British Library

Library of Congress Cataloging in Publication Data
Steel, John, 1966–
Journalism and free speech / John Steel.
p. cm.
Includes bibliographical references and index.
1. Journalism--History. 2. Freedom of speech. I. Title.
PN4855.S74 2011
323.44'5--dc23
2011025195

ISBN: 978-0-415-49325-3 (hbk)
ISBN: 978-0-415-49326-0 (pbk)
ISBN: 978-0-203-80461-2 (ebk)

Typeset in Bembo
by Taylor & Francis Books

Printed and bound in Great Britain by
CPI Antony Rowe, Chippenham, Wiltshire

For My Daughters

Contents

Table of Legislation

Table of Cases

Acknowledgements

Since first having the idea for this book a number of years ago I have been the lucky recipient of all manner of advice and guidance from friends, colleagues and acquaintances. Advice which varied from severe warnings such as 'don't do it' and 'it's not possible' to words of tepid encouragement – 'good luck', 'sounds interesting' and 'fascinating!'. To those who sounded the warnings, thanks for the inspiration; I hope I've proved you wrong. There have of course been significant contributions to both my thinking about the nature of this book as well as specific suggestions as to how the book can be improved and I thank all of the people who have had such an input. In particular Natalie Foster, Ruth Moody and Emily Laughton at Routledge whose patience and goodwill I have no doubt tested to the extreme. Significant thanks also go to two anonymous reviewers who made some very helpful suggestions as to how the book could be improved in its early stages of development. I would also like to express my genuine gratitude to Julian Petley who looked at an earlier draft of the work and provided me with numerous suggestions and ideas as to how I could improve the work. I sincerely hope that I have produced something which merits his name in the acknowledgements – though, as ever, any mistakes are all mine. Thanks also go to my friend and colleague Martin Conboy who has suffered more than most yet who's camaraderie and constant reassurance in the many 'dark times' during the writing of the book have been a constant source of inspiration and encouragement. My gratitude also goes out to friends and colleagues who directly or indirectly have made this book possible including: Karen Sanders, Mark Hannah, Jackie Harrison, Ralph Negrine, Darren Webb and Stuart Horsman. Students in the Department of Journalism Studies at the University of Sheffield also constantly keep me on my toes so I thank them for contributing to some very stimulating debates over the years. Finally I'd like to express my warmest appreciation to my partner Debbie and my daughters Jasmine and Caitlin. If it weren't for them there simply would be no work worth contemplating.

John Steel, 2011

Preface

It was during my work on the final drafts of this manuscript that revelations about the full nature of the *News of the World* phone hacking scandal were gradually being revealed by the *Guardian* newspaper. The hacking of murdered schoolgirl Milly Dowler's phone by the newspaper and its intrusion into the personal grief and tragedy of other victims of crime and even the families of service men and women killed in Iraq and Afghanistan, came as a shock to the public unable to comprehend the depths that this particular newspaper would sink. Revelations continue to come out as I write and the full scale of the hacking is still as yet unknown. Nevertheless the response by politicians, the public and from within sections of the profession itself has been that journalism in this case had gone too far. Not for the first time journalism had gone beyond the pale. 'Something needed to be done once and for all' came the cries. In reacting to the crisis the government asked Lord Leveson to set up an inquiry into standards in the press and into the relationships between the press, the police and politicians. The results of the inquiry are not due until the summer of 2012. As should be obvious from the title, this book is about journalism and free speech and in particular the role of journalism in democratic societies. There is little doubt then that the results of Leveson will have important implications for journalism and its democratic obligations which of course relate to the principles of freedom of speech, expression and the press. The claims made throughout this work are that freedom of the press is under constant pressure from without and from within. It is even more important therefore that, whatever emerges from the wreckage of 'hackgate', the relationship between journalism, free speech and democracy is enhanced and not compromised even further.

John Steel
September 2011

INTRODUCTION

Free speech under attack?

> The free press is the ubiquitous vigilant eye of a people's soul, the embodiment of a people's faith in itself, the eloquent link that connects the individual with the state and the world, the embodied culture that transforms material struggles into intellectual struggles and idealises their crude material form. It is a people's frank confession to itself, [...]. It is the spiritual mirror in which a people can see itself, and self-examination is the first condition of wisdom. It is the spirit of the state, which can be delivered into every cottage, cheaper than coal gas. It is all-sided, ubiquitous, omniscient. It is the ideal world which always wells up out of the real world and flows back into it with ever greater spiritual riches and renews its soul.
>
> Marx (1975 [1842])

Traditional historical accounts of the emergence of freedom of speech are usually framed in terms of a long fought battle between the forces of orthodoxy and repression versus the liberal impulse expressed in phrases such as freedom of thought and freedom of expression. Such accounts tend to portray the long road to freedom of speech emerging as a reaction against varieties of religious orthodoxy, with the struggle gaining momentum around the sixteenth century and continuing until democracy and the liberties it secured were finally established in America at the end of the eighteenth century and in Britain and Europe in the nineteenth century.[1] This longstanding and powerful perspective, in which freedom of speech is usually set against forces of repression and ignorance, has endured throughout the twentieth century. For example, during the last century, freedom of speech was framed in relation to the great battle between liberalism and the repressive and oppressive ideologies of Fascism, Nazism and Communism. In the context of the ideological contestations between liberal democracy and for example Soviet totalitarianism, abuse against freedom of speech was just one of the many human rights violations widely reported in the West. Soviet literary dissidents such as Mikhail Bulgakov, Alexander Solzhenitsyn and Boris Pasternak from the Samizdat movement provide us with important examples of dissent against the totalitarian Soviet state.

Yet of course even after the fall of the Berlin Wall this narrative seems to have remained. Free speech and freedom of expression are now, we are told, under threat from other repressive forces. The controversy surrounding the publication of twelve cartoons depicting the Islamic Prophet Mohammed by the Danish newspaper *Jyllands-Posten* in 2005 can be seen as one of the most controversial examples where the values of liberal democracy seem to come into conflict with another set of ideals and values. More than twenty years since the controversy surrounding Salman Rushdie's *The Satanic Verses*, the idea that Islam poses a significant threat to freedom of speech remains and to some degree has of course replaced the threat from the 'Evil Empire'. Commentators, politicians, journalists and academics warn of the new dangers to freedom of speech and freedom of the press in the light of the so-called 'clash of civilisations' – the clash between liberal democracy and Islam – which threatens not only freedom of speech but the democratic institutions in Europe and Britain.[2] Free speech, it seems according to some, is therefore still under threat.

There is no doubt that extremist, repressive and anti-democratic ideas and politics pose a threat to established freedoms and rights. Yet such a threat should be put in perspective. It exists, but focusing on the threats to freedom of speech and wider political rights coming from outside the liberal democratic tradition tends to obscure the impediments and constraints, which exist within it. More significantly, it has been suggested that radical and extremist threats to freedom of speech have actually been propagated by tensions within the liberal democratic tradition itself. As such, extremism, and particularly that of radical Islam, is conceived as a distinctly modern phenomenon closely tied to liberal democratic modernity. The implication of this is that by focusing too much attention on the threat from a minority of radical extremists, we overlook threats to freedom of speech and other political rights within liberal democratic societies. This is not to say such threats do not exist; rather, by emphasising the threat from without, we run the risk of ignoring the threat from within. Moreover, developing a more introspective analysis of freedom of speech and censorship may provide a clearer insight into the mechanisms of censorship itself. For example, as we will se in Chapter 7, the usual response when a state comes under attack from terrorism is that the state clamps down on civil liberties, as this is perceived as the necessary response to safeguard democracy. Yet as the chapter highlights, the erosion of civil liberties can indeed exacerbate the problem and precipitate more violence; moreover, democratic societies thrive on freedom of speech and expression and by undermining such liberties, the state is ultimately undermining democracy. One of the key aims of this book therefore is to focus much more on the threat from within. To explore freedom of speech and censorship in this way involves seeing censorship not merely as a distinctive set of restrictions and prohibitors practised by authoritarian states, but as something that is fluid and complex, and that can operate very effectively within purportedly open liberal democratic societies such as Britain.

And what of journalism and its relationship to freedom of speech? Where does the news media, with its long tradition of safeguarding against tyranny and nourishing democratic institutions fit into this picture of free speech under attack? It could be powerfully argued that journalism is surely now largely unconstrained given the liberalising potency of the internet and the global communication network. The news media and the journalism that sustains it have arguably never been more free and unfettered. The liberating power of the internet has removed virtually all barriers to censorship and control over freedom of expression. The website WikiLeaks, for example, offers whistle-blowers total anonymity so that they can place information in the public domain that would otherwise be restricted. At the time of writing, the website has published more than 90,000 reports, known as the 'Afghan War Diary', which according to WikiLeaks founder Julian Assange, shows the true nature of the war in Afghanistan, detailing 'the vast range of small tragedies that are almost never reported by the press but which account for the overwhelming majority of deaths and injuries'.[3] Censorship seems to have been completely blown away by the internet. As we will see in Chapter 3, however, it may be unwise to laud the internet in such liberating terms, as though it certainly offers opportunities to publish free from some forms of constraint, it also offers states and other agencies opportunities to monitor its citizens and potentially undermine democratic freedoms rather than enhance them. Moreover, in its exposé of U.S. military secrets, WikiLeaks has used traditional news media to draw attention to its whistle-blowing as *The New York Times*, *Der Spiegel* and *The Guardian* are cited as 'media partners' (see Lynch 2010). So much for the death of traditional news organisations.

And what of the news organisations themselves? For some, rather than bastions of freedom of speech, the corporate nature of news actively undermines freedom of speech as it stifles creativity and diversity, and selling us, the public, to advertisers with a pre-packaged corporate product. In other words, the principle of freedom of speech and freedom of the press, though often invoked as a component of wider liberties and fundamental freedoms, has in practice meant that press freedom is used to justify corporate aspirations of the newspaper and media market.

Aims of the book

The aims of this book are relatively simple: to provide an introduction to the ideas, principles and history of journalism and its relationship to freedom of speech and the principle of freedom of the press. The actual realisation of this relatively straightforward aspiration, as may be discerned from above, is somewhat less than simple. The central argument of this book is that journalism and its relationship with ideas of freedom of speech, freedom of expression and freedom of the press require significant examination and re-evaluation in the light of the perceived challenges to freedom of speech and freedom of the press. The book attempts to provide an analysis of journalism, freedom of speech and censorship conceptually and historically in the hope that such an analysis can reframe our thinking about the values of free and open discussion and debate in ways that enable a more nuanced and ultimately rational re-evaluation of the relationship between journalism and freedom of speech and censorship. Of principle concern to this book therefore is a re-examination of the conception of censorship.

Censorship, as I have briefly suggested, should not simply be considered as a concept that is associated with totalitarian societies and repressive regimes. Rather, as will become evident in my examination of the relationship between journalism and freedom of speech, censorship is visible. It may not be overt censorship, but it exists, dynamic, fluid, sometimes opaque yet powerful nevertheless. In stressing this point throughout the book I hope to achieve a number of things. First, I hope to warn against complacency and possible arrogance about 'our' freedom of the press in the West. As I point out more concretely throughout the book, press freedom and freedom of speech need to be considered as the realisation of more than formal and legal protection provided by the state. Second, by expanding the parameters of debate beyond the formal mechanisms of controls on the news media, I hope to demonstrate that freedom of the press and freedom of speech are liberties that have to be fought for on a continual basis, even within so-called 'free' societies. Third, I hope to extend the discussion about free speech and freedom of the press more generally from its legal and philosophical parameters. In doing so, I intend to animate theory of freedom of speech and freedom of the press and their numerous constraints in practice. Finally, in drawing on a range of approaches and theories within journalism, media and cultural studies, as well as history and philosophy, I hope to encourage debate about the limitations of our conventional conceptions of freedom of speech, freedom of the press and censorship.

Freedom of speech and freedom of the press

One of the central difficulties in discussing journalism and freedom of speech is in making the distinction between 'freedom of speech' and 'freedom of the press', which is of course associated with journalism and the news media. In dealing with this problem it is important to note that there are good historical and philosophical reasons for connecting freedom of speech with freedom of the press (Marshall 1992). As we will see in the following two chapters, the principle of freedom of speech has historically been intertwined with its realisation via the printed word. Freedom of speech has both philosophically and historically become connected to freedom of the press. Arguments for freedom of the press as a principle emerged from a specific set of historical circumstances and philosophical positions, which were bound up with the development of freedom of thought and expression.

Yet in the modern context freedom of speech is very different from freedom of the press, even though they share a similar philosophical and historical heritage. The capacity that a person has to air his or her views on a blog is of course significantly different to that of a corporate news organisation. Freedom of the press as a principle, has emerged from a specific set of historical circumstances and philosophical positions which have evolved into distinctive rights and responsibilities protected by law. Freedom of speech though protected by law is not, of course, the same as freedom of the press. Why then is this book called *Journalism and Free Speech* and not *Journalism and Freedom of the Press*? A valid question given the differences I have just stressed.

Answering this question is one of the central claims of this book as I examine the ways in which the *principle* of freedom of speech has become uncoupled from freedom of the press in practice. Freedom of the press is very different from freedom of speech, yet the two are so often conflated. This divergence becomes apparent when one focuses on the issue of media ownership and control. Within liberal democracies it is the capacity for a relatively few individuals to own and therefore control media output. As is a theme throughout this book, the overriding commercial imperatives of the news media can often serve to undermine freedom of speech in democratic societies. This is the main argument that Lichtenberg develops when she suggests that there should be some regulation of the media in order to ensure that it performs the functions appropriate to the safeguarding of democracy. Importantly for Lichtenberg freedom of speech should not be confused with freedom of the press as 'freedom of the press should be contingent on the degree to which it promotes certain values at the core of our interest in freedom of expression generally' (Lichtenberg 1987: 332). In other words

> If for example, the mass media tend to suppress diversity and impoverish public debate, the arguments meant to support freedom of the press now turn against it, and we may rightly consider regulating the media to achieve the ultimate purposes of freedom of the press.
>
> *Lichtenberg (1987: 332)*

For obvious reasons Lichtenberg is keen to distinguish rights to freedom of speech and freedom of the press; largely given the latter's commercial orientation, the press and the mass media have the capacity to stifle debate and undermine freedom of speech. Lichtenberg's argument suggests that there should be a clearer separation between arguments for freedom of speech and freedom of the press because the press, as a mass commercial operation, can and does undermine a diversity of opinion and debate.

The story of liberal democratic freedom of the press is also significantly a story in which political freedom *and* economic freedom play a starring role. As such, 'freedom of the press' should be perceived in relation to the assertion of *both* of these liberties in tandem. However, as we shall see, the advancement of economic freedom has not always benefited political freedoms. It is therefore important to recognise that freedom of the press, viewed historically, is not so much a battle between the 'forces of control and censorship as is painted by the liberal narrative' (Curran 2002), but a struggle between the democratic impulse of which freedom of speech is a component, and commercial freedom. The reason therefore that the book is about journalism and freedom of speech is firstly, to emphasise the specific character of 'press freedom' in liberal democratic societies as being primarily connected to economic freedom. Secondly, the emphasis on journalism and 'freedom of speech' is necessary in order to avoid conflating 'press freedom' as previously defined, with freedom of speech, which has an inherently democratic imperative.

Structure

In attempting to achieve these aims the book begins with a theoretical overview of the key arguments and perspectives which have contributed to the justification of freedom of speech more generally. Here I examine the specific arguments for freedom of speech primarily within the liberal political theory, as it is generally from this set of ideas that the Western democratic tradition stems. Chapter 2 moves on to explore the historical development of freedom of speech and censorship. Here we examine the specific contexts which provide the historical backdrop to contemporary debates about the limits of freedom of speech and freedom of the press. The chapter examines the particular mechanisms employed to stifle dissent via the printed word and also highlights the shift towards a particular discursive practice, which bonded our modern conception of freedom of the press to the free market and the market imperative. Chapter 3 further examines this relationship with particular emphasis on journalism, free speech and democracy. Here the democratic imperative of freedom of speech is emphasised and examined in relation to the way in which it becomes significantly undermined by the market imperative itself. Chapter 4 explores journalism in the context of new media and debates about the global public sphere. Here I examine journalism's relationship with new communication technologies and argue that too much emphasis is being placed on the 'democratic character' of new communication technologies without sufficient consideration of the ways in which democracy can be shaped. I also highlight ways in which the technology can as easily be used to stifle freedoms as enhance them.

The following three chapters deal with various forms of formal regulation and constraints pertinent to the news media. Chapter 5 examines broadcasting and the various codes which govern broadcast journalism in the U.K., while Chapter 6 looks at privacy, one of the rights that is said to compete most vociferously with freedom of the press. Chapter 7 looks at the issue of defamation law which has historically at times been used to stifle serious journalistic endeavour. The theme running throughout these particular chapters is the extent to which journalism is facilitated in its role of serving the public interest and how regulatory and legal constraints on news journalism might enhance or undermine such a notion. Chapter 8 deals with the issue of terrorism and war. Here the principle concern is to examine the idea that during times of war and conflict fundamental liberties have to be constrained and limited in order to safeguard rights and liberties in the long term. The chapter suggest that far from protecting democratic freedoms in the long term, in times of war and conflict, formal and informal controls on freedom of speech can erode such freedoms which are difficult to re-establish. Chapter 9 examines the issue of ownership which is arguably one of the most significant elements pertaining to media freedom and the democratic ideals on which it is based. Here we look at press barons, media moguls and the political economy of the media. The chapter argues that the nature of the political economy of the media places its democratic imperatives under severe strain. Indeed, the chapter, borrowing from a number of critical media perspectives, argues that a form of market censorship best characterises the political economy of the news media in the twenty-first century. The final chapter in the book emphasises the non-formal constraints on freedom of speech and freedom of the press. Here I specifically look at language and the power that language has to operationalise subtle mechanisms of censorship.

1

THE PHILOSOPHY OF FREE SPEECH

> If it be desir'd to know the immediat cause of all this free writing and free speaking, there cannot be assign'd a truer then your own mild, and free, and human government; it is the liberty, Lords and Commons, which your own valorous and happy councels have purchast us, liberty which is the nurse of all great wits; this is that which hath rarify'd and enlightn'd our spirits like the influence of heav'n; this is that which hath enfranchis'd, enlarg'd and lifted up our apprehensions degrees above themselves.
>
> *Milton (1644: 44)*

Introduction

Recent years have seen debates about freedom of speech and freedom of the press assume a new level or urgency and vigour, whether this is in relation to the primacy of freedom of speech in the wake of the hegemonic ambitions of Western states such as the United States, or in the West the so-called 'clash' of values, in which the right to offend in a 'free society' seems to sit uneasily with the multi-cultural and cosmopolitan make up of those societies. Within this context freedom of speech debates generally assume two main features: the first is a characteristic that refuses steadfastly to budge from first principles, principles that have been adapted from other eras into our democratic culture. Such principles state that freedom of speech, freedom of opinion, freedom of expression and freedom of the press are so central to our democratic institutions, that there can be no justification (other than the protection of individual liberty, property and the safeguarding of the public interest) for the state to intervene to curb such expression.

As we will see there are a number of important exceptions to this rule, but on the whole the argument suggests that principles of freedom of speech should remain intact; failure to heed this warning will inevitably compromise democracy and liberty.

With caveats against incitement and hate speech a democracy should protect even offensive speech on the basis that there should be space for all opinions and viewpoints however unpalatable some of these may be. Moreover, to curb such speech or expression is potentially damaging to the democratic principles and institutions which freedom of speech helps to serve. Durham-Peters (2005) uses the term 'hard hearted liberals' when describing those advocates who adhere to fundamental tenets of free speech doctrine.

The other set of debates tend to be less fixed and offer more of a kaleidoscopic or spectral analysis of the problem of freedom of speech. Such viewpoints suggest refinements to first principles, refinements which attempt to take into account new contexts and new ways of thinking about freedom of speech which are less rigid and much more adaptive, some would argue more relevant to twenty-first century society.

The focus of this chapter, then, is to provide an introduction to the conceptual bases of freedom of speech, and introduce the reader to the ideas that have been used to underpin the value of freedom of speech, freedom of expression and freedom of the press in the Western democratic tradition. In doing this I will set out the key themes from each of these positions and provide a conceptual overview of the area of debate. Of particular concern here will be an introduction to the range of philosophical arguments for freedom of speech that contribute to our understanding of modern notions of press and journalistic freedom in Western democratic societies. These philosophical ideas have produced principles which have helped shape our understanding of the intrinsic value of freedom of speech as a general social good in relation to servicing democratic societies, enhancing knowledge and understanding, and as a necessary component of human flourishing. In exploring these philosophical principles we are given the opportunity to scrutinise the conceptual basis of arguments for freedom of speech and highlight the tensions and contradictions that exist within and between these philosophical ideas.

It should be noted at this stage that although I will provide an introduction to the philosophical ideas and debates that relate to freedom of speech, I do not want to paint a picture of the development of freedom of speech in simplistic linear terms. In other words, though I identify certain historical and philosophical developments that pertain to debates about freedom of speech and freedom of expression, this is not a book about the inevitable march of progress and civilisation which is marked by the development of freedom of thought and expression. In other words this book is not a restatement or defence of the Whig interpretation[1] of the development of liberty of thought and expression. Rather in examining the philosophical foundations of freedom of speech in the West, I am drawing attention to the philosophical grounding on which our contemporary understanding of freedom of the press is framed. Nor does this chapter assert a 'great thinkers' approach to the topic. Certainly individuals and their ideas are identified, but this should also be seen in the context of other salient historical factors as will become evident in Chapter 2.

The chapter will proceed as follows: first, I will provide an introduction to liberalism and its philosophical foundations. This is necessary, as liberalism makes by far the most significant theoretical contribution to our contemporary understanding of free-dom of speech. In outlining liberalism in this way, I am therefore attempting to conceptually frame the main arguments for free speech that the chapter then moves on to explore. The arguments examined are: the argument relating to the operation of a fully functioning democracy; the argument relating to the advance of truth and knowledge; and the argument that relates to the flourishing of human liberty. The chapter concludes by emphasising the fundamental dislocation between freedom of speech and freedom of the press which will then be examined in greater detail in Chapter 2.

The liberal idea of freedom

Philosophically the idea of freedom, whether it is freedom of speech, or freedom of thought, conscience, expression, is most closely associated with the political ideology of liberalism. This is not to suggest that other political ideologies or belief systems do not have a conception of freedom, only that our Western ideas of freedom stem largely from the liberal intellectual tradition. As such, when discussing freedom of speech it is necessary to frame the discussion within a more general analysis of freedom in order to locate it as a concept both philosophically and historically.

Historians of political ideas generally agree that liberalism as a political ideology has its roots in the European Enlightenment when the principles of reason were asserted to provide an intellectual challenge to established authority – the monarchy and the church – during the late sixteenth, seventeenth and eighteenth centuries. This new thinking about man and his place in the universe started to challenge the existing power of society and assert the God given power of reason and human intellect as a basis for addressing social and political issues of the day. The view was that God gave mankind the power to reason and this gift should be used to determine man's own fate within a wider social contract in which rights and obligations should require protection.

Liberalism as a set of political ideals and principles developed as they were shaped and moulded by thinkers such as Thomas Hobbes (1588–1679), John Milton (1608–74), John Locke (1632–1704) and Jean-Jacques Rousseau (1712–78). Though these wri-ters should not be described as fully fledged liberals (as some of their thinking was decidedly illiberal), the ways in which their writing specifically sought to address the political turmoil and instability they encountered certainly laid the foundations of liberal ideals. New debates about the relationship between the state and the individual and the limits between the two, as well as discussions about the nature of the relationship between individuals, started to influence the political landscape of the era. Until the nineteenth century the influence of liberal thinking had helped influence significant political events such as the American Declaration of Independence from Britain in 1776 and the French Revolution in 1789. Liberal ideas had asserted the notion that political institutions should reflect the interests of 'the people' as it was the people who were the rightful owners of their destiny. As such the principle of democracy as a key ingredient of liberalism's political creed was viewed as the political system that best allowed 'the people' to have a voice in the governance of their country.

It should be noted that of course a form of democracy existed two thousand years before liberalism in Ancient Greece. Unlike liberalism, which is concerned with the relationship between the principles of democracy and ideas of individualism and individual rights, Athenian democracy was centred on the notion of civic virtue and the responsibility that members of the polis – the political community – had to one another in the governance of Athens. Athenian democracy was also direct democracy. Unlike modern democratic societies, all members of the polis (meaning men, as women and slaves could not participate) could vote on political decisions. As such, democracy for the ancient Greeks was not only about directly participating in discussion and decision-making, but also it manifested itself in the character of the people with civic virtue and obligation paramount. Moreover, democracy and liberalism are not so intertwined that they are inseparable as communitarian and socialist critiques of liberalism emphasise.

John Gray (1995) argues that there are three types of justification for liberalism which underscore its intellectual tradition (1995: 45). First is the idea, primarily emerging from the Enlightenment, that human beings possess things called 'natural rights'.[2] These rights are essential to us as human beings and 'morally prior to any social institution or contractual arrangement' (1995: 46). In other words from the moment of our birth we are considered to be in possession of rights which are natural and essential to us and which no state or individual can undermine. Michael Freeden (1991: 24) suggests that: 'For centuries rights-theorists tried to construct as invulnerable a case as possible for the existence and protection of fundamental human rights' and the development of political institutions from the eighteenth century onwards were largely framed with the protection of those rights in mind. For example, influential radical Tom Paine in his *Rights of Man* (1791) asserted that:

> Natural rights are those which appertain to man in right of his existence. Of this kind are all the intellectual rights, or rights of the mind, and also all those rights of acting as an individual for his own comfort and happiness, which are not injurious to the natural rights of others.
>
> *Paine (1791: 119)*

The second alternative justification for liberal rights according to Gray emerges in the philosophy of Immanuel Kant (1724–1804) who argued that individuals should be seen as moral rational agents who should be conceived as ends in and of themselves rather than means. This suggests that individuals should be guided in their action by a consideration of themselves and others as autonomous rational agents of equal worth. Gray suggests that Kant saw that a 'liberal society was, in effect, the only social order acceptable to persons who conceived themselves to be autonomous rational agents and ends in themselves' (Gray 1995: 50).

Kant's deontological approach to liberal philosophy should be seen in sharp contrast to the utilitarian consequentialist approach which sought to evaluate actions solely on their consequences. For Bentham, the founder of utilitarianism, the basis for formulating legal, political and moral judgements was in relation to the amount of well-being or 'happiness' which is produced among the greatest number of the population. This is the basis of his utility principle. Rather than conceiving people as ends in themselves, the utility principle claimed that all legal and political institutions, as well as the moral actions of individuals, should be designed in order to maximise utility.

Gray's third justification of liberalism relates to the contractarian approach developed in John Rawls's theory of justice (1972). Rawls put forward the principle of justice which 'gives priority to the worst off in society in condemning as unjust any inequalities which do not benefit them' (Gray 1995: 54). Rawls develops the idea of the 'veil of ignorance' which is essentially a thought experiment which enables individuals to abstract themselves from the 'real world' and imagine a society which is devoid of politics and morality – what he calls the 'original position'. The experiment also involves individuals thinking about the sort of society they would like to live in but not knowing in advance where on the social ladder they will be situated. Given that most people will not want to risk being at the bottom of the social scale, Rawls thinks that the majority of individuals will imagine a system in which the worst excesses of rich and poor are not present, in the hope that they will be able to live a comfortable and productive life. Rawls suggests that people acting rationally will tend to envisage a society that will protect them should they be one of the unlucky ones and end up at the bottom of the social hierarchy. Rawls therefore is attempting to develop a principle of liberal democracy that would ensure in practice that the worst excesses of rich and poor are no longer present as the social and political institutions that flow from this original position will ensure that such worst excesses are diminished. Rawls is ultimately concerned that people act freely but in ways that do not undermine the liberty of others. Rawls then 'accepts the moral diversity of modernity as an ultimate fact and seeks to construct principles of justice which permit rival moral traditions to coexist in peace' (Gutmann 1980: 55). In other words Rawls's theory of justice is an attempt at dealing with one of the central questions within liberalism – what are limits of individual liberty and how should these be regulated? Rawls's theory of justice attempts to balance liberty with equality and ensure that people have the maximum amount of liberty but with protections in place which ensure that the liberty of others is not undermined. Amy Gutmann suggests that Rawls's theory of justice is the 'most remarkable contemporary attempt to situate the concept of equality within a comprehensive theory of egalitarian justice' (1980: 119). This Rawlsian conception of justice then stresses the contractarian element within liberalism which emphasises a measure of restraint on liberty, usually manifest in significant amounts of welfare provision. This position would then be in stark contrast to the libertarian conceptions of liberalism which emphasised a minimal state, particularly in the economic sphere.

The brief overview of three justifications of liberalism should give us a clue that as a political and ideological creed, liberalism itself is not a settled set of principles and ideas, nor most liberals would probably argue, should it be. Arguably, all of the above elements of liberal thinking are in some ways manifest in our contemporary liberal society – for example, the conception of innate human rights that originated in the work of John Locke has become enshrined in the Universal Declaration of Human Rights (1948) and European Convention on Human Rights and Fundamental Freedoms.

However, despite their universal aspirations such conventions have been accused of being a repository of Western political thinking (Freeden 1991: 102) and as I have identified, emerge from a distinctly Western historical context and philosophical disposition. Similarly, the Kantian idea that individuals should be perceived as ends in themselves, rather than merely means to ends resonates in our recognition of individuals as autonomous agents who share equal respect and concern. Finally, the Rawlsian position that individuals have an obligation to construct social institutions that protect the weakest in society while ensuring maximum liberty for all is something that we can recognise in institutions such as the welfare state in the UK.

Toleration as a 'liberal' concept

As noted, liberalism as a set of political principles provides the basis for a wide range of religious, political and economic rights which are enshrined in constitutional codes across the world – the right to own property; the right to be free from intimidation and harm; the right to vote; the right to equal worth and freedom of conscience. Liberalism has helped shape contemporary political and legal institutions with a view to ensuring that the state does not encroach too much into the lives of individuals in ways that stifle their freedom. Moreover, liberalism has sought set out the limits of state interference in matters of individual conscience and choice. One of the ways that liberalism has sought to deal with the competing claims of individuals is in relation to formulating principles of toleration.

Toleration could be defined as a commitment to the principle that opinions and viewpoints that one might vehemently disagree with, should be permitted in a free society. Voltaire is often cited as the author of the words 'I disagree with what you say but I will defend to the death your right to say it', which is still used as a principled defence of the idea of toleration. Voltaire never actually uttered these words, rather his sentiment was more along the lines of think for yourselves and allow others to do the same. Yet the oft used quote, which was actually attributed to Voltaire by biographer Evelyn Beatrice Hall (Lee 1990), is arguably more powerful than Voltaire's actual sentiment, as toleration implies that one should tolerate the opinions of those whom you most vehemently disagree with. Toleration in the modern context could be described as much more than being indifferent to the views of others, as this implies that such views are of less worth than those one might posses; rather toleration could be defined as the recognition that the viewpoints and opinions one disagrees with have a valid connection to the identity and cultural experience of those who share that perspective. Therefore, to be intolerant is to undermine a person's identity and value as a member of the community. As we will see later in this book, this issue of toleration becomes particularly significant in relation to debates about freedom of speech and religion. The noted scholar of toleration Susan Mendus (1989: 6) points out: 'It is difficult to exaggerate the importance of religious toleration in the history of the subject.' By far the most obvious issue in relation to toleration is the extent that religions and ethical systems exhibit tolerance, the first articulate defence thereof emerging in the work of John Locke. Often cited as the originator of modern conceptions of liberalism, John Locke puts forward a pragmatic case (Mendus 1989) for freedom of opinion and freedom of conscience that has at its core an appreciation of the centrality of reason to human judgements. Locke's argument, which resonates with that of those campaigning for religious tolerance during the English Civil War, is that the church, which rightly centres on the spiritual and moral well-being of the community, should be separate from politics which should only concern itself with civil life and the protection of the natural rights of individuals. As such it was not for governments to decide matters of faith, rather it should be left to individual con-science and choice. This claim was made in relation to Locke's appeal to reason and rationality. For Locke it was just illogical to meddle in matters of faith given that it is something that is deeply held and sincerely professed. For Locke, toleration was necessary because it was rational. As Susan Mendus (1989) points out:

> [R]eligious belief is concerned with salvation, and salvation is to be attained only by genuine belief, not by insincere profession of faith. People can be threatened and coerced into professions of belief; they cannot be coerced into genuine belief.
>
> *Mendus (1989: 26)*

It is important to remember that Locke's argument was not an argument for religious diversity, rather a pragmatic and rationally grounded argument against religious intol-erance (Mendus 1989). Moreover, religious intolerance threatened civic tranquillity and as such was deemed a danger to the natural rights of men. Likewise, religious intolerance could only be justified if it were in the name of protecting the natural rights of man. As Mendus suggests 'Locke's case is thus a minimalist and pragmatic case against [religious] persecution. It is not a positive case for diversity of religious belief' (1989: 26; see also Waldron 1988).

Though toleration emerges from the liberal tradition, it may not in fact, in the modern context, be consistent with liberalism itself. Indeed Mendus argues that modern conceptions of toleration are too narrowly attached to liberalism which can lead to 'potentially illiberal consequences, particularly for those people or groups of people who are not themselves liberals' (1989: 70). The theme of 'illiberal liberalism' has also been picked up from a more avowedly Marxist perspective, most notably by Herbert Marcuse (1969), who has argued that liberal toleration within capitalist societies is in fact mythical in that it actually masks a much more deep-seated oppression than that which it is aiming to nullify. Marcuse suggests that liberal societies promote and adopt the toleration of views and perspectives only in a very limited way as freedom is only very narrowly defined. Moreover, through socialisa-tion and education we are taught to accept very narrow parameters of freedom. This narrow definition undermines real freedom as it actively serves the interests of the capitalist class. Marcuse suggests that the problem of toleration

> is not that of finding a compromise between competitors, or between freedom and law, between general and individual interest, common and private welfare

> in an *established* society, but of *creating* the society in which man is no longer
> enslaved by institutions which vitiate self-determination from the beginning.
>
> *Marcuse (1969: 101)*

As such he suggests that we are socialised into accepting a version of freedom which
is actually 'repressive' as we are necessarily limited by the socialising forces of capitalism.
Moreover, toleration in liberal societies, particularly in the news media, is presented
as impartiality which dictates that newsreaders and journalists present information
without bias or a political slant. Yet Marcuse asserts that: '[I]f a newscaster reports the
torture and murder of civil rights workers in the same unemotional tone he uses to
describe the stockmarket [...] it offends against humanity and truth by being calm
where one should be enraged' (1969: 112). Such balance actively masks the gravity of
the crime against the civil rights workers in the name of impartiality. It trivialises that
of which we should be outraged. To push the point further, the toleration afforded
to extremist political groups, particularly those on the right, in the name of impartiality,
undermines real tolerance as such groups seek to negate freedom. This was demonstrated by the fact that the tolerance afforded to Nazi and Fascist leaders in the 1930s
was the precursor to the atrocities of the Holocaust. In other words, Marcuse is suggesting that society should be intolerant of such views in the name of real tolerance
and freedom. Yet the 'repressive tolerance' practised under capitalism, only serves to
entrench existing power relations and promote further intolerance. Marcuse was
writing during a period of significant political and ideological turmoil, the student
revolts and civil rights protests of the 1960s and the crushing of dissent by both liberal
democratic societies and totalitarian states. Viewed in this context one can see that he
is attempting to challenge the notion that liberal democracies provide real freedom
through toleration when in fact, from his point of view they promote intolerance and
violence.

Free speech arguments

Frederick Schauer in his book *Free Speech: a Philosophical Enquiry* (1982) outlines a
number of distinct philosophical arguments which he suggests inform our contemporary
thinking about freedom of speech and its applicability in modern liberal democratic
societies though in principle, these arguments need not necessarily be confined to
liberalism (see also Scanlon 1979).

The arguments are: the democracy argument, the liberty argument, and the argument
from truth.[3] It should be noted that these principles do not stand alone in their
defence of freedom of speech. In other words these principles should be seen as a
starting point for discussions about freedom of speech and expression and can be
applied to different degrees and in different circumstances. As such these principles
can be seen as a basic reference point for discussions about freedom of speech, freedom of expression and of course freedom of the press. It should also be noted that
when discussing free speech arguments I am not referring to arguments that advocate
totally unrestricted speech or expression. As Warburton (2009: 8) argues freedom of

speech is a liberty not a licence; it does *not* mean the freedom to 'slander, freedom to engage in false and highly misleading advertising, freedom to publish sexual material about children, freedom to reveal state secrets', so it is worth bearing in mind that the following arguments do not attempt to justify freedom of speech without boundaries and conditions, which will be explored throughout the course of this book.

The democracy argument

The democracy argument is probably the most well known argument for freedom of speech. It stems from the view for democracies to function according to their internal logic with the public as sovereign (Schauer 1982: 35), freedom of speech is necessary as it serves a dual purpose – first as a means of informing the public about the workings of government and the activities of society's representatives, and second as a pressure valve for the public to censure government without fear of reprisal. Historically we see the spark of this view with regard the primacy of the public gaze as a servant to democratic ethos in the classical Greek tradition. Thucydides's *History of the Peloponnesian War* (1990 [circa 411 BC]) charts the gradual disintegration of Athenian democracy primarily brought about by its war with Sparta and its allies. Those who lived in the city-state of Athens saw democracy as a truly advanced form of society and government. Democracy was not perceived in terms of rights as we might advocate today, rather democracy was conceived as a fundamental component of Athenian civic life and an element of Athenians' peculiar cultural disposition towards the functioning of the polis (Haworth 1998).

In his eulogy for those who died during the first period of the war, Pericles outlines the debt of gratitude that the people owe to those who have given their lives for Athenian democracy. In reminding us, he also hints at the importance of the public gaze on the workings of a fully functioning democratic state. For Pericles Athenian democracy flourishes because of the way in which the citizens of Athens are able to openly discuss matters of public concern and have access to the decision making process. In much the same way as the democracy argument is conceived today, a fully operational democratic political body requires the flow of public information, opinion and debate. Arguably this is one of the functions that journalism, operating under the principles of freedom of the press, has provided historically (see Chapter 3).

As we will see in Chapter 2 the development of democratic institutions in France, America and Britain necessitated an informed citizenry which could not only scrutinise the workings of government as it had the capacity to act in its own interests against the interests of the people but also that the people should have the capacity to freely air their views and opinions on their elected representatives.

However, Schauer (1982) has asserted that we need to be careful when we use the term democracy, particularly in relation to discussions of freedom of speech, as democracy can be taken to mean the will of the people or the majority view. Such a majority could in principle outlaw certain forms of expression. Therefore, as a foundational principle of freedom of speech and expression, the democracy argument looks relatively weak. It seems that it only narrowly relates to matters of politics. However, if we conceive of democracy as something which moves beyond a majoritarian conception of the public, to something which incorporates fundamental principles of equality of concern and respect, then we have a much stronger conceptual basis for a democracy argument for freedom of speech.

> Equal participation by all people in the process of government is even more fundamental to the ideal of self-government than is the idea of majority power. [...] If everyone is to participate equally, then everyone must have the information necessary to make that participation meaningful.
>
> *Schauer (1982: 41)*

Schauer is suggesting a conception of democracy in which citizens have the capacity to access information and engage in informed deliberation, providing a useful foundation of a democratic justification for freedom of speech. This argument is closely associated to the work of Alexander Meiklejohn (1965) who defended freedom of speech and the First Amendment on this very basis. Similar arguments have been put forward by other liberal scholars who suggest that an active and informed citizenry operating within a constitutional framework of deliberative democracy require constitutional protection of speech and expression (see Gutmann and Thompson 1996). As we will see in Chapter 3, this notion of a deliberative active citizenry animating democracy provides a strong basis for press freedom and has been incorporated, with varying degrees of success, into journalistic ethics and practice (see Dewey 1927; Siebert *et al* 1956; Nerone 1995; Haas 2007), particularly in relation to civic engagement and public journalism (Rosen *et al* 2000). Freedom of speech, via freedom of the press, in principle at least, is said to help invigorate democracy by facilitating the deliberative process and ensuring that the two-way communication process between government and the people is not stifled. Yet Schauer reminds us that even this principle which stresses equality, is not a sufficiently independent principle of freedom of speech. Rather 'it is a reminder that *issues* relevant to self-government are especially important, and that individual interests and dignity are almost always implicated by decisions relating to the exercise of political power' (Schauer 1982: 42).

In the United States the articulation of the function of freedom of speech in a democracy is often attributed to two leading Justices of the early twentieth century – Justice Louis Brandeis and Justice Oliver Wendell Holmes. Sunstein (1993) suggests that Holmes's position on the virtue of freedom of speech is based on two key foundations. The first, and one which is similar to the ideas of John Stuart Mill highlighted below, is related to scepticism and the contestation of truth claims (Sunstein 1993: 25).

> But when men have realized that time has upset many fighting faiths, they may come to believe even more than they believe the very foundations of their own conduct that the ultimate good is better reached by free trade in ideas – that the best test of truth is the power of the thought to get itself accepted in

the competition of the market, and that truth is the only ground on which their wishes safely can be carried out.

Holmes cited Sunstein (1993: 11)

The idea is that only through a free and open debate (a free market of ideas) can we assume a greater understanding of the truth. Democracy is not the only victor in this scenario, but in principle allows for reason to overcome prejudice and superstition, falsehood to be exposed and error avoided. Such a marketplace of ideas can encourage all manner of other social goods including the discovery of truth.

However, as Sunstein and others (see Gordon 1997) have pointed out, the so-called free market does not *guarantee* that which its defenders claim. First, what is so distinctive about the market that enables it to determine truth or falsehood? Does something that is arrived at via this mechanism guarantee truth? Certainly not. A free market of ideas provides no guarantee of truth any more than a free market of goods provides the best product. It may be popular but may not be the best. Moreover, establishing 'the truth' depends on what one understands by 'truth'. Relativists and postmodernists have fundamentally questioned the idea that truth and certainty can be established.[4]

Yet of course the metaphor is perceived as useful in this context because for a democracy to thrive open and free debate is necessary (Sunstein 1993: 26). Brandeis claimed that freedom of speech was essential because of its power to cultivate a deliberative populace that would best serve democracy. Therefore, free speech is essentially a means to an end, the end being democratic government (Sunstein 1993: 27). As Sunstein emphasises, the views of Brandeis and Holmes diverge in the sense that the latter asserts a marketplace analogy which may in fact be in direct competition with the civic ideal envisaged by Brandeis. It is this latter argument that most resembles the civic dynamic of the democracy argument, and as Barendt suggests, this broader but more complex foundational argument for freedom of speech from democracy is one that enables minorities and a range of perspectives a voice, not just the majority view. However, one of the major issues with regard with freedom of speech within democratic societies is the extent to which such societies allow speech and expression which challenges or undermines the very democratic principles on which they are based.

Speech that undermines democracy

The problem most often centres around the political expression of political extremists and their use of open channels of public communication to attack, or seek to undermine the democratic principles that allow such forms of expression in the first place and which are based on the principle of equality and equal respect for all. Most Western democracies have legislation against so-called hate speech, which is classed as speech or expression which has the effect of generating hatred or contempt towards people based on the grounds of their faith, sexuality or race. The International Covenant on Civil and Political Rights article 20:2 reads: 'Any advocacy of national, racial or religious hatred that constitutes incitement to discrimination, hostility or violence shall be prohibited by law.' Yet article 19:2 of the same document proclaims that: 'Everyone shall have the right to freedom of expression; this right shall include freedom to seek, receive and impart information and ideas of all kinds, regardless of frontiers, either orally, in writing or in print, in the form of art, or through any other media of his choice.'[5] States are encouraged to adhere to this covenant yet the line between the expression of political opinion and hate speech is highly contested.

In the United States of America probably the most famous case in which the right of freedom of speech for extremists has led to calls for restrictions on extremist speech is the Skokie case. In 1977 a small group of extreme right wing extremists planned to hold a demonstration in the small town of Skokie, Illinois. Controversial enough maybe, but the main controversy about the case was the fact that the town was home to a large Jewish community, many of whom were survivors of the Holocaust. The town officials attempted to ban the demonstration and appealed to the Illinois Supreme Court to stop the demonstrators from marching on the grounds that the neo-Nazis would be inciting racial hatred against the Jewish residents of the town.[6] However, the court ruled that banning the marchers would be denying their constitutional right to free speech which is protected under the First Amendment. The key issue in this case was that the expression of a certain political opinion which preached hate towards a religious community was allowed because of the necessity of allowing all political speech in a democracy, even that which might undermine the principles of democracy. In the end, for whatever reason the marchers decided not to march, even though they were successful in court. Yet as former national executive of the American Civil Liberties Union has remarked the Nazis 'gained nothing for their movement by prevailing in Court' (Neier 2008; 23) and freedom of speech remained intact.

The case remains an important benchmark in discussions about the limits of extremist speech and expression in the U.S. because in a court of law the distinction between speech and action was reaffirmed. Speech and expression which have the intention or are likely to cause physical harm to individuals are not protected under any free speech legislation for obvious reasons. However, the debate about Skokie revolved around the issue of incitement and offence and the nature of harm caused to the residents and the wider community by such extremist language. Cohen-Almagor (2001) identifies this as the democratic catch, the idea that my freedom to express views openly in a democracy might actively undermine the rights that promote key democratic principles of equal respect for dignity and the right to live one's life without harassment. He argues that given that many residents of the town of Skokie were survivors of the Holocaust, the march through their streets would be a direct reminder of the horrors they and their families had to suffer during the Holocaust. Feinberg (1985) previously suggested that of course if the residents of Skokie didn't like it or wish to see it, they could simply leave town or close their blinds and curtains. Yet of course for Cohen-Almagor simply leaving town was not an option. They would still be cognisant of the fact that Nazis were walking down their streets with swastikas and other Nazi regalia. The offence suffered by the residents of Skokie could be so deep as to cause irrevocable psychological harm. Cohen-Almagor argues that in instances such as this the harm inflicted may in fact be as bad or even worse than the physical harm. He suggests that in certain circumstances, such as the case with Skokie, freedom of speech, even political speech such as that of the neo-Nazis, should be a contender for regulation.

Further problems related to arguments about the precise limits of freedom of speech are examined below. However, it should be noted that in the U.S., freedom of even extremist political speech is protected because of the principle that to deny a wide range of political speech, even that which is offensive to some people, might according to some (see Wolfson 1997) give the state too much power and erode the core principles of the United States Constitution. In other Western democracies, most notably those in Europe, there are specific constitutional or legal requirements which protect political speech and expression on these very grounds, though with some conditions (see Barendt 2005: 177–86).

These tensions noted, the beauty of the democracy argument for freedom of speech lies in the way in which it promotes the free flow of ideas and opinions which are the necessary lifeblood of democratic societies. Of all the principles of freedom of speech, the argument from democracy is the most closely related to the idea of press freedom given the emphasis it has on the public requirement to access the requisite knowledge and information about the workings of government. Yet as we will see in Chapter 3, though the principle is fairly sound, in practice there are a number of barriers and obstacles to the deliberative function of freedom of the press as fuel for democracy.

Truth and knowledge

According to Eric Barendt, '[T]he most durable argument [historically] for a free speech principle has been based on the importance of open discussion to the discovery of truth' (2005: 7). The idea that freedom of speech is linked to freedom of enquiry, freedom of thought and freedom of conscience is an idea that has its seeds in Milton (see Chapter 2) and continues through to John Stuart Mill's *On Liberty* (1859). Though in Chapter 2 of *On Liberty* Mill makes the specific case about the *limits* of freedom of expression, it is important to note that his arguments should be seen in the wider context of his concerns about the appropriate boundaries of the state and of the potential that public opinion can stifle individuality. Mill famously states:

> If all mankind minus one, were of one opinion, and only one person were of the contrary opinion, mankind would be no more justified in silencing that one person, than he, if he had the power would be justified in silencing mankind.
>
> *Mill (1991: 21)*

Yet on what basis does Mill make this claim? How does he justify such a position? Mill sets out four separate arguments that he thinks provide rigorous grounds for defending his 'liberty principle'. The first point Mill makes is that for us to deny someone freedom of opinion is to assume that we are infallible. Second, even if the opinion that we wish to silence may be erroneous, it may contain some element of the truth which is of value. Third, even if the opinion is true it still requires testing as otherwise it will be held as prejudice rather than informed knowledge. Finally, the opinion will be at risk of becoming 'dead dogma' if it is not open to challenge. In sum, Mill argues that if we silence an opinion or viewpoint, however obnoxious, then we are denying ourselves the opportunity of exposing that opinion as false. Moreover, even if we are one hundred per cent certain about the truthfulness of our opinions, if these are not open to question and challenge they run the risk of losing their vitality and as such we might lose sight of their essence. As Alan Haworth notes, Mill is concerned with the discovery of truth via the mechanism of liberty of thought and discussion. Prejudice and dogma are 'condemned for the way they impede the search for truth' (1998: 4).

Clearly Mill valued truth as a good in itself and saw that only through the open circulation of opinions and ideas the truth can emerge. Mill's idea that error and prejudice can be exposed and challenged by open scrutiny and questioning is one that is central to liberal conceptions of freedom of speech and informs our thinking about the value of open discussion. However, as Barendt (2005) points out, one of the central problems with Mill's truth argument is the claim that open and free discussion *necessarily* leads to the truth. Moreover, the question concerning the specific nature of truth becomes relevant. As already noted, relativists would certainly have a problem with the idea that there are such things as 'objective truths' waiting to be discovered via open debate and discussion. Haworth (1998) raises a similar objection to Mill in that he likens Mill's idea of an arena of open debate and discussion to that of a seminar, where ideas can compete with each other in a rational and calm manner. For Haworth this is not realistic as life just simply is nothing like a seminar and for Mill to suggest that rational agents come to a greater understanding and movement towards the truth, is to expect too much from the public.

In response to these particular objections it is important to remember the context in which Mill was writing. For Mill, the press itself was seen as an open arena of debate where the rational exchange of ideas and opinions was part of the convention of print culture at that time. Public discourse, albeit privileged, was indeed carried out in the open forum of the press and Mill had a long history of contributing to such debates (Wishy 1959; Rees 1985).[7] It could certainly be claimed that one of the key functions of journalism in Mill's day and today is its function, in principle at least, in allowing for public discussion and dialogue which facilitates greater awareness and understanding among its audience.

Liberty

The argument from liberty suggests that freedom of speech is an essential element in the realisation of what it is to be human and to develop to ones fullest capacities – it is an aspect of a person's self-fulfilment (Barendt 2005: 13). The liberty argument foregrounds individual autonomy and the right of individuals to express themselves according to their own tastes and concerns. Freedom of speech in this context is, of course, closely related to other liberal freedoms – freedom of religion, conscience and so on. However, as Barendt suggests, what makes freedom of speech different from these other liberties is that freedom of speech can significantly impact on other rights and liberties such as freedom of religion and conscience in that, as we have seen in the Skokie case, freedom of speech can undermine the freedom of others to live in peace in their communities. Freedom of speech then can be regarded as an 'other regarding act' (Barendt 2005: 13) and this is of crucial importance when we come to think about the limits of freedom of speech and expression.

Influential liberal philosopher Isaiah Berlin (1969) examined two versions of liberty which might be helpful in aiding our understanding of the subtleties and problems in the liberty argument for freedom of speech. Berlin argued that essentially there were two types of liberty or freedom. The first is what he called negative liberty. This is the idea that liberal states have an obligation to protect individuals from a range of harms which might undermine their ability to live their lives freely. Negative liberty is essentially freedom *from* harm – for example, freedom from intimidation, freedom from persecution or arbitrary sanction from the state. Individuals should also be protected from harms that might emerge in everyday dealings with other individuals. Therefore, negative freedom effectively places a protective bubble around individuals (and importantly their property) which in principle protects them from both state and social imposition which could undermine their liberty. This conception of freedom is arguably one all of us, in Britain at least, experience in our everyday lives. We know that our liberty could be denied us if we encroach on the liberty of others, if we steal property or physically or verbally assault someone. In relation to freedom of speech negative liberty could be seen in terms of ensuring that individuals have the right to express their views and opinions freely and openly in so far as they do not infringe on the liberties and freedoms of others to live their lives free from harassment and abuse. It is the liberal democratic state's obligation to protect and place limits on freedom of speech as a component of the protection of all the liberties of individuals.

Another form of liberty that Berlin identified is positive liberty. Rather than freedom from, positive liberty is freedom to. Freedom to see and hear and do what one likes, fully in the knowledge that one is acting on one's own agency. It is my choice as an autonomous agent to see, hear and read whatever I wish and I should have the means at my disposal to discharge these liberties. Arguably, therefore, positive liberty necessitates a social framework in which individuals are able to make any number of choices about how they live their lives – what they might do, what they might see or hear. This conception of positive liberty draws heavily on the notion of autonomy and the idea that human beings by their nature are autonomous and self-directing and that the environment in which they live should promote and underscore autonomy.

One of the key paradoxes of the liberty argument on freedom of speech is in relation to where to draw the line. In other words, what happens when positive and negative liberty collide (for example, when a person's positive freedom *to* view pornographic material conflicts with other peoples' rights *not* to have such material thrust under their noses)? Tension relates to freedom of speech as an 'other regarding act' – an act that is not solely concerned with the person doing the speaking but also may have ramifications for others in society. John Stuart Mill thought he had an answer to the problem of balancing freedom of speech with other liberties which is related to the conception of negative liberty. He argued that opinions should only be prevented from public airing when there is a significant chance that harm will result in the airing of that opinion. In other words the state or society should not interfere in matters of thought and expression unless there was a significant risk to life, limb or property. Mill uses the case of the 'corn dealer' to provide an example of the limits of free speech. He argues:

> [E]ven opinions lose their immunity, when the circumstances in which they are expressed are such as to constitute their expression a positive instigation to some mischievous act. An opinion that corn-dealers are starvers of the poor, or that private property is robbery, ought to be unmolested when simply circulated through the press, but may justly incur punishment when delivered orally to an excited mob assembled before the house of a corn-dealer, or when handed about among the same mob in the form of a placard.
>
> *Mill (1859: 62)*

This is quite a strong statement for Mill to make; that the only time the state can and should interfere with the freedom of expression of an individual is when that expression will cause imminent harm to an individual or their property. Mill goes even further than this and argues that no matter what sort of opinion a person holds and wishes to express, as long as it is within the bounds of 'common decency', it should be allowed. Mill seems to be suggesting therefore that speech or expression that 'instigates' harm to persons or property is speech that should be suppressed. What Mill is concerned with here is the specific context in which freedom of expression occurs. He uses very emotive language to paint a picture of an 'exited mob' outside the house of a corn-dealer; a 'mob' that will not have time for 'careful reflection'. Given the specific circumstances, Mill would have no objection in silencing this particular opinion. However, if the opinion is 'merely circulated through the press' then according to Mill the opinion should be 'unmolested'. So the corn-dealer example is used to specify the particular circumstances in which the state can legitimately stifle freedom of speech. For Mill, these circumstances are those in which life and liberty come under an imminent threat of harm. What is significant in a contemporary context is Mill's use of the word 'harm'. Harm here, unlike Cohen-Almagor's above, is understood as physical assault or at least the threat of assault on a person or property. As such for Mill, the limits of freedom of speech are very specific indeed.

Conclusion: Freedom of speech towards freedom of the press?

It should be evident that for the most part this chapter has concerned itself with the philosophical foundations of freedom of speech and expression with only a passing mention of freedom of the press. This has been intentional as one of the key aims of this book is to emphasise the specific differences between freedom of speech and press freedom as they are conceived, both historically and within a contemporary context.

As such the following chapter explores in greater detail the connection between the principles of freedom of speech and the principle and practice of freedom of the press. As noted in my introduction, the press itself is made up of institutions which in the West are usually large commercial enterprises, and as such arguments supporting freedom of speech for the individual or groups of individuals, cannot correspond to entities like media organisations. It is my contention that freedom of press should not be seen as merely the freedom of those rich enough to own a newspaper or media outlet to publish and be damned, rather it should be seen in the context of debates about journalism itself, its function, its history, it's purported democratic role and its often complex sense of self-identity. It should also be seen in relation to the numerous philosophical arguments about freedom of speech and it is with reference to the historical emergence of these philosophical ideas that the book now turns.

2

FREEDOM OF SPEECH AND THE JOURNALISTIC IMPULSE

Yes, we buckle on our armour of patience and perseverance – we draw forth our sword of reason, and we brave the whole host of tyranny! Defiance is our only remedy; – we cannot be slave in all: we submit to much – for it is impossible to be wholly consistent – but we will try, step by step, the power of RIGHT against MIGHT, and we will begin by protecting and upholding this grand bulwark and defence of all our rights – this key to all our liberties – THE FREEDOM OF THE PRESS – *the press, too, of the* IGNORANT *and the* POOR! we have taken upon ourselves its protection, and we will never abandon our post: we will *die* rather.

The Poor Man's Guardian (1831)

Introduction

The previous chapter was primarily concerned with examining the various philosophical defences of freedom of speech. This chapter connects the theories of freedom of speech with the notion of freedom of the press. In essence the chapter outlines the historical connection between the development of journalism and the *idea* of freedom of the press and how these have come to relate to the principles of freedom of speech and expression. The argument presented here, as throughout this book, is that though the philosophical arguments which provide the intellectual ammunition for freedom of speech and freedom of the press are compelling, the full realisation of these ideals has been limited in practice. This chapter explores some of the historical reasons for this lack of connection and suggests that journalism history should do more to take into account the fracture between the *ideal* and the *practice* of press freedom.

This chapter then attempts to examine the history of what we now understand as journalism in a way that stresses how journalism has historically been *connected* to ideas about principles of freedom of speech and expression. This is not to say that other important factors and principles have no bearing on the development of what we now call journalism. Rather, I suggest that in order to appreciate the relationship between journalism, press freedom and freedom of speech, some historical insight is required which details the way in which principles of freedom of speech and freedom of the press have became so central to the Western liberal democratic tradition.

I should point out that I do not intend to posit a particular definition of journalism, as history demonstrates this would be folly; one only need reflect on the relatively recent transformations within journalism – the Blogosphere and the impact of Twitter – to become aware of the open-ended character of journalism as professional and social practice, what Deuze calls 'liquid journalism' (Deuze 2006; see also Deuze 2005). What we find when we explore this historical aspect of journalism is that the debate about what journalism is and should be is not a modern phenomenon but has been a central feature of mediated public discourse for centuries.

The chapter proceeds with an overview of the rise of censorship and control of print during the Tudor period. To be sure, though this period did not invent censorship, the imperative to control print as a mechanism to manage politics more effectively became tightly bonded to the institutions of power. The chapter then goes on to focus on the English Civil War and particularly its legacy, with Milton providing a significant intellectual contribution to conceptions of press freedom during these turbulent times. Then the chapter moves on to explore further the emergence of the public sphere and the American and French Revolutions which galvanised the connection between the political realm and principles of press freedom, particularly in relation to the press as the fourth estate. Finally the chapter moves on to examine the development of press freedom in Britain and emphasises the very narrow conception of press freedom that emerged, a conception that remains largely intact today.

The rise of censorship and control

When we examine the historical evolution of journalism, we see that censorship has played a significant role in forging a link between the philosophical principles of freedom of speech and freedom of the press. During the Tudor period the shift towards an expanded mercantilism and competitive international trade by European states during the fifteenth century laid the foundations for an environment in which information and its exchange was vital to economic and political advantage. Political and financial competition meant that information assumed significant value and its control was central to the political machinations of the time. Up-to-date and accurate information about trade, international affairs and political and military rivalries became essential to the emergent mercantile class and political elites in a volatile and unstable international environment (Winston 2005). Though it would be another three hundred years before it became possible to receive information on the workings and proceedings of Parliament, the fact that information became an important commodity that secured those with the most up-to-date economic and political advantage meant that the control of the flow of information became imperative to those who wanted to attain or retain political and economic power. Of course the printing press in particular had made the production and distribution of information and news much more widespread and it was soon perceived as necessary to manage and control such a flow. Control of the press was seen as imperative and it was first seen as a major concern during the early Tudor period in England.

The most controversial issue at this time across Europe was the power of the Roman Catholic Church and when dissenters such as Martin Luther nailed his *95 Theses* to the door of the *Schlosskirche* in Wittenberg in 1517, the authority of the Roman Catholic Church was now openly being questioned (Copeland 2006: 5). The Catholic Church, and the priesthood as mediator between man and God, was now being publicly brought into question as the seeds of the Protestant Reformation soon spread across Europe and set a challenge to the monopoly of power of the Roman Catholic Church. The introduction of print licensing and the Court of the Star Chamber would attempt to curb the spread of dangerous ideas and enforce governmental sanctions on print. The controls would also demonstrate the power of the monarch and the ability to control dissent against the Catholic Church in Rome. These controls emphasise the perception that the emerging print culture was a potential threat to the political establishment of the day. In 1529 Henry VIII issued the *Proclamation for resisting and withstanding of most damnable Heresies*, an attempt to stop heretical writings from being imported into England. It was a list of works that were to be banned and anyone caught selling or possessing such works were to be turned over to ecclesiastical courts and charged with violation of the proclamation. Contravention of the proclamation posed a significant risk as booksellers were put to death if they were caught (Siebert 1965).

These controls continued through to the reign of Elizabeth I as the fear of print and its ability to stir up opposition and dissent became even more pronounced. As a result of this anxiety, a number of injunctions were instituted in 1559 with a view that the authority of the monarch in relation to the control of print was paramount. Licensing controls grew tighter as Elizabeth sought to continue the suppression of Roman Catholicism first begun by her father following his break with Rome. Though it was mainly Catholic literature that bore the brunt of the controls, Puritan pamphleteers also suffered. The Puritans, who were unhappy that the Reformation had not gone far enough as it retained many aspects of Catholicism, started to publish dissenting material which was critical of the established church (Copeland 2006).

The Stationers Company, which was charged with licensing all printed material, became the central mechanism of control of print over this period. It was of course a political entity in that it had loyalty to the throne; however, it also had a commercial interest in restricting the circulation of print in controlling piracy and protecting its copyright. The Stationers Company also had the responsibility for searching out and prosecuting unlicensed and seditious printing (Siebert 1965). It was within this political and religious ferment that the intellectual seeds of the English Civil War were being planted and it is during this period that print culture squarely enters the realm of politics. By the early 1640s the authority of Charles I had all but deteriorated. Power over print, in principle at least, was in the hands of Parliament. The relative chaos of new political terrain and internal squabbles within the Stationers Company meant that controls over print started to lapse. As Siebert points out:

> The freedom which the press enjoyed during this short period was due to the failure of enforcement agencies and to the pressure of other issues rather than to any belief on the part of the Parliamentarians that the press should be free.
>
> *Siebert (1965: 174)*

The English Civil War and its legacy

David Copeland suggests that our idea of freedom of the press owes 'more to the religious dissenters in the sixteenth and seventeenth centuries than of the news writers because religious issues and the right to worship according to the dictates of conscience were critical to living a full life' (Copeland 2006: 53). There is no doubt that during the years of the English Civil War print was being used as an overtly religious and political weapon. Writers and pamphleteers such as William Walwyn, Gilbert Mabbott and John Lilburn all gained notoriety at this time. The chaos at the beginning of the English Civil War, along with lapses in controls over print, meant that the early years of the war witnessed a relatively free press in which radical ideas circulated with relative ease. However, Parliament, keen to regain a measure of control over the press, established tighter controls on print, controls which focused on curbing alternative religious views and perspectives which sought to infuse secular and rational ideals of liberty of conscience and thought into the new politics of the time. The controls over print culture that the Crown once enjoyed were now taken over and reformulated for the purposes of Parliament in the new printing ordinance of 1643. The Ordinance for the Regulation of Printing (1643) meant that the role of controlling the press fell to the Stationers Company – an attempt to regain control over print, which had lapsed during the early years of the Interregnum. Failure to comply with the licensing authority would mean that publications would be seized and destroyed along with any printing equipment used to produce such material.

Throughout this period a range of arguments were heard against the tightening of controls over the press, some of which can be seen as forerunners of arguments for freedom of speech and freedom of the press today. However, one should bear in mind the specific historical context in which these calls were made and be weary of putting things into mouths of historical figures, words that they themselves would not recognise. The thrust of the arguments made by dissenters and pamphleteers were in relation to liberty of conscience and the belief that in matters of faith the state did not have authority over individual will which, after all, was a gift from God. For example, William Walwyn argued that Parliament should be 'cautious in deterring anything in this businesse of blasphemy & heresie'.[1] In an earlier pamphlet[2] he argues:

> 'Tis common freedome every man ought to aime at, which is every mans peculiar right so farre as 'tis not prejudiciall to the Common: Now because little can be done in their behalf, unless Liberty of Consciene be allowed for

> every man, or sort of men to worship God in that way, and performe Christs
> Ordinances in that manner as shall appear to them most agreeable to Gods
> Word; and no man be punished or discountenanced by authority for his opinion,
> unlesse it be dangerous to the State.
>
> *Walwyn (1644: 9)*

Arguments for religious toleration were therefore presented which sought to allow
for the dissemination of alternative religious viewpoints and perspectives based on the
idea that God himself had given man the gift of liberty to choose how he worshipped.
Government should not interfere in the spiritual matters of men; government and
maters of faith should be separate. The state on the other hand saw that the freedom
of conscience disseminated via pamphlets and other 'heretical tracts' posed a threat to
both the new constitution of Government and, from its point of view, to the word
of God.

Another dissenter who is often credited with pushing the boundaries of liberty of
thought and discussion during the years of the English Civil War is Lieutenant-
Colonel John Lilburn. Lilburn was one of the most vocal of the radicals who sought
to expose the betrayal he saw at the heart of the new Commonwealth which as he
saw it was replacing one set of unjust laws with another. Writing from the Tower of
London with his fellow agitators William Walwyn, Thomas Prince and Richard
Overton, Lilburn set out, albeit unsuccessfully, to redraw the political constitution of
England in *An Agreement of the Free People of England.*

> And being earnestly desirous to make a right use of that opportunity God hath
> given to use to make this Nation Free and Happy, to reconcile our differences,
> and beget a perfect amitie and friendship once more among us, that we may
> stand clear in our consciences before Almighty God, as unbyassed by any cor-
> rupt Interest or particular advantages, and manifest to all the world that our
> indeavours have not proceeded from malice to the persons of any, or enmity
> against opinions; bur in reference to the peace and prosperity of the Common-
> wealth, and for prevention of like distractions, and removal of all grievances;
> We the free People of *England*, to whom God hath given hearts, means and
> opportunity to effect the same, do with submission to his wisdom, in his name,
> and desiring the equity therefore may be to his praise and glory; Agree
> to ascertain our Government, to abolish all arbitrary Power, and set the bounds
> and limits both to our Supreme, and all Subordinate Authority, and remove all
> know Grievances.
>
> *Lilburn, Walwyn, Prince and Overton (1649: 2–3)*

Within this constitution would be the right of men to worship as their consciences
dictated. Furthermore, the Agreement set out to radically alter the political composition
of Parliament and ensure that those sitting in the House were truly representative of
their constituencies. Democracy as a principle was rule by the people for the people
and Lilburn and the Levellers saw that anything other than this political constitution

was against the will of God as it undermined the rationality that God had bestowed upon mankind. As such, we see in the Levellers religion and reason as the driving forces for democratic change and reform. Freedom of the press was required as it was not for the state to dictate the religious orientation of the people, but it was their choice. Press freedom was an expression of freedom of conscience and as such central to the democratic aspirations of groups like the Levellers.

John Milton

One of the key thinkers who principally identified within the Enlightenment tradition as someone who plays a significant part in the development of liberal ideas, particularly in relation to debates about freedom of speech and freedom of the press, is John Milton. Milton is seen as important in the history of freedom of expression because of his conviction that truth and reason should not be held back or constrained, and that attempts to control the circulation of ideas was both irrational and un-Godly. Milton came to write his famous attack on the licensing system *Areopagitica* in 1644 in response to the licensing authorities' attack on his pamphlets on divorce. Milton's ideas can be seen as an early form of the argument from truth. Milton's *Areopagitica* was a plea for restrictions on printing to be lifted on the basis that it was an affront to liberty, wisdom and good government, noting that 'when complaints are freely heard, deeply consider'd, and speedily reform'd, then is the utmost bound of civil liberty attain'd' (Milton 1990 [1644]: 4).

The reinforced controls that existed on print were, according to Milton, an affront to liberty and truth and of benefit to no one but those who sought to hold back the human spirit. Milton argues that such restrictions

> will be primely to the discouragement of all learning, and the stop of Truth, not only by disexercising and blunting our abilities in what we know already, but by hindering and cropping the discovery that might bee yet further made both in religious and civill Wisdome [sic].
>
> *Milton (1990 [1644]: 7)*

So liberty of conscience and the circulation of opinions would enable the truth about God to be known to all. However, it is well known that Milton's purported liberal temper was somewhat selective and malleable. For Milton, as with other dissenters, liberty of thought and expression was not a universal right and such liberty should only be for those of a 'civilised disposition' and not be given to Catholics and heathens. Moreover, given that in 1651 he agreed to act as an official censor for Cromwell (Winston 2005), one might forcefully argue that Milton's status as a champion of freedom of speech is fatally undermined. Despite this fundamental flaw, as we saw in Chapter 1, the relative power of the argument from truth remains a powerful philosophical principle for freedom of speech and Milton's ideas remain significant primarily because of the emphasis he placed on the relationship between the advancement of truth and the free exchange of ideas via public debate.

'News' and the public sphere

The political turbulence of the seventeenth century stimulated a desire within sections of the population for information and knowledge about events that were directly affecting their lives (Raymond 1996). However, the appetite for information about one's circumstances has of course been a feature of all societies in one form or another. The development of news, or what we might discern as news, became more formalised in England well before the advent of printing in the fifteenth century (Conboy 2004). Ballads and newssheets provided information, gossip and rumour within a developing network of information flows as the feudal system and its growing mercantile classes required. This class demanded information that would enable them to attain and maintain commercial advantage, something that has been a feature of news since this period. Information therefore became a functional necessity of the emergent mercantile classes. Among the early forms of news were the Corantos, essentially digests of news and information on trade and politics that were first published in the Netherlands in the fifteenth century. These started to appear in England as early as the 1620s and, as Conboy (2004) points out, though these newssheets did not contain any information about domestic politics (as this was illegal), they did provide information for a limited elite public keenly interested in foreign affairs and trade. What the popularity of the Corantos demonstrates was a desire for information to be provided at regular intervals so as to chime with the specific circumstances of the day. Hence we have the notion of periodicity (Somerville 1996) which enabled news to establish itself as a component of culture (Conboy 2004; Carey 1989).

Following the restoration of the Crown in 1660 the idea of news both as an element of cultural identity and a reflection of political and economic interests became much more firmly established. Politics came to dominate public discourse. Whether it was in relation to continued debates about the limits of religious toleration or the controversies about the extent of Royal Prerogative, public discourse on matters of significance began to establish itself more firmly outside the local and regional. As Briggs and Burke (2009: 81) maintain, 'In Western Europe, from the Reformation onwards, the fragmentation of religious as well as political authority had made it impossible for governments to fully control printing.' This period during the late seventeenth and early eighteenth century has been conceived as an era in which public discourse on matters of direct significance to bourgeois interests started to develop. This public sphere, it is argued, grew in order to sustain the growth in both political and economic terms of a new bourgeois class (Habermas 1989). It was out of an appetite for political and economic news that the public sphere therefore started to emerge, with European bourgeois interests being the dominant voice at this time as they sought to wrestle power from the Monarchy and the Church.

In 1712 a tax was introduced under the authority of Queen Anne which meant that all printers and publishers of newspapers in England would be liable to pay a levy on newspapers and pamphlets, on advertisements, on paper and on registration (Siebert 1965: 311). This legislation was brought in to both exert some measure of control over print and therefore arrest the spread of political dissent and to limit the numbers of printers, thereby helping to maintain a monopoly over print (Siebert 1965). Winston (2005) suggests that the stamp tax was essentially a vehicle to quash the growth of Whig journalism and Whigism more generally as it was starting to make important gains politically. However, the tax was limited in its effectiveness given that it was difficult and expensive to enforce and could easily be avoided by newspapers simply changing their format and size to avoid the tax. They could also of course raise their prices or charge more for advertisements (Winston 2005). Another option was simply to refuse to pay the tax, though this did not address the other key mechanism open to the authorities – to prosecute for seditious libel.

Though the eighteenth century saw further attempts to impose post publication taxation on newspapers, Michael Harris suggests that by the latter part of the century the 'form and character of the newspaper had been established by a series of adjustments focused in the first half of the century' (Harris 1978: 97). These adjustments effectively concerned the balancing of political interests with those of commerce. Indeed more recently Martin Conboy has suggested that from 1712 we see the development of journalism as a 'pragmatic negotiation' (2004: 66) concerning the demands of three key constituents important in the framing of journalism at that time. The first of these is the readership, who were starting to advance a sense of themselves as a 'public'. This public was conceived as being made up of a constituency of increasingly powerful private individuals. The second important element in the development of journalism at this time was the growth in the power of advertisers and those wishing to cash-in on the expansion of print; as such, the commercial opportunities that newspapers offered were significant. Finally, we see politicians themselves who were effectively caught between the need to court the public, and therefore legitimise their position of power, and yet open themselves up to criticism in the press. What we see developing at this time was the recognition by politicians that a press that was compliant and not too noisy could be a useful resource in the management of political and economic affairs.

Intellectually the idea of a free press was connected to the ideas of Locke which stated that men were born free and arbitrary government was against natural law and God. Locke, as we saw in Chapter 1, was interested in the scope and limit of government power over man. Locke suggested that men have natural rights which should be protected by consensual agreement between man and the state. The legal expression of this in England was the Bill of Rights which was passed in 1689 which contributed to the development of the idea of Parliamentary sovereignty. For the state to arbitrarily limit man's natural rights was to go against God and the natural order of things. This idea that liberty was paramount and should be protected by a higher authority that had the consent of the people to wield that authority, becomes much more resonant in the political discourse of the early eighteenth century and particularly in print – for example, in Cato's letters, which steadfastly related the principles of liberty of the press to broader natural freedoms. Cato was in fact the pen name of John Trenchard and Thomas Gordon who agitated against the Walpole government which had effectively sought to manage dissent in the press by outright bribery of journalists, and the gradual buying off of newspapers (Winston 2005). In a letter in the *London Journal* in 1720 Gordon and Trenchard argued: 'This sacred Privilege is so essential to free Government, that the Security of Property, and the Freedom of Speech, always go together.' The letter continues: 'Whoever would overthrow the Liberty of the Nation, must begin by subduing the Freedom of Speech' (Winston 2005: 760). What we see developing at this time are two sides of a political divide that would be fundamentally important in the history of British political life – the gradual liberalising or Whig emphasis on greater representation and free trade, and their opponents, the traditional Tory landed classes. The formation of this distinctive political sphere had a significant impact on the development of the wider public sphere which would be evident in the broader debates about politics and political rights. These debates would crystallise the connection between public discourse and the emergent political sovereignty of the people; conceptions that would be much more fully realised in the revolutionary upheavals of France and America.

American and French Revolutions

The conceptual and political shifts that started during the Enlightenment – notions about man and his place in the universe – impacted significantly on the intellectually lead upheavals which culminated in the French Revolution in 1789, and before that, the American Revolution in 1776. One hundred and seventy years prior to American independence from Britain, the British colonies in Virginia promised a new life for those wishing to escape religious persecution and the prospect of a long and arduous war. In the 1620s the Virginia Company used print to tempt people to make the journey across the Atlantic and start a new life, free from the threat of war, economic ruin, high taxation and religious orthodoxy (Copeland 2006). The anxieties of the 1620s and 1630s, where the idea of religious freedom was an anathema to the Crown and its agencies of enforcement and control, would be left behind as the promise of a new life in which Puritan religious values would be realised. As Copeland somewhat romantically suggests 'when Puritans and others sailed across the Atlantic with the baggage required to begin a new life, they also brought with them all that had transpired in the development of liberty of conscience up to that point' (Copeland 2006: 105). However, the Puritan ethic which developed in America at that time was a long way from the Enlightenment vision of freedom of conscience, toleration and democracy that the Levellers were to envisage. This would come much later, though it would begin in New England, where the tight connection between church and government would be questioned (Copeland 2006).

In America newsletters had started to appear from the mid-to-late seventeenth century (Mott 1941), but arguably the first American newspaper was Benjamin Harris's *Publick Occurances Both Foreign and Domestick*, published in Boston in 1690. It did not get off to a great start as the newspaper was victim of licensing regulation, a legacy from the Mother country:

> The Governour and Council having had the perusal of the said Pamphlet, and finding that therein is contained Reflections of a very high nature: As also

sundry doubtful and uncertain Reports, do hereby manifest and declare their high Resentment and Disallowance of said Pamphlet, and Order that the same be Supressed and called in; strickly forbidding any person or persons for the future to Set forth any thing in Print without Licence first obtained from those that are or shall be appointed by the Government to grant the same.

Publick Occurences, Both Foreign and Domestick *(Harris 1690)*

Harris's publication was an attempt to provide the people of Massachusetts with information and news that had proximity to their everyday experiences. In this sense the news provided in *Occurrences* was such that it sought not only to inform but also generate a sense of geographical and community based around the idea that 'people realise God's hand in everyday events' (Copeland 2006:136).

According to Mott (1941) the first American newspaper that was continually published and without subject to prosecution was the *Boston News-Letter* with other titles such as *The Boston Gazzette* and the *New England Courant* following soon after. As with their English counterparts, these newspapers sought to provide information on trade, foreign affairs and stories of human interest that, according to Mott (1941: 16) provided entertainment which became a function of American journalism thereafter. With this development, as well as its political and economic orientation, news became much more of a commodity than it had been in the past because of the particular and distinctive way in which it framed its audience and represented the interests of its readership. The steady growth of competition among newspapers and the end of licensing in England first in 1679 and then again in 1695 meant that pre-publication licensing in Massachusetts became untenable by the 1720s. However, to say that the press was free is a vast overstatement as controls over print remained via post publication control usually in the form of prosecutions for seditious libels. The new commercial environment of the colonial press meant that print became used as a weapon that had both political and economic imperatives, yet its control by those who governed was seen as necessary in order to protect the status quo.

The growth of print at this time enabled debates to take place within the public realm. Social and political debates were had within this new environment and the recognition that those governed had a right of reply to the institutions and mechanisms of government started to penetrate public political discourse. Freedom of the press was starting to be perceived as an expression of the relationship between the government and the governed in the social contract identified by Locke.

However, prosecutions for seditious libels had the effect of undermining that social contract and the Zenger trial in 1735 seemed to encapsulate the sense that public had the right to ascertain and publish the truth and to criticise improper government (see Copeland 2006; Stephens 2007). It seemed, following Zenger's acquittal by a jury on charges of seditious libel, that newspapers were gaining public licence at least to criticise government as long as this criticism was shown to be truthful and not directed towards individuals. However, it was the imposition of taxation, and the stamp tax in particular that would provide newspapers with the central role in the American Revolution.

As we have seen, a stamp tax on the press in England was put in place in 1712. By 1765 a similar tax would now be liable on printers and publishers in the American colonies. The prospect of such a tax caused uproar in the colonial press and dissent against the imposition of this and other taxes grew, stimulated by debate and critique among the press in the colonies. As Stephens notes, not only was this tax imposed on the press by a political body that did not represent them (and therefore had no political legitimacy), but also it was a significant threat to the commercial interests of newspapers as well (Stephens 2007: 166). This economic point is also picked up by Uhm (2008) who suggests that central to the concept of the people's right to know which helped underscore arguments for freedom of the press, was the idea that the public should be made fully aware of the financial demands and debts placed on them by the British government.

> The American Revolution, therefore, was a call to arms for a broader political freedom that included economic protection from excessive tax taxes and overblown debts to British creditors. [...] it can undoubtedly be seen as a rallying call for achieving financial independence as a way of fulfilling the emerging conception of popular sovereignty that was closely tied to radical Whig ideology.
>
> *Uhm (2008: 396–97)*

Therefore, we can observe the strong economic argument which helped shape the republican sentiment and demand for access to information that is seen as central to this day as 'publication of congressional proceedings was especially deemed necessary because they are closely tied to financial transparency of pubic funds' (Uhm 2008: 399). However, of possibly greater importance in the shaping of the revolutionary sentiment was the role that the press had in developing the conception of popular sovereignty that Uhm highlights above. Stephens (2007) argues that it was not just this critique of the British authorities by the American press that forced the issue over British rule and American independence. Critique, argument and exposition are all well and good, but this can only go so far in undermining political power. The role newspapers have in identifying and defining communities of interest in which they speak to and on behalf of – 'the public' – in this case the American public, was a crucial factor in legitimising the revolutionary response to illegitimate British rule. Indeed David Waldstreicher (1995), echoing Michael Bakhtin's conception of the 'carnivalesque', has highlighted the way in which public celebration, festivity and performance during the revolutionary period, underscored the development of American national identity, something which was also expressed via the print culture of that time. The seeds of American national identity can therefore be traced back to the culturally reinforcing relationship between print culture and the people which fuelled the requirement for such a culture. It is this role in reflecting, and at the same time reinforcing identity, that the press were able to provide the public with an insight into an increasingly shared set of values and experiences which the press attained for itself during the revolution in America in the late eighteenth century.

Copeland (2006) suggests that given their experiences with British colonial rule, American people saw the particular value of press freedom in that it could guarantee protection against similar autocratic and arbitrary government. Indeed he notes that the Constitution of the United States, in its formulation of the Bill of Rights, prioritised freedom of speech and freedom of the press as indispensible to the wider liberty of the people. The First Amendment, which states that 'Congress shall make no law [...] abridging the freedom of speech, or of the press; or the right of the people peaceably to assemble, and to petition the Government for a redress of grievances' is, of course, the enshrinement of that guarantee.

The press during the French Revolution also played a significant role in developing and articulating a specific notion of French identity that had its foundation in ideas of citizenship and conceptions of the public. Moreover, Chapman (2008) suggests that the initial aspirations of the French revolutionary press were to develop the parameters of, an albeit bourgeois, public sphere that was egalitarian in essence and civic in outlook. A central facet of the reconstitution of politics during the French revolution was the realisation of the idea that legitimate governance occurs when the public has full knowledge of the activities of the assemblies – a realisation of the democracy argument in its infancy. Gough (1988: 7) maintains that before the Revolution there were significant controls over print as licensing and prior censorship were the norm, although these measures were not always effective. Moreover, 'censorship had come under increasing attack [...] as Enlightenment-based demands for freedom of intellectual expression' took hold.

As in the United States, press freedom was seen as an important element of wider political freedom. Following the Revolution the controls that had existed on the press had vanished with the old regime. The French press before the Revolution was largely prohibited from drawing attention to domestic affairs. Following the Revolution, the press was transformed as 'the campaigning journalist was no longer the detached observer of events, but a participant in them, using his newspaper not as an analytical mirror held up to the face of reality, but as a weapon in political campaigns' (Gough 1988: 36).

Popkin (1990: 27) notes that 'for the most part, when the French called for freedom of the press in 1789, they were thinking of a system like that in England, where prior censorship and licensing had been abolished, but where authors and publishers could be prosecuted for libel, blasphemy, and obscenity'. As such press freedom became an embodiment of the new political constitution in which public life became represented in the press. Newspapers, according to Popkin, 'served as the Revolution's real "public space," its national forum for political debate' (Popkin 1990: 180). It is this notion of the press as acting in the interest of the public and as an organ of public debate within a democratic community that press freedom starts to become more firmly established in the later eighteenth century. At this time, it is argued, we start to see the emergence of the press as a component of the public sphere and as a necessary component of democratic life. Here then we see the emergence of the fourth estate function of the press and it is to this aspect of the press that I now turn.

The 'idea' of the fourth estate

Contrary to traditional notions of the development of the liberty of the press, there was no single unifying spark and linear pattern of 'progress' that finally came into rea-lisation once formal controls of the press were lifted by the middle of the nineteenth century. Rather, what we see are various struggles for *particular* rights and liberties – of thought, conscience and religious freedom – merging with struggles for greater levels of economic independence and political representation. These struggles com-peted with established power and through a process of negotiation, compromise and political expediency, gained the formal freedoms that enabled liberty of the press, along with other freedoms and rights, to be established as cornerstones of democratic societies. Yet given the complexity of the historical emergence of 'press freedom', as James Curran (1978; 1997; 2002) and others have suggested,[3] the traditional liberal view of the emergence of freedom of the press ignores and omits important historical elements of its development. These elements once evident help to shed light on the rupture between the principles of freedom of speech and their application as the practice of press freedom.

It was Thomas Carlyle who attributed the phrase 'Fourth Estate' to the father of modern Conservatism Edmund Burke when he noted:

> Burke said there were Three Estates in Parliament; but, in the Reporters' Gallery yonder, there sat a Fourth Estate more important far than they all. It is not a figure of speech or witty saying; it is a literal fact – very momentous to us in these times.
>
> *Carlyle in Barendt (2009: 6)*

This 'literal fact' emphasises the perceived importance that journalism and freedom of the press has to the proper running of democratic societies. In the United States the primary function of the First Amendment was to allow for a 'fourth institution out-side of government as an additional check' on government (Barendt 2009: 6). As such journalism's 'watchdog' role has, as we have seen since the institutionalisation of democratic rights and liberties, been seen as paramount.

Wilkes and his legacy

In historical terms, the relationship between journalism and democracy seemed to crystallise following the Wilkes controversy in the late eighteenth century. John Wilkes was an agitator, contrarian and, he thought, a man of the people. He was also MP for Aylesbury. Wilkes edited a pamphlet called the *North Briton*, first published in 1762, which sardonically goaded the power and privilege of both the Tories and the Whigs. The main target of Wilkes's ire, however, was the First Lord of the Treasury Lord Bute. Bute was loyal to King George III as it was widely claimed he was sur-reptitiously trying to undermine the hard won liberties of England by promoting Royal prerogative and increasing the power of the Monarch (Barker 1998). In April 1763, issue No. 45 of *North Briton* was published and caused uproar in its attack on Bute. Wilkes was subsequently arrested on charges of seditious libel, though he was released not long after citing Parliamentary privilege. The Wilkes affair and the furore that surrounded it emphasises the emerging relationship between the press and political scrutiny. Wilkes is particularly important as Martin Conboy suggests, because he had an appeal that spanned the social spectrum. He suggests that he 'employed the tactics designed to appeal to the lowest common denominator which were to become the hallmarks of succeeding generations of popular journalism' (Conboy 2002: 36). Liberty of the press was increasingly seen as providing the people with a voice. Hannah Barker (2000: 151) maintains that Wilkes, though having no great radical agenda, 'was able to persuade the English people that his personal cause and that of English liberty were one and the same'. Though Wilkes has been cast as an important figure in the development of rights of representation and press freedom, we should be careful not to see Wilkes as a romantic and heroic figure that individually took the vanguard of liberty against the vestiges of the *Ancien Regime*. Wilkes was a product of his time and shaped by the social and political turmoil of the eighteenth century. Indeed, as Gilmartin citing Brewer (1976) suggests, the character of political dissent that was evident at the time of Wilkes was already in place as there was an

> alternative political 'infrastructure' of organisational and communicative resources, extending from London to the provinces and from the 'parliamentary classes' to growing 'political nation', developed gradually over the course of the late eighteenth century.
>
> *Gilmartin (1996: 30)*

There is no doubt that Wilkes and the controversy surrounding his trial set the broader context in which later struggles for press freedom played out. During the latter parts of the eighteenth century the stirring of radical ideas that found their expression in the American and French Revolutions gained momentum and vigour across Europe. The Wilkes affair was undoubtedly historically important in focusing attention on the link between the narrow political constituency of Parliament and the public at large. This attention would become even more acute during the nineteenth century as the radical ideas of men such as Tom Paine gained prominence and significance. The key arena in which these ideological struggles would take place was via the press and is to these struggles in this period we now turn.

The 'struggle' for press freedom

At the turn of the nineteenth century Britain was a place of significant political turbulence and change. The burgeoning Empire and technological developments in agriculture and industry placed Britain at the heart of the modern world. In the realm of politics, Britain was not yet a full democracy and it would be the press that would play an important role in eventually helping to widen the political franchise and ensure democratic accountability of those in Parliament. During the early years of the nineteenth century, the press would be at the forefront of democratic reform, fighting for the rights of those who were disenfranchised and against the system of taxation which deprived so many people of the opportunity to learn about the world via the pages of the newspaper. Once political reform came and press freedom was guaranteed, the legacy of the press as championing the rights of ordinary people was set as the press would continue to keep a check on the powerful to ensure that democracy thrived. This is the gist of the conventional story of the 'struggle' for press freedom. The reality is, however, somewhat different.[4]

Certainly at the turn of the century, Britain was in a position of significant power; like many other European nations, this was built largely on Imperial expansion and exploitation of foreign resources. However, Britain was also a place of great anxiety, particularly for the political elite as ideas about democracy and liberty, ideas which sparked the revolutions in France and America, started to influence radical thinking in Britain and soon found their way into print, with radical pamphlets and newsletters circulated in taverns, coffee houses and at public meetings. Inspired by the works of Tom Paine, publications such as Thomas Wooler's *Black Dwarf*, William Sherwin and Richard Carlisle's *Sherwin's Political Register* and *Republican* and William Cobbett's *Political Register*, all developed a style of political rhetoric that challenged the political status quo and appealed to a mass audience (Conboy 2004).

The weakening of controls during the eighteenth century, along with the victories of Wilkes, had enabled radical ideas to spread via pamphlet and newsletter, and it was with this in mind that the government brought in the Six Acts of 1819. The Acts, also known as the Gagging Acts, were effectively six pieces of legislation which sought to suppress radical ideas and political insurgency and made it an offence to commit seditious and blasphemous libels, which were in effect anything that the censors viewed as being critical of the government or the church. Prosecutions for seditious libel increased significantly after the introduction of the acts with radicals and agitators risking imprisonment or deportation for their crimes. Another part of the legislation was the introduction of the 'stamp tax' which would impose a levy on all newspapers and periodical publications (Wickwar 1928). Thomas (1969: 37) notes that the tax 'was intended to discourage political opposition by imposing a stamp duty of a penny a sheet on newspapers and two shillings a sheet on one copy of each edition of a pamphlet which was more than half a sheet'. The idea behind the stamp tax was that it would raise the cost of newspapers and pamphlets and so limit their access to the masses (Curran and Seaton 2003). The growth of political dissent emerging during the early nineteenth century sought to attack the privilege and corruption in the House of Commons, and to strive for greater political representation, and the Gagging Acts seemed to reinforce the notion among the wider public that democratic reform was required.

This sentiment enabled a range of oppositional interest groups to coalesce around key issues, namely greater parliamentary representation and the abolition of controls over the press. Hollis (1970) notes that during the period of the 1820s and 1830s there developed a set of political allegiances between working class and middle class reformers that sought to push for reform. Arguments against control of the press assumed a number of forms from a variety of quarters, yet all of these arguments attempted to undermine the credibility and justice of the prevailing system. However, though their aims seemed to correspond to one another, the ultimate political ambitions of the middle class reformers undermined the democratic ideals of the mass working class movement for political reform. Further discussion of this point is required as it has a significant bearing on the nature of the freedom of the press that would develop after it was formally achieved in 1855.

In relation to debates about freedom of the press, ideas were primarily articulated in terms of calls for an end to the stamp tax which was perceived as a 'tax on knowledge' and a hindrance to greater scrutiny and critique of government. Moreover, it was the circulation of ideas and knowledge, particularly for the labouring classes and the poor, which would enable them to overcome their circumstances and raise themselves out of poverty. As Joseph Hume MP suggested to the House of Commons in 1831, he was 'against all laws which prevented the circulation of truth, and laid imposts on knowledge'.[5] Moreover, 'a tax on knowledge or the spread of information, was injurious to both individuals and to the community at large'. Hume knew of 'no legitimate way of opposing opinions but by arguments; and that opinion that could not be met by argument must be a sound and just one'.[6] Discussion and debate, it was argued, all contributed to the stock of knowledge and contributed to the greater good of all. A stamp tax was a hindrance to the accumulation of wisdom among the people and would ensure good government did not prevail. However, the 'taxes on knowledge' arguments, which were articulated mainly by middle class reformers, were essentially economic arguments against government taxation on the press. In other words, not only were these reformers against the stamp tax, but also all taxes that were seen as inhibiting to the profit motive. Moreover, by appealing to mass movements that called for greater representation and political reform, such arguments acted to cultivate acceptance among the working classes of the virtues of the new science of political economy – capitalism (Steel 2009).

Following the Reform Act of 1832, which extended the political enfranchise to a greater number of middle class voters, and the reduction of the stamp tax in 1836 from 4 pence to 1 pence, much of the radical democratic fervour that preceded the reform declined. As Curran and Seaton (2003) note the reduction of the tax and the extension of the franchise in the 1830s, rather than liberating the press actually undermined its democratic potential as the legislation created greater competition among the press which forced those with fewer resources out of business. Therefore, the democratic aspirations articulated by newspapers and pamphlets operating illegally under the stamp tax were wiped out of existence. With them went a voice that was representative of the wider working classes. Though campaigns against the tax continued until its final abolition in 1855, with organisations such as 'The Association for the Repeal of the Taxes on Knowledge', the bulk of the arguments used to undermine the rationale for the tax were in relation to their anti-market tendencies. With the reduction of the tax in 1855 it seemed that the 'struggle' for freedom of the press was finally over, yet in reality press freedom was only narrowly defined in economic terms. Chalaby (1998) suggests the period immediately following the removal of controls on the press is one in which journalism itself became a significant economic force as the press shifted from its role in representing the people, to one of generating profit. The press therefore became industrialised and with it journalism became commodified and professionalised. This did not occur over night after the removal of the stamp tax, rather the 1840s and 1850s was a period in which journalism developed as a distinctive idiom which shifted its focus from that of speaking on behalf of the people, to speaking to the people. Chalaby argues that before the demise of the formal controls of the press Britain saw essentially two types of publicist: the bourgeois and the plebeian, the former publishing in the interests of the middle class, the latter in the interests of the working classes, both writing for distinctive constituencies with separate interests and aims in journals, newsletters, pamphlets and newspapers (Chalaby 1998).

Chalaby chooses to refer to these individuals as publicists, because he contends that *journalism* as a professionalised set of practices did not exist prior to the ending of the economic controls over print. In other words, it was not until the expansion and intensification of commercial newspaper publishing under the principles of capitalist accumulation, that journalism actually came into being. As noted, the end of the controls over the press effectively wiped out any representation that the working class had. This 'victory' of the middle class liberal press, according to Chalaby, had two important effects: first, to shut out the working class from the public sphere; second, to define the political and ideological parameters of journalism as a discursive field (Chalaby 1998: 32). The result was a discursive field – journalism, which was bonded to the dominant institutions and ideology of capitalism.

A number of significant issues emerge from Chalaby's analysis which have important implications for the idea that journalism embodies the fourth estate. First, if Chalaby's analysis is correct then journalism's function, as it came into being within the frame-work of capitalist production relations, is inherently and necessarily tied to maintaining and securing those relations. As such, journalism as a mechanism for generating profit, rather than as a means of safeguarding democracy, becomes journalism's *raison d'être*. Therefore within the parameters of this analysis, the phrase 'freedom of the press' loses any essentially democratic imperative as it is usurped by the all-encompassing profit motive. Freedom of the press becomes freedom for news organisations to compete in the market. To curb freedom of the press is therefore to curb capitalist enterprise. It is within this context that press freedom, as I maintain in the following chapters, has come to be understood and articulated. I argue that the commercial imperative of the press continues to undermine the democratic imperative despite the common linguistic turn which allows freedom of speech to be so associated with freedom of the press.

Conclusion

The purpose of this chapter has been to provide an historical overview of the development of what might generally be understood as freedom of the press. It has sought to historically contextualise the development of the *idea* of freedom of the press and the relationship of this idea to particular historical circumstances and political struggles. From the austere controls on print during the Tudor period to the liberal 'victory' of freedom of the press in the nineteenth century press, I have attempted to highlight the range of mainly official and political methods, and the rationale behind such measures, that were established to limit and control the press. It should be clear by now that such controls were felt to be necessary because of the increasingly important role that print gained in disseminating and propagating critical and dissenting ideas. However, I have emphasised the notion that the *idea* of press freedom largely remained unrealised, as freedom of the press as a principle became welded to the practice of capitalist accumulation and enterprise. As such, in historical terms at least, the so-called 'victory' of freedom of the press should be understood more specifically in relation to market freedom, which, as Chalaby rightly points out, changed the character and dynamic of what we now recognise as journalism. The remainder of this book will be devoted to exploring the notion that the *idea* of freedom of speech and its relationship to the *principle* of freedom of the press is one that is perpetually undermined. Though we live in an era in which freedom of speech and freedom of the press are guaranteed by international convention and national legal requirements, freedom of speech remains under attack.

3

JOURNALISM AND THE DEMOCRATIC IMPERATIVE

Ordinary citizens, though occupied with the pursuits of industry, are still fair judges of public matters; for, unlike any other nation, regarding him who takes no part in these duties not as un-ambitious but as useless, we Athenians are able to judge all events if we cannot originate, and instead of looking on discussion as a stumbling-block in the way of action, we think it an indispensible preliminary to any wise action at all.

Thucydides (411 BC)

Introduction

Of all the overlapping philosophical principles that underpin conceptions of freedom of speech and freedom of the press, the idea that journalism should function to safeguard the institutions and principles of democracy is by far the most enduring. As we saw in Chapter 1 the democracy argument for freedom of speech is a principle which is central to Western philosophical thinking about the role of freedom of speech in stimulating an active and informed citizenry and as a means of holding its representatives to account. In Chapter 2 we examined the historical development of journalism's role within this framework as embodying the so-called Fourth Estate and explored the notion that the philosophical ideas which emerged in response to specific historical circumstances over time contributed to the development of principles which have come to connect freedom of speech and eventually freedom of the press, with democracy – the democratic imperative of journalism. Anderson and Ward (2007: 39) suggest that debates about role of the news media in democratic societies tend to 'vary between two extremes'. This polemic is essentially animated by those who see the liberal news media as performing their democratic function in that they are supplying their audiences with what they want, and those who see commercial considerations effectively undermining the public sphere to such a degree that democracy becomes contorted and degraded. In other words on one side of the debate is the argument that the commercially driven media adequately services the democratic imperative and allows a plurality of voices and opinions. The commercial imperative of the market 'makes the press a representative institution' (Curran and Seaton 2010: 326). On the other side of the debate the argument tends to focus on the media's role in 'dumbing down' political debate and 'sensationalising' politics with its emphasis on 'hyperadversarialism' and personalisation (see McNair 2000: 1–13).

Of course journalism exists and has existed in a variety of forms as both a reflection and reinforcing element of culture and identity (Carey 1989; Anderson 1991), as entertainment (Conboy 2002), as a weapon of defiance and critique (Atton 2002), as well as a means for making all money (Greenslade 2004), yet of course the dominant liberal view of journalism sees its prime role in safeguarding democracy. In order to do this journalism must be unfettered, as far as is possible, from government control. Of course there are numerous examples of journalism serving the interests of democracy and acting as a 'Fourth Estate' against political corruption and misdeed. Woodward and Bernstein's exposure of the Watergate tapes for the *Washington Post* in the 1970s is probably the most famous of all the examples of investigative journalism exposing government corruption. Before Watergate the publication of the 'Pentagon Papers', initially by the *New York Times*, brought to light classified details and top secret information about the conduct of the Vietnam War (Bollinger and Stone 2002). More recently in the U.K. MPs' abuse of their expenses allowances was exposed by the newspaper press and became a key issue of the 2010 general election.[1] Indeed there is a long history of investigative journalism, which demonstrates the power of quality journalism in exposing the corruption and abuse of power (de Burgh 2008; Pilger 2001). However, though one of the key functions of journalism has been to safeguard against abuses of power and wrongdoing, it is a matter of debate whether or not journalism adequately functions in this capacity on a consistent basis. The purpose of this chapter then is to explore the issue of 'freedom of the press' specifically with regard to its relationship to democracy and examine some of the factors which impact on journalism's capacity to fulfil its democratic obligations.

The first part of the chapter will explore the relationship between journalism and democracy by analysing the role of the media. Here the deliberative model of democracy is fore-grounded as I suggest that it is such a model which most closely relates to the effective functioning of news journalism in democratic societies. The role of commercial speech and advertising in particular is central to this discussion as I examine how and why commercial speech in the United States came to receive almost as much protection under the First Amendment as individuals. Though this argument is built on in later chapters with regard to media regulation in Britain it is necessary here to closely examine the relationship between First Amendment protection for commercial speech as it offers an insight into the way in which, primarily via advertising, commercial imperatives of commercial enterprises became protected within the sphere of constitutional democratic rights in the United States. The second part of the chapter moves on to explore political communications and looks at changes which have occurred in the communication of politics which have led some commentators to argue that democracy is being fundamentally compromised. Finally, I point to the relatively recent observations from a prominent philosopher that address the very foundations of the relationship between news media and democratic societies.

Theorising journalism and democracy

Democracy of course comes in various shapes and sizes (see Held 2006). Anderson and Ward (2007: 47) draw on Stromback (2005) and identify four main types of democracy: procedural, competitive, participatory and deliberative. Each model has its own emphasis and with its own distinctive relationship with journalism and the media. Given that there are so many different types and approaches to democracy and therefore different ways in which the media engage with democracy, before we venture further it is worth briefly looking at ways in which media systems and their relationship with democracy have been theorised. In their book *Comparing Media Systems* (2004) Hallin and Mancini have suggested that the most useful way of analysing the relationship between the news media and democratic political systems is to separate them into three separate groups or models which reflect their particular cultural and historical characteristics. These are the Mediterranean or Polarised Model, The North/Central European or Democratic Corporatist Model and the North Atlantic or Liberal Model. They suggests that the distinctive historical and cultural development of journalism and democracy can be largely incorporated into these models and used to understand their different functions and their different relationships more accurately. For example, Hallin and Mancini suggest that in the Mediterranean model 'liberal institutions, including both capitalist industrialism and political democracy, developed later' (2004: 89) and as such have cultivated a different set of political orientations and structures as well as distinctive relationships with the media. Similarly the Democratic Corporatist model, which encompasses states such as Germany, Austria and Switzerland with their similar historical, religious and cultural histories, 'played a particularly important role in creating a common culture and common public sphere in Northern and Central Europe' (2004: 143). Finally the authors point to the model that will be most familiar to readers of this book – the North Atlantic Liberal Model – which stresses the distinctive historical development of democratic institutions alongside the emergence of the news media. Though stressing obvious historical, cultural and social differences within the countries mentioned,[2] the authors emphasise the role that political parallelism has played in the development and continuing operation of the system. Political parallelism can be described briefly as the level in which the news media is neutral from political institutions. For example, in Britain, where the press is politically partisan (press-party parallelism), the levels of political parallelism is said to be higher than say in Canada or Ireland. As Hallin and Mancini suggest, weak levels of political parallelism correspond to higher levels of journalistic neutrality and presumably a stronger fourth estate role for the news media. This, of course, is significant when we examine the role of the press in Britain in offering support for political parties, as we shall see below.

In terms of the different approaches to democracy, it is clear that contemporary democratic theory, as Carter and Stokes (2002) suggest, faces a range of challenges, from issues of group rights, multiculturalism and identity politics and their associated rights (Kane 2002), to gender and citizenship (Frazer 2002) and the challenges of nationalism (Canovan 2002). In response to such challenges, the authors have pinpointed a number of directions for democracy which could go some way in addressing the problems we potentially face. Such solutions include associative democracy (Carter 2002), transnational democracy (McGrew 2002) and social democracy (Plant 2002). However, with regard to the role of news media in complementing liberal democratic institutions, Warren (2002: 196) argues that deliberative democracy offers a 'commitment to the notion that political decisions are better made through deliberation than money and power'. He suggests that deliberative democracy relates explicitly to already existing democratic and media institutions; arguing that 'democratic institutions serve not only to distribute power in the form of votes, but also to secure the connection between the power to make decisions and equal participation in collective judgement' (see also Gastil 2008). In other words deliberation is as important as voting in democratic societies and it is in respect of journalism's role in cultivating this deliberative ethos that we now turn.

Journalism and deliberation

As we have seen in principle, the press functions to provide both the means by which civic engagement can occur through its capacity of sufficiently informing the public about matters of social and public importance, and also providing, though not exclusively, the spaces in which public debate can occur. Yet the news media's capacity and obligation to provide an arena for civic debate is not uncontested. During the 1920s in the United States a debate emerged which centred on the role and function of the press and its capacity to inform and cultivate civic debate. Walter Lippmann's studies of the American public (1955 [1922]; 1925) led him to conclude that for the most part, the realms of politics and the deliberations of public life were too complicated for the average American to comprehend. Complex arguments and debates about law, policy and regulation should not be the concern of everyday citizens as modern life already confronted Americans with too much information for them to make adequate sense of politics. Moreover, as a forum for debate and deliberation, the media is ill disposed to adequately provide for the airing of all opposing ideas and arguments as 'the men who regularly broadcast the news and comment on the news cannot – like the speaker in the Senate or in the House of Commons – be challenged by one of their listeners' (Lippmann 1955: 129). In other words the media simply cannot provide a genuine open arena of debate. Journalism therefore has to re-evaluate its role and rather than seeking to provide a forum for the exchange of ideas, it should 'translate the technical deliberations and actions of political leaders and experts into a publicly accessible language to inform, as best as possible, a citizenry incapable of governing itself' (Haas 2007: 7).

In *The Public Philosophy* (1955: 14) Lippmann asserts that given the twentieth century's turbulent history of war and international turmoil, it is clear that modern democracy has not lived up to its expectations and that 'people have acquired power which they are incapable of exercising, and the governments they elect have lost powers which they must recover if they are to govern'. In other words according to Lippmann, the original principles of democracy have been withered away because people have lost sight of their essence and vitality. For Lippmann liberal democracy 'cannot be made to work except by men who possess the philosophy in which liberal democracy was conceived and founded' (1955: 160–61). Lippmann's misanthropy and paternalism reflects an almost Platonic disregard for the capacity of the public to engage in civic debate. Clearly Lippmann expresses an unabashed contempt for the masses.

Lippmann's pessimism about the capacity of 'ordinary folk' to engage with politics much beyond the casting their vote, is contrasted with that of John Dewey. Though Dewey was concerned about public engagement in political discussion, he was less pessimistic than Lippmann about the public's capacity to engage in debate and democratic deliberation. For Dewey, rather than merely simplifying political information, it was the role of journalism to fuel political debate and engagement. As Haas (2007: 8) has pointed out, so influential were Dewey's concerns about the role that the media should play in American democracy, they were absorbed into the 1947 Hutchins Commission Report on Freedom of the Press which was set up to look into the democratic functioning of the press and which noted that journalism should

> (1) provide a truthful, comprehensive and intelligent account of the day's events in a context which gives them meaning; (2) serve as a forum for the exchange of comment and criticism; (3) project a representative picture of the constituent groups in society; (4) be responsible for the presentation and clarification of the goals and values of society; and (5) provide full access to the day's intelligence.
>
> *Hutchins Commission cited in Haas (2007: 8)*

This deliberative function of journalism and the news media is as far from Lippmann's prescription as could be.[3] Journalism and the news media more generally should facilitate open and informed discussion in matters of public concern. According to Sunstein (1993) such a notion emerges from what he terms a 'Madisonian' conception of free speech which links the process of public deliberation with properly functioning democracy. This 'Madisonian'[4] conception of free speech explicitly links the notion of freedom of speech to the proper workings of a 'particular conception of democracy' (xvii). Here then is the deliberative function of free speech in which 'the people' have the capacity to openly discuss and debate matters of public importance. In this sense discussion should not be 'abridged' as this would undermine the very foundations of the democratic system. Free Speech here is the cornerstone of democratic government. Sunstein's main argument is that the Madisonian conception of free speech has been largely forgotten and replaced by a conception of freedom of speech based on the 'marketplace of ideas' which underscores particular economically orientated justifications for media freedom. He argues that this conception of freedom of speech is one that prioritises commercial speech and as such can actually undermine the deliberative dynamic of freedom of speech. He notes that the marketplace model in which commercial speech is protected under the First Amendment is something that is a relatively recent phenomenon and emerged during the 1980s. Before then the conventional view was that the media had an obligation to encourage debate and discussion as a requirement of a properly functioning democracy. The Federal Communications Commission stated in 1949 that 'the development of an informed public opinion through the dissemination of news and ideas concerning the vital public issues of the day' was one of the main functions of broadcasting (Sunstein 1993: 4). Yet 'for the most part, the system of free expression in America is now approaching a system of unregulated private markets' (1993: 17).

The view is that as with economic markets, they function best when left alone by the state. Through the 'invisible hand'[5] the market regulates itself and this is how it should be. Sunstein, however, rightly asks the question of whether 'unregulated markets actually promote a well-functioning system of free expression' (1993: 18). Following the Madisonian conception, Sunstein argues:

> Politics is not supposed merely to protect pre-existing private rights or to reflect the outcomes of interest group pressures. It is not intended to aggregate existing private preferences, or to produce compromises among various affected groups with self-interested states in the outcome. Instead it is designed to have an important deliberative feature, in which new information and perspectives influence social judgements about possible courses of action. Through exposure to such information and perspectives, both collective and individual decisions can be shaped and improved
>
> *Sunstein (1993: 18–19).*

As noted Sunstein is suggesting that the modern application of First Amendment law has shifted unhelpfully in favour of protecting the commercial interests of news organisations and media corporations. An important question therefore is why and how has this occurred? In order to answer this question it is necessary to examine more closely the relationship between First Amendment law and commercial speech.

Commercial speech and free speech

As we have seen there is a significant difference between freedom of speech for media institutions and freedom of speech for individuals, yet because freedom of the press and freedom of speech are so often conflated, any perceived attack on press freedom is seen as an attack on freedom of speech and expression more generally (see Chapter 9). In short free speech and freedom of the press become blurred and this ethical and constitutional grey area has allowed commercial organisations to exploit free speech rights to their full advantage, particularly in the United States. Freedom of speech for individuals and for media organisations is protected by the First Amendment; this, however, has not always been the case and it is only relatively recently that corporate bodies' rights to freedom of speech and freedom of expression have been given such protection.[6] Such protection is, of course, most significant in the area of advertising.

Commercial speech and advertising

As one might expect there are restrictions on commercial speech which prohibit false advertising or other deceptive business practices (Zelezny 2010: 524) with advertising overseen by the Federal Trade Commission (FTC) as well as state level advertising regulators (Belmas and Overbeck 2011: 549). This noted that commercial speech in the U.S. did not receive any special protection from government until 1975. Until that time commercial speech was not generally thought to be worthy of special protection in the same way as political speech given that commercial speech did not have the same social and political status as political speech or other forms of expression. However, in 1975 the case of *Bigelow v Virginia* seemed to shift the emphasis in favour of allowing protection for some forms of commercial speech, especially if such expression was thought to have a wider social value. *Bigelow v Virginia* centred on the rights of an abortion referral service to place an advert in the *Virginia Weekly* newspaper. The managing editor of the newspaper was originally convicted for promoting abortion which was illegal under Virginia law; however, the conviction was overturned as it was considered that it was not legitimate for the state of Virginia to ban information about lawful services in the state of New York. Banning the advertisement was deemed in contravention of First Amendment law which asserts the rights of newspaper readers to receive information about abortions which were legally available in other states. It was considered therefore that there was a wider social interest in allowing such services to be advertised in the press and as such the advertisement was perceived to function beyond mere commercial interests.

A similar case was heard the following year in which Virginia Supreme Court's prohibition of the publication of pricing for pharmaceutical drugs was deemed unconstitutional and ran counter to the First Amendment protection of free speech. It was successfully argued that the First Amendment protected givers *and* receivers of information, in this case about pricing policy of pharmaceutical drugs. In other words the court viewed such speech as having a public health value and therefore should be protected within the 'marketplace of ideas'. The issue here seemed to be some confusion about just what exactly constituted commercial speech, a question which continues to be a very difficult question for First Amendment scholars. The judge in *Virginia State Board of Pharmacy v Virginia Citizens Consumer Council Inc.* Justice Blackmun 'asserted that the very obscurity of the category of commercial speech meant that it could not entirely be without First Amendment protection' (Post 2000: 7). Moreover, the judge argued that it was in the public interest for consumers to have information at their disposal that would enable them to make informed decisions about products in the market. This allusion again to the marketplace signifies a slight shift in emphasis towards the notion that the market itself has some preordained moral value and that to deny people the ability to choose in the open market was deemed unconstitutional.

Another landmark case, which aided the development of First Amendment protection of advertising and commercial speech, was the case of *Central Hudson Gas and Electric v Public Service Commission of New York* (447 U.S. 557). The case centred on the New York Service Commission's attempt to prevent the advertising of utilities which it argued went too far in promoting the consumption of resources given the environmental cost. Originally the New York Court of Appeals upheld the ban citing conservation and energy preservation as taking precedence over free speech. However, the U.S. Supreme Court overturned the decision noting that such a ban on advertising would have only a minimal impact on energy consumption and Central Hudson Gas and Electric should not have their First Amendment rights violated in this instance (Belmas and Overbeck 2011: 554). More significantly, however, the *Central Hudson* case set out the criteria which the courts could use to evaluate any future government attempt to restrict advertising:

1. whether the expression is *protected by the First Amendment* (if it involves deception or unlawful activities, it is not protected by the First Amendment and may be banned without considering this text);
2. whether the claimed *governmental interest that justifies the restrictions is substantial*;
3. whether the regulation *directly advances the governmental interest* in question; and
4. whether the regulation is *more broad than needed* to fulfil the governmental interest.

Belmas and Overbeck (2011: 554) emphasis original

Belmas and Overbeck note that the *Central Hudson* test 'has been cited in hundreds of cases since it was handed down in 1980 […] as both state and federal courts have had to rule on a variety of government restrictions on advertising' (2011: 544).

Finally in the 1990s the United State Supreme Court, in the case of *Liquormart v Rhode Island* (517 U.S. 484), 'reaffirmed the First Amendment protection of commercial speech [as it] handed down a decision on liquor price advertising that was so broad it appeared to give commercial speech almost the same First Amendment protection as noncommercial speech' (Belmas and Overbeck 2011: 549). The Court argued that 'a state legislature does not have the broad discretion to suppress truthful, nonmisleading information for paternalistic purposes' (*Liquormart v Rhode Island* 517 U.S. 484: 510).

Though the relationship between advertising and the First Amendment is highly complex and not without significant points of contention, it should be clear that there has been a shift over the last thirty five years from a situation where advertising received no special protection to one where it receives almost as much protection as individual expression. There are a number of perspectives as to why such a shift has occurred. On the one hand it could be argued that commercial speech and advertising is an important component of civil life and to deny or restrict access to the consumer would therefore undermine individuals' rights to choose and have access to the range of choices available in the market. Post suggests that such protection underpins the idea 'that citizens may acquire information from commercial speech that is highly relevant to the formation of democratic public opinion' (2000: 11). As such from this perspective it is the right of receivers to have access to information which seems to have been the driving force in the development of how commercial speech came to be taken much more seriously in First Amendment jurisprudence as it is considered an important aspect of their rights as citizens to be in possession of as much information about goods and services as possible.

However, more critically and in line with Sunstein's comments above, some commentators argue that commercial speech has come to be protected by the First Amendment because of the increasing centrality of the free market ethos (especially since the 1980s) in all aspects of American life. Such values, which are of course tied to individual notions of entrepreneurship and property rights, resonate through American culture and history and this cultural mythology has empowered corporations and commercial bodies to appropriate the language of free speech for their own commercial gain. As John Keane has noted:

> The marketeers' case for the rights of corporate speech resonates in a culture which remains under the spell of early modern individualism, of the kind which fuelled arguments for 'liberty of the press'. [...] It is ironic that this prejudice has strengthened the constitutional hand of large corporations, who have taken advantage of the First Amendment, which turns a blind eye to corporate power by prohibiting only federal and state governments from abridging free speech.
>
> *Keane (1991: 83–84)*

This analysis therefore suggests that it is the democratic right to freedom of speech for individuals which has been appropriated by corporate interests for commercial gain. Moreover, contrary to Post's observations regarding consumer choice 'advertising encourages a general shift away from diversity of coverage towards the packaging of "product lines" into "light entertainment" [...] Advertising commercializes the structure and content of programmes' and 'privileges corporate speech' (Keane 1991: 81–83). In other words it acts against diversity rather than stimulating it. One might conclude therefore that such a shift has led to the deliberative component of democracy being significantly undermined.

In the news media this is because in the drive for competitive advantage, news media organisations tend to focus on scandal and gossip regarding the rich and famous. Celebrity culture drives much public debate. In politics and public affairs coverage is often sensationalised and trivialised thereby demeaning any meaningful political or civic engagement in politics and public life. Again Sunstein suggests that 'if we give broadcasters unrestricted property rights and then immunize them from government control, we may compromise both quality and diversity in broadcasting' (1993: 53). In other words it could ironically be that it is the First Amendment, because of its relatively recent shift in emphasis towards the protection of commercial interests, which actively undermines the mechanisms for deliberative democracy.

In contrast to Anderson and Ward's suggestion that the deliberative model is 'a little too far into the theoretical world and away from the reality of everyday life to be considered as a practical alternative' (2007: 47), I contend that the deliberative ideal is something that should be central to debates about freedom of speech and freedom of the press and to give up on it is to provide tacit support for Lippmann's degraded view of so-called 'common people'. Yet what of the political institutions themselves? Do they not bear some responsibility for stimulating public debate and discussion of politics? In exploring these questions it is necessary for me to now turn my attention to the communication of politics.

Political communication and the democratic deficit

In recent years there has been increased focus on the processes and practices used by government and political parties and institutions to communicate to the wider public. Though not an especially new field of inquiry, historic and structural changes to the ways in which governments, parties and political institutions utilise the media, has led to closer attention on the processes, practices and relationships between political actors and institutions and their communicative practices. Negrine (2008) has suggested that there has been a significant transformation in the field of political communication which in part has come about through increasing professionalisation of the practices and processes of communicating politics. In other words 'professionalization suggests an ongoing process where structures and practices are continually revised and updated in order to make them more "rational" and more "appropriate" for the conduct of politics at any particular point in time' (Negrine 2008: 2) As Sanders (2009) notes, there are a number of definitions 'political communication' (see Chaffee 1975; Blumler and Gurevitch 1995; McNair 2007) though for the purposes of this book, I see no reason to depart from her relatively straightforward definition of Political Communication as a field of study that 'is concerned with communication and its role in political processes, systems and institutions' (Sanders 2009: 19).[7]

Losing the faith

Recent years have witnessed growing disenchantment with party politics with voter turn out in the 2001 U.K. general election being the lowest since 1918 at 59.4 per cent. Despite a gradual increase in turn out in 2005 and 2010,[8] deceit over the Iraq War, government mismanagement and complicity in the economic decline, along with an almost endless list of transgressions in the so-called expenses scandal, there remains widespread disillusionment of traditional politics among the public.[9] As Couldry et al (2007: 179) notes 'this is an age of declining participation in the electoral process and declining institutional legitimacy'. Not only, it seems, do we have little faith in our politicians, but also we seem to hold long-established political institutions in contempt. In short for many people politics seems to be primarily inhabited by self-serving individuals who have little interest in serving the public. As Colin Hay suggests, for the vast majority of the public, '[p]olitics' is a dirty word, a term that has come to acquire a whole array of almost entirely negative associations and connotations in contemporary discourse. Politics is synonymous with sleaze, corruption and duplicity, greed, self-interest and self-importance, interference, inefficiency and intransigence. It is, at best, a necessary evil, at worst an entirely malevolent force that needs to be kept in check.

Hay (2007: 153)

Much of the blame for this general level of public disenchantment with politics has been attributed to the transformation of political communications over the past thirty years. No longer do we have journalism having opposing agendas to those of politicians – the classic conflict model – but we see the two sides operating in mutually beneficial or even collusive ways (Blumler and Gurevitch 1981). In this sense journalism is not perceived as something which exists outside the political context in order to provide scrutiny and ensuring accountability, rather it operates too closely with political actors in ways which undermine journalism fourth estate role. Peter Oborne (1999, 2007) has suggested that in Britain in recent years we have seen the emergence of a distinctive class of actors whose appearance has signalled a break from the established relationships between journalists and politicians. Not only is this something that damages the integrity of journalism but also the proper functioning of Parliamentary democracy itself.

Manipulation of political debate

First, in his study of the rise of New Labour and its chief of communications Alastair Campbell, Oborne notes the rise of what he terms 'the Media Class' which he suggests differed significantly from journalists a generation before which had an essentially deferential attitude towards politicians and the House of Commons. Though this deference started to wane in the 1960s it was not until the 1980s that it 'emerged as a fully fledged force on the national stage' (Oborne 1999: 117). Now journalists in Westminster had less deference and more power. Moreover,

> [t]he Media Class became an elite at Westminster. It suddenly became the case that journalists, now for the most part graduates, were cleverer, more self assured, far better paid and very much more influential than most of the people they were writing about. The brightest and the best were going into the media, by contrast it seemed the dunderheads who went into politics.
>
> *Oborne (1999: 118)*

We see therefore that the media itself and political journalism in particular has assumed a more dominant role in the communication of politics and reporting the affairs of government. Oborne suggests that traditional forms of reporting politics by the gallery reporters who reported almost verbatim the debates within the Chamber became a thing of the past. Now political correspondents and sketch writers don't bother with verbatim accounts but provide coverage which is polemical and sharp

(Oborne 1999: 118). Such coverage has both empowered and emboldened journalists to the degree that some of them have become media personalities in their own right. Oborne argues that the Media Class also had a new set of values which would determine how they would write about politics: '[T]hey would prefer the short-term to the long-term, sentimentality to compassion, simplicity to complexity, the dramatic to the mundane, confrontation to the sensible compromise' (1999: 119). According to Oborne such a simplification of politics benefitted the architects of New Labour as they sought to reinvent and rebrand their party after disastrous electoral defeats in 1979, 1983, 1987 and 1992. As such, however, it is important to note that the changes were not just occurring within journalism. The way in which politicians related to the media and to journalists was also starting to change. Politicians knew that a much more proactive and at times assertive relationship with journalists, editors and of course newspaper proprietors would be beneficial to their success. Though New Labour came to be seen as the party of spin and media manipulation, the changes in political communications during the Thatcher era under Bernard Ingham (Franklin 2004: 39) and developments in political communications further afield (Negrine and Papathanassopoulos 1996) should also be seen as contributing to this change in relations and change in the balance of power between journalists and politicians.

However, the most significant revolution in government communications emerged after the election of the New Labour government under Tony Blair in 1997. In its years in opposition the Labour Party suffered a battering by the largely Conservative supporting press. The Labour leader from 1980 to 1983 Michael Foot received a particularly hard time from the press. Whether it was in respect of his personal attire and appearance, his left wing politics or even that he was somehow a KGB 'agent of influence' (Cohen 2003: 140), he was vilified particularly by the Murdoch press (Greenslade 2004: 452). Similarly his replacement Neil Kinnock suffered at the hands of the right-wing press with the *Sun* famously proclaiming of the 1992 general election result 'IT'S THE SUN WOT WON IT' for the Conservatives (Greenslade 2004: 606–21).[10] Following the resignation of Kinnock after the election and the death of leader John Smith in 1994, the architects of 'New Labour' Peter Mandleson, Tony Blair, Gordon Brown, Phillip Gould and Alastair Campbell (Oborne and Walters 2004) sought to transform the way in which the party would be portrayed in the press. Given the hostile treatment the party had received from a largely Conservative supporting press, a new approach to managing the media was perceived to be an essential to the reinvigoration of Labour's electoral chances (Gaber 2004). One of the key factors in this would be to secure the support of Rupert Murdoch who's *Sun* had been so vitriolic towards previous Labour leaders. Oborne and Walters (2004: 129) note that it was both Alastair Campbell and Tony Blair's belief that securing the support of the *Sun* 'was a necessary, and possibly sufficient, condition of Labour victory at the general election' and secure his support they did. Following a meeting with Murdoch at the Australian resort of Hayman Island which would reassure Murdoch that New Labour would be 'submissive' to News International (Cohen 2003: 146) the Murdoch press warmed to Blair's New Labour who subsequently won the 1997 election by a landslide.

Once New Labour was in government it set about changing the structures and procedures of government communication which acted to further centralise power in No.10 and court its new friends in the press (Franklin 2001; Franklin 2004). As Raymond Khun (2007: 187) has noted 'ministers and their special advisers were constantly engaged in seeking to harness the media in the task of promoting the government's achievements to the electorate through positive imagery generation and symbolic management'. Osborne suggests that the Blairite machine was particularly adept at 'client journalism' in which 'deceit, bullying, favouritism' were key instruments alongside 'the ruthless exchange of privileged information in return for the support of key newspapers' (Osborne 2007). Charges of spin and 'control freakery' (Jones 2004) reached their height following the Blair government's decision to follow George W. Bush's lead in the search for Weapons of Mass Destruction (WMDs) in Iraq in 2003 in what has now become a well-documented episode in the history of Tony Blair's premiership.

Though there is no doubt that New Labour took the dark arts of spin to new heights, it would be mistaken to blame the orchestrators of the New Labour project for the appearance of spin in the first place. As Karen Sanders (2009: 29) has noted, the 'dark arts' of spin have been around 'for as long as there have been humans interested in exercising social influence'. Though as she suggests, spin came to prominence during the presidential election campaign of Bill Clinton in 1992, Sanders maintains that:

> Spin doctoring is the anti-thesis of letting the facts speak for themselves. It aims to manage and shape impressions and perceptions in a way most favourable to the communicators cause. The professionalism and perceived effectiveness of communication experts [...] raised questions about the integrity of political communication and the consequences for public discourse and democracy.
>
> *Sanders (2009: 30)*

Moreover, an increasing reliance on Public Relations (see Davis 2002; Davis 2007; Davies 2008; Lees-Marshment 2004) and the professionalisation of political communication seems to have led to greater levels of public mistrust in politicians and political institutions. However, some commentators have argued that the media too has to take much more responsibility for public mistrust in politicians and disengagement from politics. For example, John Lloyd (2004) has suggested that the media themselves should take some of the blame for increased public dislocation from politics. Contrary to Osborne's Media and Political Class thesis, Lloyd argues that the honourable journalistic trait of scrutinising politicians has gone too far and the relationship between politicians and the news media has gone beyond healthy adversarial engagement and turned into an almost cynical lust for political blood on the part of the journalists. For Lloyd this is problematic on a number of levels as it not only encourages much greater scepticism of politicians among the public, it also undermines important journalistic practices that are essential for accurate and objective reporting, the fall out from the Gilligan affair being a case in point. Similarly, Russell has recently suggested that the news media are increasingly too quick to judge and castigate MPs who step out of line

On the main news and current affairs programmes, thoughtful probing and questioning have increasingly been replaced by a tendency to harangue every interviewee as if they are already guilty of errors of judgment and deserve to be caught out. Interviewers are hunting for weakness, or contradictions, rather than illumination. It is an easy position to adopt. It makes for entertaining, gladiatorial radio or TV, and it produces headlines for programmes. But its wholesale application has become an utterly destructive part of our collective life.

Russell (2010)

Yet is it accurate to blame the media for civil disengagement in politics? As Norris (2000: 17) has pointed out, much of the work within political communications that suggests widespread malaise and civic disengagement in politics rests largely on 'assumptions about the audience' and how they make sense of the messages. Yet she goes on to examine 'extensive evidence' which points to opposite trends in which 'use of the news media is positively associated with a wide range of indicators of political knowledge, trust, and mobilization' (2000: 17). Moreover, as McNair (2000: 39) suggests with regard to Britain 'the political public sphere [...] is larger, denser, and accessible to more people than at any point in Britain's cultural history, and it continues to expand'. However, more information does not automatically mean more open and accountable political institutions as we shall see.

A 'crisis of trust'?

In her 2002 Reith Lectures philosopher Onora O'Neil examines what she terms the 'crisis of trust' which is seemingly apparent in many Western democracies and in Britain in particular. O'Neill initiates her discussion by drawing attention to the reported decline of public trust in traditional institutions – the police and legal profession, medicine and healthcare and of course politics. Yet, O'Neill contrasts this reported crisis in trust with the fact that actions speak louder than words. In practice trust is something we demonstrate on a daily basis as we go about our lives and in our dealings with others. Moreover, 'the evidence suggests that we still constantly place trust in many of the institutions and professions that we profess not to trust' (O'Neill 2002).[11] She goes on to note that though there may be questionable evidence for a crisis of trust, there is significant evidence for a 'culture of suspicion', which ostensibly emerges from an overreliance on audit trails and a broader culture of accountability which has become increasingly fashionable in Britain. O'Neill argues that such a culture leads to defence strategies within the professions which may in fact obscure rather then enlighten. More significantly she argues that such a culture has failed to make inroads into public lack of trust of institutions. Rather than trust being enhanced, it seems that the culture of accountability has eroded levels of trust and generated fear and suspicion of professionals and professional bodies.

Importantly O'Neill is not calling for the end of accountability, rather an end to the current vogue in accountability methodology which sets targets from above and enforces them arbitrarily. What is required is a form of 'intelligent accountability' which depends on some measure of 'self-governance within a framework of financial or other reporting'. O'Neill adroitly links this culture of accountability to the abundance of information at our disposal which, it seems, allows public bodies and institutions to be held fully accountable and open to public scrutiny; if anything she suggests, trust should be attainable in such a culture, yet of course it seems even further away. She notes 'this high enthusiasm for even more complete openness and transparency has done little to build or restore public trust. On the contrary, trust seemingly has receded as transparency has advanced'; moreover, 'transparency can produce a flood of unsorted information and misinformation that provides little but confusion unless it can be sorted and assessed [...] the very prospect of a "free and open encounter" is drowning in the supposedly transparent world of the new information order' (2002). Yet of course the majority don't have the resources to manage the information overload and separate fact from fiction, speculation from analysis and we depend on journalism to provide a truthful and accurate picture of the world which then allows us to make informed decisions about how we live our lives. In other words we need journalism to provide us with the resources with which we can give our informed consent. In addressing the crisis of trust O'Neill asserts that what is needed is a 'more robust public culture in which publishing misinformation and disinformation, writing in ways that others cannot hope to check, is limited and penalised'. This is not an attack on freedom of the press, if anything she argues 'freedom of the press can and should be an accountable press'. Freedom of speech and expression for individuals does not amount to freedom of the press. Institutions should not have the same rights as individuals. Freedom of the press should mean the freedom to uncover truth and challenge accepted norms in the Millian sense, not to spread misinformation, half-truths, deception and lies. This can only lead to an absence of trust and therefore ultimately be damaging for democracy and civil society. The absence of trust in the press and in the politicians they report on undermines the very notion of informed consent which is the cornerstone of democracy. Rights come with responsibilities and such responsibilities and obligations are all too easily ignored by the press.

> A free press is not an unconditional good. It is good because and insofar as it helps the public to explore and test opinions and to judge for themselves whom and what to believe. If powerful institutions are allowed to publish, circulate and promote material without indicating what is known and what is rumour; what is derived from a reputable source and what is invented, what is standard analysis and what is speculation; which sources may be knowledgeable and which are probably not, they damage our public culture and all our lives.
>
> O'Neill (2002)

Conclusion

It has been the purpose of this chapter to move beyond the theoretical and historical discussions of Chapters 1 and 2 and further examine the relationship between journalism, freedom of speech, freedom of the press and democracy. Of principle concern has been to highlight the relationship between journalism and democracy and emphasise a number of ways in which this relationship has been conceived. We see that there are good historical and practical reasons for journalism and democracy to be self-reinforcing; moreover, recent technological innovations have meant that journalism is arguably in a far better position than it has ever been to function according to its democratic imperative. However, this will be all the more difficult as long as the tension between the liberal (market) dynamics of the media and their democratic obligations remain. Given their specific historical development, the commercial imperatives of news media organisations necessarily have a tendency to undermine a genuinely democratic and deliberative public sphere. Journalism for the most part is too bound to the commercial imperatives of the market to fully provide a genuine public sphere in which deliberation and debate, free from the constraints of the market can occur. Freedom of the press is central to the proper functioning of democracy, yet the commercial dynamic tends to be underplayed, largely at the expense of democracy itself. So what of the future? The picture painted here looks like a very pessimistic evaluation of the state of journalism and its relationship with democracy. One of the ways in which some commentators have seen a way over-come some of the constraints highlighted above is by looking at the development of the global and local public sphere which is re-invigorated by new media and a new emphasis within journalism. It is to these debates we now turn.

4

JOURNALISM, NEW MEDIA AND THE GLOBAL PUBLIC SPHERE

> Now in our age we are all disillusioned with politics and this machine organising
> principle has risen up to become the ideology of our age. But what we are discovering
> is if we see ourselves as components in the system, it is very difficult to change the
> world. It is very good way of organising things, even rebellions, but it offers no ideas
> about what comes next [and] leaves us helpless in the face of those already in power in
> the world.
>
> Curtis (2011)

Introduction

Discussing the contemporary technological media environment with my students
I am always struck by the relative nonchalance with which they talk about so-called
'new media'. To them it is not new, digital technologies have been around since
before most of them were born. Rather, the technologies they surround themselves
with – mobile phones, notebooks and tablet computers – are ever evolving. For
them, it's not new media, it is just a technological tweak from what they had before:
a smarter phone, a quicker laptop. Nor is it anything to be marvelled at, it fits so well into
their lifestyle and their work almost as if it was an extension of themselves as individuals and as students of journalism. Moreover, the technologies connect them into a
network which can be used for communication and information. For some of course
such technologies can be used to liberate or at least challenge prevailing power.
However, as the quote from Adam Curtis above suggests, we should be wary of
investing too much power in the technology itself. This 'machine organising principle' to which Curtis refers is, of course, the notion of the networked society to which
we are all infinitely connected. Curtis sounds a warning, however, that we should
not invest too much in the power of technology to liberate us, as this comes at the

expense of developing new ideas about how to change society. This chapter examines some of the debates about journalism and technology with particular reference to the conception of the global public sphere as much is often made of technology's power of reinvigorating the public sphere and shaping new political contexts. We will begin by exploring the conception of globalisation and how some authors view new information and communication technologies as both drivers of globalisation and as saviours of a degraded public discursive space. Following this we move on to discuss new media and journalism in more detail and analyse the ways in which some authors have argued that such technology radically alters journalism in practice and in nature. Here we will examine the WikiLeaks phenomenon, the debate about which is still raging as I write. The chapter then looks critically at some of the more optimistic claims of those who cite new media technologies as the key drivers of a reinvigorated public sphere. Here I explore what Morozov (2011) terms the dark side of internet freedom where repressive and even democratic states use internet technology in particular to monitor its citizens and crack down on dissent. Finally, I assess whether or not the much-lauded democratising power of the internet and journalism's utilisation of the internet for democratic purposes is yet to be fully realised. Even in an era where a leaked cable on WikiLeaks can cause red faces in the corridors of power it is suggested that we should view the relationship between new media and the new context of journalism far more critically.

Globalisation and the reinvigoration of the public sphere

Globalisation is not an easy term to get to grips with as there are some significant disagreements among scholars as to what it means and indeed when (and if) it first emerged as a process. Thankfully for us, it is far beyond the scope of this book to venture in to this territory too far, suffice it to say that some scholars have placed the birth of globalisation as far back as the sixteenth century (Wallerstein 1999), others see its emergence during the later twentieth century (Held *at al* 2005; Held and McGrew 2003) while some question the usefulness of the term altogether (Rosenberg 2000; Hafez 2007). Within the social sciences the phrase 'globalisation' can be traced to the debates in the 1950s and 1960s concerning the ending of the industrial age and the start of the new information age (see Webster 2002). It was during the 1980s and 1990s, however, that the phrase entered common discourse as rapid developments in information and communication technologies took place. In raw descriptive terms, globalisation might be described as the process which drives capitalist production and consumption across national boundaries and which is unhindered by factors such as location or geographical distance. Bluntly, in the economic realm, globalisation can be seen as a term which denotes the concentration *and* expansion of financial and productive markets on a global, rather than local or national scale as well as the interconnectedness of these markets. Some of the most obvious things that animate globalisation, the things that make it apparent to us that we live in a world in which globalisation is evident, are the ways in which societies have become increasingly interconnected – not just physically with advances in communication and information technologies (though of course this crucial) but materially and culturally as well.

Globalisation is also said to be apparent in relation to the increasingly diluted power of nation states, particularly in relation to economic and foreign policy. Institutions such as the United Nations, the International Monetary Fund and the World Bank assume an overarching position over nation states to such a degree that they can sanction states if they fail to comply with their resolutions and terms and conditions. Corporations too operate globally with media companies having particular global resonance which can also exert forms of pressure on the legal and political frameworks of traditional nation states (Hertz 2001). Such global corporations can also impact on cultural life as brands and the promotion of certain lifestyles associated with particular brands permeate national boundaries and diverse cultures. Sport, cinema, music and other cultural and artistic endeavours are no longer constrained by national borders. With the help of global corporations and a global media infrastructure almost anyone can enjoy a Bollywood film or a U2 video. Very generally then, as Webster suggests, globalisation 'signals a growing *interdependence* and *interpenetration* of human relations alongside the increasing integration of the world's socio-economic life' (2002: 68).

It could be suggested therefore that the capacity for global communication and interconnectivity provide us with a perfect opportunity to observe globalisation in action as global media organisations, unbound by limitations of space and time, enable greater interconnectivity and democratic deliberations within what is purportedly an emerging global public sphere in which the media and news journalism are arguably taking a key role.

Globalisation, journalism and the news media

Given the purported magnitude and significance of globalisation, one would expect it to have profound consequences for journalism and the news media, not only in terms of its structure, organisation and operation, but also in relation to the norms and values that inform journalistic practice. In recent years there has been significant scholarly attention within journalism studies on the 'impact' of globalisation on journalistic practice and its ethics and norms, what Reese (2008) refers to as global logics of journalism.

> Transnational ownership, non-national technological reach, extra-national diasporic communities, and supranational governmental forms have weakened the connection between journalism and its traditional nation state base, leading to increasingly 'global logics' within journalism.
>
> *Reese (2008: 240)*

In other words Reese is suggesting that globalisation is actively shaping journalism in a way that uncouples it from its traditional national base. He suggests that three particular trends are apparent in journalism which demonstrate this.

The first trend is in relation to the ways in which 'reach, interconnectedness, and virtually real-time properties of globalised media contribute to our experiencing the world as a whole, shaping the intensity and nature of that experience. This evolving media system creates what I describe as the global news arena' (2008: 241). Globalisation and the technological developments in media and communications has fostered the development of a 'global news arena' in which an 'alignment' of news values and norms facilitate the notion of 'single community' to engage with each other in an emerging global news arena' (2008: 241). Journalism therefore helps to construct representations of the world that are not constrained by narrow parochialism as they become much more global in their orientation and outlook.

Second, Reese suggests that 'journalism as a practice and interpretative community, is adapting to this emerging global news arena and increasingly must navigate between its traditional "vertical" orientation within whatever nation state it is carried out and a "horizontal" perspective that transcends national frameworks' (2008: 241). So journalism is being forced to adapt and reorientate its gaze outwards and become much more global in its outlook; journalism should therefore adopt a much more cosmopolitan stance. Not, however, in a way that compromises its local and national obligations, rather local issues should be reflected upon within a much wider global framework. Of course the term 'glocalisation' is the label most associated with this 'interplay between the global and the local' (2008: 244).

Third, Reese suggests that such developments are impacting on journalism to develop a culture of journalism which is more in tune with globalisation (2008: 241). In other words within this new context we see the emergence of a new set of professional norms and ethical values which transcend national and cultural boundaries and become globalised. The conventional journalistic values of 'objectivity', 'balance' and 'impartiality' are establishing themselves as central pillars of professional journalism in areas of the world that have not gone through the developmental phases that journalism has in Britain or the United States. The professionalisation of journalism in places from Nigeria (Yusha'u 2010) to Mexico (Peña Corona Rodríguez 2010), though arguably not as stable or advanced as some countries in the West, has arguably led to a gradual democratising force in the developing world. Moreover, the existence of international organisations such as 'Reporters Without Borders' and the 'International Federation of Journalists' which advocate transnational journalistic ethics and speak out against threats against press freedom seem to support Reese's view of the growth of a global logic of journalism.

> As a result of [the] changes in political, cultural and other spheres in society, there are new social actors, agents and interfaces emerging that confront journalism with new expectations that may be remarkably different from those to which traditional journalistic routines are ready (or even willing) to respond.
>
> *Heinonen and Loustarinen (2008: 236)*

Yet there are significant tensions between the range of competing ethical and normative values and those that drive the essentially Western liberal tradition. Indeed it may not be possible or indeed desirable to attempt to mould the vast range of ethical principles and values which exist into a 'one size fits all' ethical system. Moreover, the central problem of the globalisation of journalism and the news media remains within Reese's analysis, that being the fundamental driver of globalisation – capitalism – is arguably the force that compromises and distorts the deliberative capacity of journalism to act as an important element of the democratic public sphere. This is not to say that journalism itself cannot adapt to specific contexts in such a way that it corresponds to both contexts. Instead of speaking of global journalism (Berglez 2008), it might be more appropriate to speak of global 'journalisms' with regional adaptations to essentially dominant core principles such as objectivity, balance and a commitment to the democratic imperative.

New media and journalism

As noted, technological developments in information and communication are seen as emblematic of globalisation. It could be powerfully argued that the twenty-first century era of the internet and global satellite communications has heralded a new age of democratic deliberation and engagement in politics and social affairs. In relation to journalism, it has been argued that globalisation and new media in particular are having a profound impact on the very essence of journalism and its democratic imperative. Pavlik (2009) maintains that the new media age has 'reshaped' journalism in four significant ways. First, new technology has impacted on the ways in journalists go about their work. Long gone are the days when journalists simply relied on a telephone, pencil and notepad to cover a story. The World Wide Web of course has enabled journalists to conduct research at the click of a mouse. Similarly, email, blogging and micro-blogging have enabled journalists to communicate with vast audiences as well as access incredible amounts of information from leaks and tip offs to breaking news stories. Advances in technology have also meant that journalists can record store and send images, audio and text relatively simply and almost instantaneously (Deuze 2006). Second, Pavlik argues that the new technology has impacted on the structure of journalistic institutions and organisations. Newsrooms are being reorganised in order to accommodate the convergence of new media technologies in ways that facilitate the rapid production and dissemination of news. The development of new technologies for disseminating and consuming news content with e-readers such as Amazon's 'Kindle' and Apple's 'iPad' has provided news organisations with new opportunities to converge media content and deliver it free or via subscription.

Third, new media is enabling journalists to produce new content forms, from web-based newspapers containing video and audio, to blogs and micro blogging. Pavlik suggests that blogging in particular has enabled a form of participatory journalism in which the traditional gate keeping roles within the established and traditional media can be bypassed (see Domingo *et al* 2008; Newman 2009). Finally, new media is reshaping the relationships 'between and among journalists, journalistic organisations, and their many publics' (Pavlik 2009: 643) which he suggests has implications for greater levels of citizen engagement and involvement in both the consumption and production of media and its capacity for deliberation and discourse.

Moreover, given that anyone with access to technology and a little know-how can theoretically call themselves a 'journalist' the technology has the capacity to blur the professional distinctiveness of journalism as a profession or craft. The boundaries between professional journalism and so-called citizen journalism have arguably become blurred in no small part because of the ease of access to the public sphere afforded by the new technologies. As Fenton (2010: 11) has suggested: 'The social actors involved in the construction of news have expanded and extended outside of the newsroom resulting in the expansion of the locus of news production.' According to some commentators then, not only has new media technology impacted on the very essence of journalism and its relationship with itself and the public, but also it has expanded the deliberative capacities of a great mass of people across the world. Whether fighting local injustice or issues of global significance, digital communications technologies have purportedly enabled a new form of political participation which offers a much needed challenge to both the entrenched and established 'old' political order and to the hierarchical systems of control and management of media and communications (Atton 2002; Downing 2001).

In relation to the control of the media environment, some have argued that the transformations that new media has forced on traditional media, has liberated communicative processes and undermined long-standing mechanisms of control and censorship. For example, Brian McNair (2006) argues that as a result of the significant advances in communications technologies, we are witnessing a dramatic and significant shift in power away from essentially elite controlled media towards a more democratic and open system of access to media. McNair's position is that advances in communications technologies have heralded a new chaotic era in which elites no longer have the capacity or power to control information as the media has become more diffuse and random and as such it is able to transcend the control systems of the past, whether in terms of formal censorship or control of information by large media corporations.

Similarly, Wessels (2009: 105) suggests, 'One advantage of the Internet is that its interactivity makes it possible for citizens to request information, voice their opinion, and request a personalized answer from their representatives'; moreover, 'the interactivity of the Internet can facilitate the re-engagement of citizens in collective civic action that may feed into the political process'. Liberal democracies ultimately benefit from this chaotic media environment as information management becomes much harder to achieve and power becomes more diffuse. Again Wessels (2009: 122) notes in areas of welfare, health provision, education, local government the internet 'could support a more informed and participative public that could push to ensure high quality and inclusive services. For politics more generally, the internet is seen as a potential important antidote to contemporary political malaise with new opportunities for civic engagement and political participation. The internet can provide the public with access to Parliament and their elected representatives (Coleman 2004) as well as fora for democratic discussion and debate (Coleman 2007). Moreover, in non-democratic states such as Iran and China, new media and its chaotic environment have the capacity to challenge oppression and expose the abuse of human rights (see Sreberny and Khiabany 2007; Allen and Thorsen 2009).

Not only is government and institutional abuse of power more likely to be exposed given this relatively new communication environment, but also the media itself is more likely to be confronted and its authority as gatekeeper of information challenged (see Singer 2007). So traditional hierarchical structures of power in which the media itself has been located can be challenged and subverted by the enhanced capacity for almost anyone to engage. No longer do we have a media monopoly in which only the privileged few can participate in discussion and debate. Instead, we have a true marketplace of ideas in which hierarchy and news values can be transcended. Moreover, rather than being silenced or prevented from engaging in the new public sphere, critical and sometimes even radical perspectives on politics and media are given space within conventional media contexts. For example, the critical works of Naomi Klein, Michael Moore, Morgan Spurlock and Robert Greewald[1] compete in an open marketplace with mainstream media (McNair 2006: 89). In other words to say as some critical media commentators suggest, that societies are effectively sold short by conventional media whose search for market advantage undermines the democratic potential of the media, is to ignore the vast amount of critical and even anti-capitalist media that capitalism itself enables to reach a global audience. Indeed it could be argued that a more open media environment which has been facilitated by new information and communication technologies has enabled a new era of journalism in which public debate and engagement on a global scale – a global public sphere – has become a reality rather than a mere possibility.

WikiLeaks controversy

WikiLeaks describes itself as a 'non-profit organisation dedicated to bringing important news and information to the public'. It provides whistleblowers within powerful organisations an opportunity to get information into the public domain without fear of reprisal or exposure. In November 2010 with the help of *The Guardian* newspaper in the U.K.; *Le Monde* in France; *The New York Times* in the U.S. and *El Pais* in Spain, WikiLeaks began publishing a series of secret U.S. diplomatic cables from its embassies around the world. Earlier that year it had released what it called the 'Iraq War Logs' which consisted of 391,832 reports and documents about the Iraq war and its subsequent occupation. The documents, which include field reports and planning documents provide a hitherto prohibited insight into the U.S. military's thinking and approach to the war and subsequent occupation. Similarly, WikiLeaks published its 'Afghanistan War Logs' which was again based on secret U.S. military documents and communications about the U.S.'s involvement in Afghanistan from January 2004 until December 2009. WikiLeaks founder Julian Assange suggested that the documents demonstrate the true nature of warfare and that the public had the right to know about what the U.S. government was doing in Iraq and Afghanistan. It was, however, the leak of the U.S. diplomatic cables between the State Department and its embassies around the world which has ignited the most recent controversy surrounding WikiLeaks and its founder Julian Assange. The cables, which date from 28th of December 1966 to February 2010, provide information about U.S. spying missions; complicity in corruption and torture; lobbying for U.S. corporations, and embarrassing disclosure which expose the discrepancies between the U.S.'s real and public persona. Among more controversial revelations include directives from U.S. Secretary of State Hillary Clinton that U.S. diplomats around the world should gather personal details, sensitive computer information and even 'genetic material' in the course of their diplomatic work. There was also the revelation that some Arab nations had lobbied the U.S. to attack Iran and that China had made contingency plans for the possible collapse of North Korea.

The reaction and response to WikiLeaks has been divided. In the U.S. there have been calls by the Obama administration for Assange's arrest, however, on what charge it is still not clear.[2] There have even been calls from some on the political right for Assange to be 'pursued by with the same urgency we pursue al Qaeda', given that he is an 'anti-American operative with blood on his hands'.[3] This is despite the claim by senior state department officials, in a what seems to be a direct contradiction to the U.S. government, that the leaked cables have caused any significant or lasting damage to U.S. diplomacy (Harris 2011). Nevertheless the U.S. government is seeking his arrest prompting his lawyers, who are fighting an extradition request to Sweden on charges of sexual assault, to argue that Assange is facing possible detention in Guantánamo Bay or even execution if he is forced to face charges in Sweden.[4] Supporters of WikiLeaks and Assange suggest that he is being persecuted because he has stood up to U.S. militarism and exposed the hypocrisy and corruption at the heart of American power. John Pilger, for example, has suggested that the attacks on Assange are a 'direct response to an information revolution that threatens old power orders, in politics and journalism' (Pilger 2011).

It could be argued that the disclosure of the secret cables has done nothing more than expose the realities of the murky world of international diplomacy. The fact that states with the capacity to spy on their allies do so should be no surprise. Indeed this is arguably one of the key functions of the diplomatic service. Moreover, that officials at times express less than glowing views of some of their opposite numbers should again come as no surprise. Embarrassing it may be, but politically damaging? Possibly not. Yet there have of course been some significant political repercussions to the release of the cables which may have long lasting affects. For example, Morgan Tsvangirai (the power-sharing Prime Minister of Zimbabwe and former opposition leader) has been severely undermined by the release of cables where he privately urges Washington to continue sanctions against Zimbabwe while publicly opposing them. The release of the cables and the subsequent exposure of Tsvangirai has led to calls by his political opponents for him to be prosecuted for treason.[5] Indeed *The Guardian* newspaper has since come under fire for publishing the cables and potentially undermining an already fragile political coalition and endangering the life of Tsvangirai.[6]

What does the WikiLeaks controversy tell us about journalism free speech in the era of new media? Given the day-by-day unravelling of this controversy and the fact

that its significance is still yet to play out, it is difficult to reach any sustainable con-
clusions about WikiLeaks. Yet, given that the release and publication of the cables has
come under sustained attack by the U.S. which has even 'encouraged' private companies such as PayPal, Mastercard and Visa to withdraw their services to the website,
we should not underestimate the potential longer term ramifications, particularly with
regard erosion of privacy and free speech rights. The basis of this particular commercial backing for the U.S. stance on WikiLeaks seems to be that the companies are
in agreement with the U.S. that WikiLeaks is essentially an illegal operation which is
threatening the national security and lives of Americans. The withdrawal of services
has prompted revenge cyber attacks on these organisations in what was termed
'Operation Payback' with apparently only limited success (see Addley and Halliday
2010). The U.S. Department of Justice is also in the process of attempting to pressure
Twitter to release private information about account holders who are active supporters of
WikiLeaks. This is potentially a serious threat to privacy in the name of protecting
freedom despite claiming to respect and uphold the rights of citizens and press freedom around the world (see also below). So arguably the WikiLeaks controversy
exposes the tension related to trying to balance individual liberty with state security,
an issue that is discussed in greater detail in Chapter 8. Related to this is what the
WikiLeaks controversy tells us about the role of newspapers in managing leaks and
other sensitive or highly charged information. Of course the release of the diplomatic
cables has been done with the significant help of newspapers and incidentally, only
those newspapers who have negotiated agreements with Julian Assange to publish the
material, though this is now a matter of contestation (see Ellison 2011). Moreover,
the material has not, as was widely reported been 'dumped' on the internet.
As Greenwald (2011) has suggested, for the most part WikiLeaks has only been publishing cables 'which its newspaper partners first published'. Moreover, it is the editorial
judgement of the newspapers and the skill of the journalist which turns the WikiLeaks
data into 'great copy' (Preston 2010). Of course newspapers have a commercial
interest in publishing the data and will seek to do so on their terms, even if it leads to
a souring of their relationships as has occurred between Assange and *The Guardian* editor
Alan Rusbridger. Yet as Ellison (2011) has suggested the relationship between
newspaper and whistleblower in this instance is one which exposes a primal
tension within journalism: that between journalism acting as a mere conduit of raw
information and that of mediator. Yet of course journalism has never been about
acting as a mere conduit of information; it has always attempted to contextualise and
editorialise – WikiLeaks is no different. Whether it will maintain the upper hand in
its attempt to retain control over information and its mediation to the public remains
to be seen.

Global public sphere: reality or illusion?

How then are we to evaluate claims about the reinvigoration of the public sphere
and by extension of freedom of speech and democracy? There is certainly no doubt
that new media technologies have facilitated the expansion and intensification of

media production that have diminished the constraints of both space and time. Arguably, we have more media, greater access to media and the ability to produce and publish our own media content on a global network, and we have greater freedom to express our views and ideas. Yet the question of whether or not society has become more democratic as a result of this proliferation is an important one. Converged media and its capacity to disturb and unsettle established media conventions and processes (at the time of writing and probably for some time to come) are still being worked through (Fenton 2010). Yet though we assume that the internet allows us all access to the new marketplace of ideas, some commentators argue that public deliberation and democratic debate is in no better health than it was before the advent of new media technologies, in no small part because of the commercial imperative that continues to drive such initiatives (Golding 1998).

Another criticism of the globalisation of communication as a component of democratisation is that it offers a picture of global communications that is fundamentally Western. It sees the values of globalisation: the market, liberal democracy, fragmentation of national boundaries and nation states as providing a positive framework to 'combat the forces of authoritarianism and control' around the globe (McNair 2006: 210) yet it also offers a mirror image of Western society which might not be appropriate for other cultures. John Street (2001) has suggested that the power and global reach of a relatively small number of media organisations have the capacity to pressure states and societies into conforming to Western ideals of commercialism and individualism. As such fundamental democratic principles may be placed under pressure given the commercial drive of global media organisations. He suggests that such commercial ventures 'reflect an ambition to provide a complete media package and represent an ability to control and manage cultural production – whether news or entertainment' (2001: 165). This can impact significantly on cultural and even national identity with a form of cultural homogenisation taking place. Globalisation can 'squeeze out local culture' and 'produces homogeneity: the same ideas and values, the same films and songs, carried to all parts of the world' (2001: 174). Contra the analysis of McNair globalisation becomes a form of cultural imperialism which, with the aid of new media technologies, may have a significant impact on identity and culture.[7]

Though the evidence for media globalisation might seem overwhelming, critics argue that the notion of media globalisation is nothing more than a powerful myth. For example, Kai Hafez (2007) argues that rather than the media providing us with examples of globalisation in action, a more focused analysis of the media highlights the fact that the 'myth' of media globalisation is based on very shaky foundations. The fact that so-called global media organisations so strongly reflect national agendas testifies to the continuing relevance and power of the nation state. The so-called 'CNN effect' which is supposed to emphasise global 'media diplomacy' over and above national diplomacy, ignores the power of nation states to set agendas as we see in relation to the framing of 9/11 and the subsequent invasion of Iraq. For Hafez 'the media *follow* rather than *lead*. The true strength of the media consists not in its capacity to influence politics, as evoked in the CNN effect, but in the affirmation and legitimation of national politics' (Hafez 2007: 54).

A number of critics have also argued that new media technologies have not heralded a new age of democratic deliberation and greater political participation and engagement. On the contrary, they argue that the process of globalisation has merely entrenched existing power structures as powerful media organisations have come to dominate the new media environment in much the same way as they dominated the old as patterns of media ownership have not altered dramatically as a result of technological proliferation. Nor have democratic societies necessarily become more democratic given technological advances in communications. Though there may be capacity for greater deliberation and debate, its realisation is largely constrained. However, before we examine the internet's impact on journalism and democracy in democratic societies, it is worth considering its use in states in which are decidedly undemocratic. As we will see, claims about the democratising power of the internet in this context may also be somewhat wide of the mark.

Democracy and the internet: China and Iran

In China vast sections of the internet are blocked or restricted by the Chinese authorities which has an army of official internet monitors and volunteers checking websites, blogs, forums and email (James 2009). The so-called 'Great Firewall of China', which is officially known as the Golden Shield Project,[8] has led to human rights organisations criticising U.S. technology firms such as Google, Microsoft, Yahoo and Cisco for developing much of the technology that has enabled the Chinese state to attempt to censor internet use within their borders (Bambauer 2006; Amnesty International 2006). In terms of control and surveillance, Fallows (2008) has analysed a range of mechanisms through which the authorities are attempting to control internet use by the Chinese public. From physically managing the cable services entering China (slowing the network or shutting it off altogether) to 'tapping' internet searches to seek out undesired search terms and redirect the results, and blocking certain search terms (such as 'Falun Gong' or 'Democracy Movement'), China is developing a system of control which is 'constantly evolving and changing in their emphasis, as new surveillance techniques become practical and as words go on and off the sensitive list. They leave the Chinese internet public unsure about where the off-limits line will be drawn on any given day' (Fallows 2008). In 2009 over 15000 websites were closed down and over 5000 arrests were made following an anti-pornography campaign (Reporters Without Borders 2010).

In 2010 plans were also afoot to pre-install software on all personal computers sold in China with the programmes 'Green Dam' and 'Youth Escort' being installed to fight against internet pornography. Facing a range of opposition from bloggers, technology corporations (including American company Cybersitter who are suing the Chinese authorities for piracy), and media freedom pressure groups, the Chinese authorities seem to have backed down from the plan. At the time of writing Google is in the process of terminating its operations in China following cyber attacks on its computer system which are thought to have originated from within China, and increased criticism from freedom of speech groups for its cooperation with Chinese censorship since it arrived in China in 2006. *The New York Times* reported in 2010 that Google has increasingly been 'constricted' by the Chinese authorities in its attempts to obstruct Google's Gmail system, limit certain search terms and block access to various websites (Markoff 2010).

On a technical level, the attempts by the Chinese authorities to control internet use are somewhat limited as there will always be ways for the committed activist to bypass technological constraints instigated by the authorities. Yet of course as there are numerous other ways in which governments of authoritarian regimes can combat internet activism, from surveillance techniques which can identify trouble makers and their allies, to even participating in online fora and misdirecting and misinforming its members, authoritarian states need not direct their energies at blocking and removing material online. Information cascades in particular can be used to spread false or misleading information which given the viral nature of the internet can reach millions of users in a short space of time.

Morozov (2009; 2010) has argued that though the internet can have the potential to push forward democratic change, many of the claims made on behalf of its democratising potential at the moment are very wide of the mark. Of course groups can organise, petition and agitate online, but what are the significant impacts of such activism? Moreover, the internet can be used – by both repressive states and other anti-democratic movements and criminals – to stifle dissent and undermine progressive movements. During the Green protests in Iran in 2009 internet and mobile phone technology was widely used to organise the demonstrations and provide the outside world with pictures of the agitation. Yet 'despite all the political mobilisation facilitated by social media, the Iranian government has not only survived, but has, in fact become even more authoritarian' (Morozov 2010). Morozov goes on to suggest:

> The changes currently taking place in Iran are far from positive: a catastrophic brain drain triggered by the recent political repressions, a series of violent crackdowns on politically active university students who have chosen to remain in the country, the persecution of critical bloggers, journalists and editors, the appointment of more conservative ministers to the government, and mounting pressure on dissident politicians. From this perspective, the last six months could be taken to reveal the impotence of decentralised movements in the face of a ruthless authoritarian state – even when those movements are armed with modern protest tools. [...] The big question [...] remains: 'what do we really gain if the ability to organise protests is matched (and, perhaps, even dwarfed) by the ability to provoke, identify and arrest the protesters – as well as any other possible future dissidents?'
>
> *(Morozov 2010)*

To be sure, journalists and net activists have succumbed to overt pressure to conform and moderate their dissent. An exhaustive list of journalist and activist casualties is far beyond the scope of this book, however, according to *Reporters Sans Frontières* thirty journalists and seventy-two 'netizens' are in Chinese gaols for expressing their dissenting views online. The *Committee to Protect Journalists* (CPJ) states that activists critical of the Chinese authorities such as Kunchok Tsephel Gopey Tsang, the manager of *Chomei* a Tibetan cultural website, face gaol sentences of up to fifteen years (CPJ 2009). In Iraq Sardasht Osman was found shot dead in May 2010 after having received a number of death threats relating to his contributions to online news websites *Sbei, Awene, Hawlati* and *Lvinpress* (CPJ 2010). In April 2010 the CPJ challenged the authorities in ten countries to seek justice for murdered journalists. Countries such as the 'Philippines,[9] Sri Lanka,[10] Pakistan, Russia and Iraq have the world's worst law enforcement records when it comes to deadly violence against the press'. The cases include thirty journalists who were killed in the Philippines during an ambush on a political convoy; Anna Politkovskaya who was shot dead in her Moscow apartment building in 2006, and Lasantha Wickramatunga, a journalist in Sri Lanka, who was attacked by a mob. At the time of writing no prosecutions have been made.

Sadly the list is almost endless as journalists around the globe face intimidation, torture and death at the hands of those who would prefer it if they kept quiet. Examples such as these should remind us that censorship manifests itself in not so subtle forms. The murder and intimidation of journalists by repressive regimes, criminal gangs or terrorist organisations is as much an affront to democracy as any state oppression practices by the former Communist or Fascist regimes of the twentieth century. The scale might be much less in the twenty-first century, but the damage to democracy is no less significant.

Internet in democratic societies

It is not just authoritarian states that pose a threat to freedom of speech and deliberation online. Hosein (2010) suggests that U.S. and European governments too have enabled law enforcement agencies to develop widespread surveillance of the internet including the 'retention of location, call and email transactional data for up to two years'. Not only are such measures an invasion of privacy but also can they can stifle freedom of expression and freedom of speech. Hosein argues that dissenting voices and political movements have perversely become more at risk because of the vulnerabilities embedded within the technology of the internet itself as large amounts of personal information can be made available to the authorities. He suggests that widespread surveillance can also undermine journalists' commitment to protect sources as internet surveillance can be 'used to discover the identities of journalists' sources by gaining access to telephone and email logs so surveillance [and] creates a hostile environment for free speech'. Curran and Seaton (2010: 266) also point out that commercial websites collect and 'aggregate' information about users which can then be sold on to other commercial enterprises. Rather than a place of anonymity, they argue that the internet 'has become a glasshouse (although many people appear to be unaware of this when they go online in the privacy of their homes)'.

Joachim Frenk (2008: 179) has suggested that though some forms of regulatory censorship and surveillance are widely accepted in order to curb extreme web content such as child pornography, rape and 'snuff' videos, and other violent and extreme content, such control 'may serve to justify far-reaching limitations of citizens' freedoms and privacy'. While few people would have a problem with controls which are aimed at protecting the young and the vulnerable, as Curran and Seaton (2010: 266) maintain, such mechanisms undermine the view that the internet is beyond control. Moreover, as with other forms of formal censorship and control, regulatory mechanisms of censorship and the use of online surveillance can generate much more subtle forms of 'constitutive' censorship in which internet users may well internalise the invisible eye of the authorities and modify their online behaviour, even if such behaviour is perfectly legal and appropriate. For critical journalists, political dissenters and activists, and even law abiding citizens this is particularly worrying.

With regards claims about the deliberative capacity of the internet Cass Sunstein (2006; 2007) has explored the potential of the internet as a deliberative and critical political environment which ideally could not only act as a check on power but also infuse democratic institutions by providing a hitherto largely silent public with a significant voice. He has analysed recent technological developments with regard to social media and online news media and evaluated their potential to contribute to democratic deliberation. Rather than finding spaces in which free and open exchanges of ideas and values takes place, Sunstein suggests that the internet has acted to generate a multitude of 'enclaves' in which like-minded individuals engage in a largely insulated level of debate and discussion. Such spaces could of course relate to issues that are mundane or extreme, the point is that the web is increasingly occupied by those who streamline their activities and the information they access, to conform to their own interests and prejudices. For example, Sunstein suggests that websites, discussion boards and blogs devoted to topics from gun control, anti-abortion, sports and celebrity gossip, to extremist and even terrorist content, provide those who are interested in such topics spaces within which they can discuss the issues with like-minded individuals. Following friends and celebrities on Twitter may give the impression that one has more of a connection with the individuals that one is following; however, this is usually within the confines of the specific interests of those who are doing the tweeting and the receivers of the tweets. Similarly, Facebook or MySpace groups tend to generate a coalition around specific interests or values, whether they are political, social or personal. As such the internet is not so much a space for democratic deliberation, more an arena of atomisation and polarisation of interests and beliefs. This, of course, has significant implications for democracy as if society becomes more and more atomised and polarised, the possibility of meaningful deliberative democratic engagement becomes harder to achieve.

It could be argued then that the new media marketplace of ideas, which as we know, contributes much to the conceptual basis of the role of freedom of speech and freedom of the press in democratic societies, has not yet been significantly enhanced by new media technologies. Moreover, as Davis (2010: 122) has suggested, so far the expectations placed on new technologies and their democratising potential 'have remained largely unfulfilled'.

Journalism and the 'communication revolution'

As discussed above, debates about new information and communication technologies have been largely concerned with the democratising power of these technologies primarily in relation to their capacity to undermine formal mechanisms of censorship and control and in the contribution they make to a more deliberative polity. As we have also seen there are a range of criticisms of the democratising potential of the internet which largely focus on the as yet unrealised ambitions of cyber optimists as well as the contention that new technologies bring with them new mechanisms of control, surveillance and censorship. Yet what has been missing from this discussion thus far is a critical analysis of the ways in which journalism has engaged with these technologies and the impact this has had on journalism and its democratic component. Fenton (2010) notes, drawing on the work of Curran and Winston on technological innovation in media and communications, that even though there have been significant changes in the ways in which journalists work and in the material they produce,

> [w]e should remember that the history of communications technology shows us that if innovative content and forms of production appear in the early stages of a new technology and offer potential for radical change this is more often than not cancelled out or appropriated by the most powerful institutions operating within the dominant technological and social-political paradigms.
> *Fenton (2010: 13)*

As such, whatever the potential of new media, this view suggests that its democratic or radical potential is absorbed into the prevailing system and as such has a tendency to become neutralised as a means through which social change can take place. If we look at the experience of journalism we can discern a range of factors that have led some analysts to conclude that journalism is in fact in a much worse position in relation to fulfilling its democratic function than it was before the advent of the new information and communication technologies of the digital era. It is worth examining specific areas in some detail and I will borrow from Pavlik's (2009) framework mentioned above to highlight some of the problems with his essentially optimistic view of the impact of the internet on journalism.

First, in relation to the ways in which journalists go about their daily work there is no doubt that the internet has had an impact. Unfortunately it is often being relied on as a source of information for journalists instead of one of a number of tools that journalists can utilise as they go about their jobs. For example, Phillips (2010) has examined the increased pressure faced by journalists to produce stories within a specific timeframe. Journalists have of course always worked to tight deadlines, but Phillips suggests that because of the specific time pressures that journalists face, coupled with the depletion of sources which employers suggest is made up for with greater reliance on digital technologies, journalists tend to resort to relying on 'known hierarchies and news values' (2010: 100). As such the intense and increased commercial pressure placed on journalists can serve to constrict their practice by forcing them to rely on a relatively narrow source pool or worse, to 'cannibalise' copy from other news organisations and official reports. What this produces is something strikingly similar to that outlined by Sunstein above, a narrowing of perspective and a homogenisation of news content (Conboy and Steel 2008).

Second, in relation to the view that the internet has impacted on the structure of news organisations; there is no doubt that news organisations have had to accommodate convergence and restructure and reorganise their operations accordingly. Yet it is largely in response to the rarefied economic climate and the panic induced by the prospect of being left behind that such alterations are made. The shift in emphasis to online 'converged' content has largely been in response to increasing economic demands on the newspaper industry and pressures to cut costs. The intensification of competition among news organisations has meant that technology is adopted not as a boon to greater democratic or enlightened journalism, but more as an opportunity to cut costs and expand markets (Davis 2010).

Pavlik also suggests that the internet has enabled new content forms for journalists and non-journalists alike which blur the boundaries of journalism, freeing them up and allowing greater scope for more participatory journalism. However, as Singer (2005) suggests, the traditional gatekeeping role that journalists and news media organisations continue to occupy shows little sign of being eroded. Indeed she suggests that 'journalists and media organizations remain unwilling to relinquish or even share their gatekeeping role' (2005: 192). As such the capacity for relationships between journalists and the public to be reshaped with a view to greater levels of citizen engagement and involvement in media production that is uncoupled from the commercial imperative seem somewhat exaggerated (see also Curran and Witschge 2010).

Conclusion

It has been the purpose of this chapter to examine the relationship between journalism, new media and the emergence of the public sphere on a global level. The issue of freedom of speech is central here as on the surface at least as technologies seem to be facilitating a shift towards greater levels of transparency, openness and deliberation which can circumvent mechanisms of control and censorship, particularly within repressive regimes. However, we have also seen that some of the democratising claims made by some celebratory accounts of the technology tend to ignore the complex dynamics at play. Technology can be used to liberate and challenge oppression, but it can also used to reinforce existing power, both in democratic and non-democratic societies. Moreover, it is often argued that the ways in which politics can be enhanced by such technologies have tended to focus far too heavily on the 'potential' of the technology itself with little reflection on the sorts of democratic ideals and aspiration that might be met. Real progress would no doubt involve rethinking the nature of our democracy and looking at how technology can best serve these new ideas. I would argue therefore that technology should not be the central focus of discussion, rather energies should be devoted to new thinking about the nature and function of democracy and the public sphere and how technology and journalism might fit into this realm, rather than the other way around. We have also seen how technology has been embraced by journalism in its attempts to stay a step ahead of its rivals and exploit potential new markets. However, journalism seems reluctant to adapt and reorientate its core rationale as it struggles with the keeping hold of editorial power and control in the mediation process. How it will continue to adapt to this constantly changing context remains unclear, but adapt I'm sure it will.

5

REGULATING BROADCAST JOURNALISM

I don't have to tell you things are bad. Everybody knows things are bad. It's a depression. Everybody's out of work or scared of losing their job. The dollar buys a nickel's worth, banks are going bust, shopkeepers keep a gun under the counter. Punks are running wild in the street and there's nobody anywhere who seems to know what to do, and there's no end to it. We know the air is unfit to breathe and our food is unfit to eat, and we sit watching our TVs while some local newscaster tells us that today we had fifteen homicides and sixty-three violent crimes, as if that's the way it's supposed to be. We know things are bad – worse than bad. They're crazy.

Network (1976)

Introduction

The above extract from the on-air breakdown of fictional TV news anchor Howard Beale, played by Peter Finch in the 1976 film *Network*, brings into sharp focus our expectations of newsreaders and broadcast journalists – namely, that the news media in democratic societies are not generally at liberty to disseminate information which is inflammatory, inaccurate, defamatory or offensive. Though as we have seen journalism has developed a set of general principles which are orientated towards often competing objectives – to hold the powerful to account and to generate profit – it must nevertheless do so within a set of parameters which are intended to ensure that it meets the highest standards. Of course journalism does not always conform to such demands, yet in the U.K. there exist both statutory and voluntary regulatory frameworks which are intended to ensure journalism corresponds to its central claims and ideals. The present chapter and the one that follows are primarily concerned with the regulatory codes and guidelines that pertain to journalism, with broadcast journalism being centred on here, and print in Chapter 6.

First, we will explore the broader context of regulation regarding freedom of expression before moving on to examine the principle of Public Service Broadcasting (PSB) which has historically shaped the broadcasting regulatory environment in the U.K. and continues to prompt debate about the nature and scope of broadcast regulation in Britain. From this we will look specifically at the regulatory frameworks which apply to broadcast news which are the Ofcom Broadcasting Code and the BBC's Editorial Guidelines and examine the specific requirements made of the broadcast news media. It is important to stress that this chapter is primarily concerned with rules concerning the regulation of broadcast news and does not therefore pay attention to the guidelines which apply to the wider media. Here we will focus on issues of accuracy, impartiality and fairness, harm and offence, crime and anti-social behaviour and the issue of privacy.

Regulation in context

The liberal democratic conception of freedom of the press of course is not unconstrained. 'Freedom of the press' does not give the news media licence to publish or broadcast whatever it likes. In liberal democratic societies, freedom of the press, in principle at least, tends to be balanced in relation to other rights in the recognition that freedoms can often conflict and clash. Press freedom therefore is generally conceived to exist within legal and regulatory frameworks which are intended to ensure that the news media fulfils its democratic obligations in a responsible manner and which attempts to create a working balance between free speech rights and other competing rights such as privacy.

Though the news media have developed historically to perform a range of functions, arguably the most important is to ensure democratic accountability and to facilitate the public sphere. Core values of sincerity and accuracy within particular spatial and temporal locations (Harrison 2006) are generally perceived therefore to be the minimum requirements of news journalism. Regulatory frameworks are perceived as essential in order to ensure the news media meet these requirements.

Freedom of speech and freedom of expression are also of course asserted in principle in a range of international codes and conventions on human rights. Within these conventions generally, the right to freedom of speech is emphasised as one of a number of 'inalienable' fundamental human rights which are posited as essential to all human beings irrespective of race, class, gender or religion. We also see that the rights of freedom of speech and expression come with safeguards against abuse, the protection of national security, public order, health and morals and so on. Such protocols specify rights to individual conscience and rights to privacy and it is often in relation to these seemingly competing rights that much of the controversy concerning the limits of freedom of speech and expression revolve. Such protocols are intended to specify a minimum standard of protection which should be afforded to all people but with limits which are intended to safeguard the interests of others. In addition to balancing out freedoms between individuals, these freedoms are also framed in relation to the protection and security of the state as such freedom of speech is protected only until it threatens the national interests or life and well being of its citizens (see Chapter 8).

Historically international conventions were drawn up in response to the crimes against humanity committed during the Second World War and the tyranny inflicted on millions of people by authoritarian and totalitarian regimes. The principle asserted in the Universal Declaration of Human Rights is that the inviolable nature of fundamental human rights are protected by international agreement to which all states have a requirement to safeguard and promote. Within national boundaries, different countries have different constitutional arrangements for the protection of freedom of speech and expression and freedom of the press. In the United States, as we have seen, the First Amendment of the Bill of Rights is intended to protect the fundamental right to free speech and expression and freedom of the press. In Germany, 'freedom of expression, press freedom, and other related freedoms are guaranteed [...] by Article 5 of the Basic Law' (Barendt 2005: 59). In France Article 11 of the Declaration of the Rights of Man and of the Citizen 1789 also protects freedom of thought, opinion and expression (Barendt 2005: 67). Within European countries, Article 10 of the ECHR also provides protection of freedom of speech and expression. Until the Human Rights Act (1998) freedom of speech in Britain was given no special protection. In other words there was no specific constitutional safeguard which asserted or protected freedom of speech. What did exist, specifically with regard to broadcast media, was the public service ideal which was established in law and set the regulatory environment of the broadcast media in the U.K., one which continues to this day.

The public service ideal

Gibbons (1998: 56) notes that there are numerous interpretations of the concept of public service broadcasting but two in particular are distinct, the first

> is the idea of universality, in the geographical sense that the material which is produced should be available throughout the country, and in the consumer sense that it should cater for all tastes and interests. The other feature is the idea of cultural responsibility, that material should have the object of informing and educating the public, offering a high standard of quality, as well as entertaining them.
>
> *Gibbons (1998: 56)*

Such an emphasis highlights the fact that the historical evolution of the press was in stark contrast to that of the broadcast media; a contrast has been highlighted by Nichols (2000), who has examined the relationship between the BBC and the newspaper sector during the inter-war years, and suggests that it was an 'uneasy competitive relationship'. The conception of Public Service Broadcasting (PSB) has evolved significantly since John Reith, the first director general of the BBC. Reith's vision for the BBC was to provide a service that would reflect the national interests and be independent from both government and commercial pressures. Though the

British Broadcasting Company was originally set up as a commercial enterprise, difficulties managing the licences and dissatisfaction among wireless manufacturers who were struggling to make a profit from the radio sets, led to the setting up of the Crawford Committee on Broadcasting in 1925. The committee was charged with considering 'the future development of British broadcasting' (Crisell 2002: 24). The Committee put forward the argument that the British Broadcasting Company would not be able to serve the national interest adequately and as such a 'Public Commission operating in the National Interest' should take its place (cited in Curran and Seaton 2010: 105).

Crisell (2002: 18–19) maintains that Reith's view was that the service would have five key elements: to broadcast to everyone in Britain who wished to listen; to maintain quality and high standards; to operate as a monopoly as competition would undermine quality; to be funded by a licence fee which would ensure that the size of a programme's audience would not determine its cost; and finally to be independent 'institutionally and editorially' from both commercial pressures and from government. Tracey (1998: 16) has suggested that '[a] key assumption behind public service broadcasting [...] is that broadcasting entails important moral and intellectual questions and ambitions which are separate from any technological or financial considerations'. It was this high ideal that Reith sought to achieve, providing high quality programmes that would appeal across the social spectrum of society, unconstrained by considerations of profit or loss.

Curran and Seaton (2010: 106) maintain that the formation of the BBC as a 'Public Service Utility' stemmed largely from Britain's experiences of the First World War and the assertion that a form of centralised planning of the distribution of resources (as the BBC was perceived) would provide the most efficient means of management and organisation. Commercial imperatives were rejected largely because they could not guarantee the standard of service that Reith and the Crawford Committee had envisaged. The market was just too unpredictable. It would also potentially limit its geographical scope and undermine Reith's power within the corporation and more widely (Curran and Seaton 2010: 107).

The development of the commercial sector in the 1950s and the ideological and political assaults from the 1980s (Curran and Seaton 2010; Golding and Murdoch 2000) have had a significant impact on the public service ethos of the BBC. Though the BBC continues to maintain its relative independence from government via the particular mechanisms with which it is governed and regulated, the notion of public service is becoming increasingly difficult to discern. As Gibbons (1998: 63) notes the single monolithic conception of public service is something that is fluid and ever changing, particularly as 'new forms of programme delivery are developed, enabling audiences to become more differentiated' within a much wider market environment. Nevertheless public expectations that broadcasters be impartial and conform to high standards of journalism has become deeply embedded in British culture, primarily through the development of the principle of public service broadcasting. Gibbons maintains that this ethos emerged from a recognition in the 1920s that 'there was a public interest in communication which required special protection' (1998: 56). The broadcast media has to devote a proportion of its output to fulfilling public service principles which, according to Petley,

> were intended to keep out certain forms of content deemed undesirable or harmful […] others were designed to regulate *into* the system qualities generally regarded as positive, such as, in programming terms, impartiality, independence, originality, innovation, and diversity, and in terms of ownership, plurality and public accountability, as it was assumed that plurality of ownership was necessary in order to safeguard diversity – and independence – of content.
>
> *Petley (2009: 127)*

Finally, it should also be noted that broadcast regulation in the U.K. perceives the medium as particularly powerful and as such requires special attention with regard to harm and offence and the protection of children and vulnerable people. As we will see below, the immediate nature of broadcasting, particularly live broadcasting, necessitates strict compliance in order to safeguard the public and serve their interests.

Communications Act 2003

The market-orientated ethos has become increasingly dominant since the 1980s and 1990s. During this period the regulation of the commercial sector was highly fragmented (Kuhn 2007) with a number of regulators taking responsibility for particular areas of communication. Prior to the Communications Act 2003 the commercial U.K. broadcast and communication sectors were regulated by five separate bodies: the Independent Television Commission (ITC); the Broadcasting Standards Commission (BSC); the Office of Telecommunications (OFTEL); the Radio Authority and the Radiocommunications Agency (Smith 2006). Such fragmentation was perceived as problematic given the rapid technological changes affecting the sector along with increasing regulatory complexity. Moreover, in light of this regulatory complexity the formation of a single regulatory body – Ofcom – could be seen in terms of an attempt by government to reflect the converging nature of the telecommunications sector and to ensure that the regulatory environment became clearer for stakeholders, broadcasters and communications providers. The idea was that a specific authority such as Ofcom which could integrate its functions would be better placed to deal with the increasing complexity of the sector. Ofcom has a statutory obligation to regulate the content of television, radio, satellite and mobile communications technologies and to ensure that 'a wide range of high quality television and radio programmes are provided' (Ofcom 2010).[1] It also has a responsibility to ensure that competition thrives while at the same time seeking to ensure that broadcasting standards and public service commitments are met by the independent media sector. As Kuhn (2007: 129) notes: 'Ofcom has responsibility for ensuring a competitive marketplace in communications media and also monitors the application of "light touch" content regulation in the broadcasting sector.' However, Smith (2006) suggests more critically that rather than merely simplifying the communications and broadcast environment, it was the combination of a number of factors which heralded the establishment of Ofcom and shaped its remit and focus, factors including commercial media interests, New Labour's commitment to a free market ethos, a 'turf war' between regulators (principally the ITC and Oftel) and inter-departmental 'bargaining' between rival departments of government (Smith 2006: 937). If one examines the social and economic shifts taking place during the 1980s and 1990s it is possible to discern a distinctive move towards the development of deregulatory context, or what Petley (2009) terms 're-regulation', in which the market would play an increasingly significant role. The 2003 Act and the setting up of Ofcom can be seen in terms of the continuation of a trend towards greater deregulation of the media which began in the 1980s and continued well on into the 1990s (Curran and Seaton 2010).

Regulatory mechanisms

With regard the framework which regulates broadcast news media there are two mechanisms – Ofcom's Broadcasting Code which has responsibility for the regulation of the commercial sector but which also includes some responsibility for the BBC (see below); while the Editorial Guidelines of the BBC set out the principles on which the BBC is based and function as a guide for producers, editors and journalists so as to ensure that BBC news fulfils its public service remit as set out by the Royal Charter and Agreement.

Broadcasters who fail to comply with or breach the Code are censured usually in the form of the publication of 'findings' which determines why and in what circumstances the broadcaster has breached the Code. Serious or continued breaches could bring statutory sanctions which can include a financial penalty or having their licence revoked (Ofcom 2009: 3). In addition to the publication of adjudications, the BBC, in areas which Ofcom has responsibility (see later) is also liable to fines of up to £250,000 if it is found in breach of the Broadcasting Code. It is important to stress that these codes and frameworks are not solely concerned with identifying the limits of what the news media can broadcast or offer directives on its news gathering practices, they also set out important frameworks concerning the function of the news media and the responsibilities it has to the public. Thought of in this way these regulatory codes might be seen in terms of, at least in principle, facilitating the highest standards of journalism as well as setting out the particular boundaries journalists and producers should be aware of.

In the preamble to the Code Ofcom sets out the legislative background to the Code which includes the Human Rights Act 1998 and the European Convention on Human Rights, particularly Articles 8, 10 and 14. The Code itself is divided into ten sections: protecting under-eighteens; harm and offence; crime; religion; due impartiality and due accuracy and undue prominence of views and opinions; elections and referendums; fairness; privacy; commercial references in television programming and commercial references in radio programming. The most significant sections for journalism are the sections on due impartiality and due accuracy and undue prominence of views and opinions; elections and referendums; harm and offence; crime and anti-social behaviour, and fairness and privacy.

The BBC and Ofcom

Until the Communications Act 2003 the BBC was principally governed by the Board of Governors who were responsible for ensuring that the organisation met its statutory obligations. However, as Fenwick and Phillipson indicate, the Deed of Amendment of 4 December 2003 makes

> significant changes consequential to the 2003 Act. These, crucially, make the BBC subject [...] to external regulation – by OFCOM – and to a system of sanctions for breach of obligations now binding upon it, including the new, comprehensive Broadcasting Code.
>
> *Fenwick and Phillipson (2006: 854)*

In short the 2003 Act states that Ofcom has powers to 'regulate the provision of the BBC's services and the carrying on by the BBC of other activities for purposes connected with the provision of those services' (Communication Act 2003: 198.1). As Fenwick and Phillipson note, this means that the BBC also has to observe Ofcom's Broadcasting Code in relation to certain aspects of its output.[2] Importantly for broadcast journalism in the U.K. The BBC is *not* subject to Ofcom regulation in the areas of accuracy and impartiality, though it does cover the BBC in respect of fairness (see later).

The Communications Act 2003, therefore, 'has opened up the BBC to Ofcom's powers in a wide range of circumstances'; as such the BBC is 'now subject to almost all aspects of Ofcom's Broadcasting Code' (Feintuck and Varney 2006: 51). Though Ofcom has increased its influence over the BBC the organisation continues to operate by virtue of a Royal Charter and Framework Agreement which is granted by government. The Charter and Agreement comes under review by government every ten years and sets out the powers of the BBC Trust which replaced the Board of Governors in 2007. The Trust was set up in order to ensure that the BBC's policies and the management of complaints against the organisation would have greater independence and more fully represent the interests of the public. The previous system was of course subject to serious rebuke from Lord Hutton in his report in 2004,[3] and the subsequent Neil Report (2004) which was an attempt to 'learn the lessons' of the Gilligan affair (Neil 2004). In 2007 Ofcom published its Memorandum of Understanding which among other aims sought to 'establish the principles and practices which will apply to dealings between the Trust and Ofcom' (Ofcom 2007a).

BBC Editorial Guidelines

The fundamental elements driving the BBC's Editorial Guidelines are the Royal Charter and the Agreement which ensure the editorial independence of the BBC and provide the key drivers for the Guidelines. The Charter, which is next due for renewal in 2016 'sets out the public purposes of the BBC, guarantees its independence, and outlines the duties of the Trust and the Executive Board' (BBC 2011b). The Agreement which is an agreement between the Secretary of State for Culture,

Media and Sport and the BBC, 'provides detail on many of the topics outlined in the Charter and also covers the BBC's funding and its regulatory duties. The Agreement is an important constitutional document because together with the Charter, it establishes the BBC's independence from the Government' (BBC 2011b). Moreover, the specific function and purpose of the BBC is set out by the Charter and Agreement in its public purpose which include: sustaining citizenship and civil society; promoting education and learning; stimulating creativity and cultural excellence; and representing the U.K., its nations, regions and communities (Department for Culture, Media and Sport 2006: 2–3).

As Chairman of the BBC Sir Michael Lyons notes the 'public expect the information they receive from the BBC to be authoritative, and the Guidelines accordingly place great stress on standards of fairness, accuracy and impartiality' (BBC 2011: 1). Director-General Mark Thompson notes that the Guidelines will help the BBC's employees 'make the best possible content to the highest standards' (BBC 2011: 2). It is important to note that the Guidelines are meant as such – guidelines – which means that they are intended to offer a framework within which the BBC are expected to adhere so as to produce the highest quality output to the widest possible audience. The Guidelines also emphasise specific editorial roles and responsibilities as well as the principles or 'standards that all BBC output must meet' (BBC 2011: 9) which should conform to the overall principles.

As a public service provider the BBC of course is not constrained or compromised by the commercial imperatives which most other media organisations are subject to. The very nature of the funding mechanism of the BBC, which is generated from the legally enforced TV licence fee, ensures in principle that the BBC is forced to focus on the breadth of its audiences' needs and requirements. This means that the BBC, while catering for mainstream and popular tastes, also has a responsibility to produce content which appeals to all sectors of society. In other words audience figures are *not* the driving force behind content, which are a factor for other media organisations, rather the organisation's commitment to public service broadcasting as we have seen above. However, it is important to recognise of course that the BBC operates within a global and commercially driven media environment, where the drive for audience figures and the generation of profit provide the central dynamic. The BBC has an interest in commercial activities overseas and as such recognises the importance of the BBC as a brand, with all that it stands for.

Mandatory referrals

All of the particular areas covered in the Guidelines are subject to mandatory referrals which offer guidance in relation to what scenarios or issues should be referred upwards to the Director of Editorial Policy and Standards and/or Programme Legal Advice. The system is also intended to enable transparency and ensure managerial oversight on particular dilemmas facing the production team. The specific policing of the policies and Guidelines is undertaken by the Editorial Complaints Unit (ECU) with appeals being the responsibility of the Editorial Standards Committee (ESC).

These bodies seek to ensure that the BBC adheres to its Charter and Agreement obligations and provide a vehicle for complaints against the BBC with regard its output. The Editorial Guidelines centre on the following: Accuracy; Impartiality; Harm and Offence; Fairness and Consent; Privacy; Reporting Crime and Anti-Social Behaviour; Children and Young People; Politics, Public Policy and Polls; War, Terror and Emergencies; Religion; Re-use and Reversioning; Editorial Integrity and Independence; Conflicts of Interest; Interfacing with Audiences; The Law, and Accountability. The following section offers a summary of the key sections of the Guidelines which are relevant for news media workers at the BBC and which are not covered elsewhere in this volume.

Requirements of news media

Accuracy, impartiality and fairness

Accuracy in reporting is one of the fundamental requirements of journalism. To be credible, journalists and news organisations must ensure that the stories they produce are based on accurate information. In explaining the precise terms of the Code Ofcom asserts that the phrase 'due' is perceived to be 'an important qualification to the concept of impartiality' (Ofcom 2011: 23). The meaning of 'due impartiality' does not require broadcasters to devote an equal amount of attention to all views or perspectives or even that the range of perspectives be covered. Rather the notion of due impartiality requires broadcasters to be aware of the specific context in question and make judgements about the nature of the programme and audience expectations. The Code stresses that in relation to the news there are also special impartiality requirements which relate to 'matters of political or industrial controversy and matters relating to current public policy' (Ofcom 2011: 24). The Code states that:

> Programmes [...] must exclude all expressions of the views and opinions of the person providing the service on matters of political and industrial controversy and matters relating to current public policy (unless that person is speaking in a legislative forum or in a court of law).
>
> *Ofcom (2011: 24)*

Special attention is also given to ensuring that broadcasters do not give 'undue prominence' to some views and opinions in their programming particularly in relation to coverage of matters of political or industrial controversy or matters relating to current policy (Ofcom 2011: 27). During election periods or referendums (see Section 6), Ofcom requires licence holders to also observe special impartiality requirements which are intended to ensure that broadcasters do not give undue prominence to a particular party or candidate and ensure that parties and candidates are covered with due impartiality and accuracy.

The BBC Guidelines state that: 'All BBC output, as appropriate to its subject and nature, must be well sourced, based on sound evidence, thoroughly tested and presented in clear, precise language' (BBC 2011: 14). The Programme Standards Code, which are set and reviewed by Ofcom, lays out the key requirements of broadcasters. In relation to the requirements of news broadcasters the Standards Code Section 2(d) deals with news programmes and places a requirement 'that news included in television and radio services is reported with due accuracy' (Communications Act 2003: Section 2(d)).

Similarly, the principle that higher standards of journalism require particular attention to impartiality in reporting ensure that 'audiences should not be able to tell from BBC output the personal prejudices of our journalists or news and current affairs presenters on matters of public policy, political or industrial controversy, or on "controversial subjects" in any other area' (BBC 2011: 28). Section 10 of the BBC Guidelines on Politics, Public Policy and Polls reinforce this commitment to impartiality in reporting politics, as does Section 11 which covers War, Terror and Emergencies (see also Chapter 8).

Finally under the provisions of the Broadcasting Act 1996 all broadcasters, including the BBC, must comply with Section 107 of the Fairness Code which relates to 'unjust or unfair treatment or interference with privacy' (Broadcasting Act 1996 Sec. 107) and the Programme Standards Code of the Communications Act 2003 (Section 319).

Though the guidelines emphasise the importance of accuracy and impartiality in reporting, there have always been charges, particularly from governments, of breach of 'due accuracy and impartiality'; probably none more so vigorous than those from the Blair government and Alastair Campbell in relation to its coverage of the build up to the war in Iraq in 2003 (Kampfner 2004). Though the Gilligan affair and its aftermath remains a sensitive issue for the BBC it has been subject to criticism in the past. One area which has historically and continues to generate significant controversy and difficulty for the BBC is in relation to charges of bias in its coverage of the conflict in the Middle East and in particular, between Israel and Palestine. Such has been the nature of the accusations that former Director of News Richard Sambrook commissioned the Balen Report to investigate allegations of bias against the BBC. However, the report, which completed in 2004, has not been made available to the public, a decision which has generated some significant controversy. In January 2005 the BBC received an FOI request from a Mr. Steven Sugar for a copy of the report which the organisation declined on the grounds that the report was not covered under FOI regulations. According to the Freedom of Information Act 2000 the BBC was not compelled to make public information 'held for the purposes of journalism, art or literature' (Freedom of Information Act 2000: 53). The Balen Report, it argued, was held for the purpose of journalism. Following an unsuccessful appeal to the Information Commissioner, Sugar wrote to the Information Tribunal to appeal against the judgement made by the Information Commission that the he did not have jurisdiction 'to further consider the issue' (Hirsch 2009). The Tribunal upheld the request 'saying that the Commissioner did in fact have jurisdiction to consider the issue, and that the Balen report did not fall within the "purposes of journalism" exception' (Hirsch 2009). In February 2009, following decisions by the High Court and the Court of Appeal, The House of Lords overturned the Court of

Appeal decision relating to matters of jurisdiction and that the High Court should judge the meaning of the terms 'journalism, art and literature' in relation to the remit of FOI. The subsequent judgement by the High Court, later upheld by the Court of Appeal, ruled that the BBC was under no obligation under the terms of the FOA to publish the report.

More recently a BBC *Panorama* programme entitled 'Death in the Med', which was broadcast in August 2010, focusing on an Israeli Defence Force (IDF) assault on an aid ship heading for Gaza, the BBC's Editorial Standards Committee upheld a number of complaints which centred on issues of accuracy and impartiality. Though the committee noted that the programme overall had met the required standards of 'due accuracy' and 'due impartiality', complaints were upheld which centred on particular issues where accuracy and impartiality were undermined.[4]

Another issue which generated significant controversy for the BBC was its decision in 2009 to broadcast an episode of its flagship television programme Question Time which included the leader of the far-right British National Party (BNP) Nick Griffin. Though Griffin had appeared as a guest on other BBC radio and television programmes, his appearance on this programme prompted widespread criticism of the BBC. Senior government figures, anti-fascist and anti-racist groups argued that allowing the BNP to appear would give them an air of respectability they did not deserve and that the BBC was providing a platform for fascists. For example, former Home Secretary Alan Johnson refused to appear on the show as did Peter Hain the then Secretary of State for Wales. Hain argued that if it allowed Griffin a platform, the BBC would contravene its own anti-racist and equal opportunity policies. Moreover, the BNP was not a legitimate political party given that it was in breach of the rules regarding its policy of white only membership. The campaign group Unite Against Fascism also protested against Griffin's appearance on the show.

Of course the debate about whether or not Griffin should appear on the programme centred around the tension of allowing extremist parties a public platform to air their views set against the rights of minority groups to be protected from such views. The argument put forward by former Labour Mayor of London Ken Livingston was that when extreme right-wing organisations such as the BNP get airtime they appear more credible and concessions such as this only advances their cause (Livingstone 2009). A *Guardian* comment by Jim Wolfreys (2009) noted that similar mainstream television appearances benefitted the far right in France. Moreover, fascist parties such as the BNP clearly seek to undermine the democratic rights and liberties of ethnic and religious groups in society and as such should not be provided with a platform to espouse their views. This tension highlights what Cohen-Almagor terms the 'democratic catch' (2001) in which the exercise of freedom of speech can undermine the rights and liberties of target groups and which, in his view cannot be justified.

In response to such criticism, director general Mark Thomson asserted the BBC's commitment to impartiality and argued that the BBC had a responsibility to allow the public to 'hear the full rage of political perspectives' and if it did not allow the BNP to appear, he argued, it would be in breach of its 'central principle of impartiality' (Booth 2009) He suggested that it was a matter for Parliament to ban the BNP if it saw fit, but the BBC had a responsibility to allow the representatives of legal political parties airtime. Griffin's appearance on the flagship television programme did little to bolster support for the BNP, despite complaints from some viewers and Griffin himself that he was subject to unfair treatment by the broadcaster.[5] In an attempt to contextualise the debate surrounding Griffin's appearance on the programme Brendan O'Neil (2009) has suggested that the argument about Griffin's appearance had little to do with debates about freedom of speech but were instead related to an elite desire for political and moral validation in the absence of any meaningful political sentiment or ideas on their part. Griffin, O'Neil suggests, played the 'voodoo doll' who was subject to a 'cultural lynching' and 'calculated [...] moral distancing' by those involved. Under the spotlight in an open forum of debate in the Millian sense Griffin's odious moral and political sentiments were on show for all to see; however, less apparent according to O'Neil, was any meaningful political vision offered by his political opponents.

Linked to the principle of impartiality is the notion of conflict of interest and the BBC Guidelines stress that advice and guidance on impartiality should be read in conjunction with the section on Conflict of Interest that '[e]xternal activities of individuals working for the BBC must not undermine the public's perception of the impartiality, integrity, independence and objectivity of the BBC. Nor should they bring the BBC into disrepute' (BBC 2011: 155). The notion of a publicly funded organisation and its employees gaining pecuniary or other advantage because of their particular profile or position is one that raises difficulty for the organisation. The guidelines in particular prevent news presenters and journalists from 'undertak[ing] promotions, endorsements or advertisements for any company, outside organisation or political party' (BBC 2011: 157). In a recent judgement relating to charges of a conflict of interest of one of its newsreaders, Moira Stuart, relating to her work for HM Revenue and Customs' tax return campaign, the BBC judged that there was no conflict of interests as Mrs Stuart was promoting a public service rather than a particular product or service (Plunkett 2010).

In its commitment to accuracy and impartiality, the Guidelines also emphasise BBC's obligation 'to be fair to all – fair to those our output is about, fair to contributors, and fair to our audiences. BBC content should be based on respect, openness and straight dealing' (2011: 52). In addition to its own guidelines the BBC is also under an obligation under the Ofcom Broadcasting Code to 'avoid unjust or unfair treatment of individuals or organisations in programmes' (Ofcom Rule 7.1). The Guidelines specify the requirement that informed consent should be obtained where possible[6] and that contributors to programmes should be 'appropriately informed about the planned nature and context of their contributions' (BBC 2011: 52).[7]

Harm and offence

Media are of course liable to the same legal sanctions as members of the public in relation to the limits of freedom of expression and in particular, regulation relating to the incitement to religious or racial hatred have been strengthened in recent years via the Racial and Religious Hatred Act 2006. Media organisations have to be particularly explicit about the particular boundaries of their output so as to frame their content within what are considered 'generally accepted standards' which are drawn from the 2003 Communications Act. The BBC Guidelines and Ofcom state explicitly that they 'must apply generally accepted standards so as to provide adequate protection for members of the public from the inclusion of offensive and harmful material' (BBC 2011: 36). Specifically the use of the 9pm watershed and TV scheduling are intended to signal that programmes broadcast after the watershed are not suitable for children and are intended for an adult audience. Of course the regulation recognises that 'the nature of news means that it is not always possible to avoid showing material that might distress some of our audience before the watershed' (BBC 2011: 40). Considerations of audience expectations also play a role within the Guidelines which recognise the requirement for editors and programme makers to justify use of graphic images which should always be prefaced with a warning. With regard to online news content then clearly the watershed cannot apply, as such the BBC Guidelines state that '[a]ny content immediately accessible one click from the Home Page should normally be suitable for a general audience, including children' (BBC 2011: 41).

Crime and anti-social behaviour

Reporting crime and what has more recently been termed 'anti-social behaviour' has always, it seems, been a feature of journalism since the time of Northcliffe (Conboy 2004). Broadcasters' emphasis on serving the public interest is highlighted as a guiding principle in their coverage of crime. Similarly, the notion of balance is stressed with the use of deception and intrusions against privacy only permissible within the organisation's commitment to public service broadcasting. The Code also stresses general prohibitions against investigative reporting which involves 'deception and/or intrusion, [and which] must be clearly editorially justified and proportional' (BBC 2010: 83). The Guidelines in particular offer a blueprint for staff with regard to reporting crime; dealing with criminals, perpetrators of crime as well as victims and witnesses of crime and in respect of investigations into crime and anti-social behaviour (BBC 2010: 83).

Broadcasters and privacy

The scope with which journalism and the news media have to legitimately delve into the private lives of individuals in the name of the public interest is one of the most difficult questions for journalism. Of course the wider legal context is informed by Articles 8 and 10 of the European Convention on Human Rights (ECHR) and the Human Rights Act 1998, which guarantee individuals the protection of the rights to privacy and freedom of expression respectively. The Ofcom Broadcasting Code makes explicit that the section on privacy (and the preceding section on fairness) 'apply to how broadcasters treat the individuals or organisations participating or otherwise directly affected by programmes, or the making of programmes, rather than to what the general public sees and/or hears as viewers and listeners' (Ofcom 2011: 37).

The emphasis is placed on the implications for participants or those affected by the programme rather than wider public sentiments. The BBC's Guidelines on privacy are heavily informed by Section 8 of the Ofcom Code and stress that decisions relating to privacy should be made with an overriding concern for the public interest. Though conceding that no definitive statement exists as to the exact nature and scope of the public interest (see Chapter 6), the Guidelines specify the following indicative priorities: exposing or detecting crime; exposing significantly anti-social behaviour; exposing corruption or injustice; disclosing significant incompetence or negligence; protecting people's health and safety; preventing people from being misled by some statement or action of an individual or organisation, and disclosing information that assists people to better comprehend or make decisions on matters of public importance (BBC 2011: 65). The Guidelines also assert the notion that there is a public interest in freedom of expression itself. The Ofcom Code places emphasis on the notion of 'warranted' and infringement in which the broadcaster would be required to 'demonstrate that the public interest outweighs the right to privacy' (Ofcom 2011: Sec. 8: 38). The definition of public interest here broadly corresponds with those set out in the BBC's Guidelines.

Given significant differences in the regulation relating to the print and broadcast media it should be no surprise that that in relation the regulation concerning privacy, there is a similar level of divergence. As Chris Frost notes:

> Ofcom receives and adjudicates complaints from the public about TV and radio programmes but its powers to punish are much tougher than the PCC's since it can insist on publication of its adjudication, but also levy fines, impose conditions on licence holders or even revoke a licence to transmit for serious breaches.
>
> *Frost (2010: 384)*

Possibly given the specific statutory foundation of these controls, matters relating to invasions of privacy tend to be fewer than those in the press. Frost notes that since 2004 'licence holders have been fined a total of £13.145 million for 52 breaches of Ofcom's code', with the majority of complaints relating to media standards (Frost 2010: 384). However, he goes on to indicate that on average Ofcom annually receives less than half the number of fairness and privacy complaints than the PCC over the same period with the bulk of the complaints relating to fairness, a principle that the PCC does not account for in its guidelines (Frost 2010: 385). Yet despite the relatively low number of complaints to Ofcom concerning invasions of privacy, there remain some anomalies in respect of Ofcom's regulatory framework and the introduction of the Human Rights Act (1998). The anomalies concern the apparent inconsistency in U.K. law in relation to the 'system of complaints and post-broadcast sanctions [which] does *not* (sic) satisfy the requirements of Articles 8 and 13 of the Convention'[8] (Fenwick and Phillipson 2006: 880).

Fenwick and Phillipson (2006) point to the ruling in *Peck v UK*, which from their perspective highlights the failure of U.K. law. In August 1995 photographic stills of

CCTV footage of a man holding a knife on a public street were printed in local newspapers and shown on both Anglia Television and the BBC. The man, a Mr. Peck, had attempted suicide and was clearly identifiable from the footage, despite claims by the owners of the CCTV footage – Brentwood Council – that they had sought to protect Mr Peck's identity. In 2003 the European Court of Human Rights held that though the CCTV recording was not an infringement under Article 8, the release of footage by the local authority to the press without his permission and without sufficiently concealing his identity *did* constitute a breach of his rights. The failure of the council to adequately protect Mr. Peck's identity and the failure of the courts to provide for an 'effective remedy' (Fenwick and Phillipson 2006: 862) for the invasion of privacy demonstrates the 'manifestly unsatisfactory response to the finding that the U.K. had violated Articles 8 and 13' (Fenwick and Phillipson 2006: 880).

Online environment and privacy

There are also issues in regard the regulation of online content, some of which comes under the jurisdiction of both the PCC and Ofcom. Frost (2010: 387) points out that in relation to the regulation of the respective sectors 'regulatory bodies are taking very different lines in their regulatory decisions about essentially the same activities'.[9] This, of course, can only lead to confusion and inconsistency with regard to the broader regulatory *and* legal environment and two separate, though two related developments are significant in emphasising the problematic nature of the current approach. The first has been the publication of the Neuberger Report in May 2011 which sought to address concerns about the perceived prevalence of interim injunctions and so-called super-injunctions in the wake of the Trafigura and John Terry cases (see Chapter 6). The second has been the attempt, via the use of a gagging order, by a Premiership footballer to prevent the disclosure of his identity in relation to an alleged affair he had with a reality television personality. Though his name was widely circulated on the social-networking site Twitter, newspapers and broadcasters were not permitted to disclose his identity. However, following the publication by a Scottish newspaper the *Sunday Herald* of a front page photograph of the well-known player with the word 'Censored' obscuring only his eyes, Liberal Democrat MP John Hemming used parliamentary privilege to name the player in the Commons, thereby circumventing the gagging order and according to some abusing his parliamentary privilege to deliberately break the law (Brogan 2011; Toynbee 2011). Hemming's actions have drawn attention to the conflict between parliament and the judiciary with regard to privacy law which the Prime Minister David Cameron has promised to examine. Moreover, this case not only highlights the general confusion and inconsistency relating to the protection of privacy in English law, but also elites anxiety about the power of technology with Lord Neuberger himself conceding that modern technology was seemingly 'out of control' (Bowcott 2011). However, it is not the technology which is the key concern for elites, rather those who use it, as Tim Black argues: 'It's our freedom to speak our minds online, to negotiate our own relationships, that terrifies the fusty judiciary, not the shiny new technology itself' (2011).

What is clear is the unsustainable legal framework governing the press and broadcast news in matters relating to privacy and the anxiety this has created for Parliament and the Judiciary and their respective powers and responsibilities. The recent furore surrounding privacy highlights tension between Parliament and the Judiciary and their specific roles in relation to the development and application of U.K. law in the context of the application of ECHR via the Human Rights Act in particular. Of course, it is too early to tell whether or not the most recent debate about privacy will have implications for the regulatory codes and frameworks which relate to the broadcast media on matters of privacy. What is likely to remain intact, however, is the particular emphasis on public interest which the guidelines suggest are the overriding factor where matters of infringement of privacy are concerned.

Conclusion

In his 2009 MacTaggart Lecture, News Corporation's James Murdoch lambasted the BBC and the regulatory frameworks of the media in Britain and Europe which he argued stifles competition and limits choice. Likening broadcast regulation to a form of anti-Darwinian creationism, Murdoch suggested that the regulatory environment of Britain acts 'as an impingement on freedom of speech' which contrasts sharply with this history of press freedom from 'the broadsides of the Levellers, [...] the thundering 19th century *Times*, to *The Sun* fighting for the rights of veterans today' (Murdoch 2009: 13). Murdoch's sentiments resonate with those of his father Rupert who gave the MacTaggart Lecture in 1989. As Keane (1991) notes Rupert Murdoch's speech harked back to the struggle for press freedom that was fought against state censorship and oppression. Keane suggests that such emotive language 'typifies this extraordinary revival of the old language of liberty of the press' (1991: 53) in the cause of attacking state-regulated media and asserting the principles of market rationality. In other words the seemingly timeless trope is trotted out that freedom of the press is stifled if the rationality of the market is interfered with in any way. The market is the arbiter of freedom in all its varieties, or so the argument goes.

During the summer of 2011 Rupert Murdoch's News Corporation looked set to receive the go-ahead to gain full control over BSkyB. If the purchase had gone through, it would have been evidence of a continuation of trends which gained momentum in the 1980s and 1990s, towards a more fully developed market-orientated model of broadcasting regulation, and a signal of the acceleration of the long slow death of the public service ideal. However, shocking new revelations about the extent of the *News of the World*'s phone hacking practices condemned this move to the dustbin and thwarted the Murdoch empire's attempts to further penetrate the British broadcasting landscape.

6

PRIVACY AND THE PUBLIC INTEREST

Instantaneous photographs and newspaper enterprise have invaded the sacred precincts of private and domestic life; and numerous mechanical devices threaten to make good the prediction that 'what is whispered in the closet shall be proclaimed from the house-tops'.

Warren and Brandeis (1890: 195)

Introduction

The words of Warren and Brandeis uttered over a hundred years ago remain relevant, especially following the shattering revelations about the extent of the *News of the World*'s phone hacking activities. Technology and greed did indeed enable the invasion of the 'sacred precincts' of the private lives of the family of Milly Dowler, the murdered schoolgirl whose mobile phone was hacked by employees of the newspaper while she was still missing. By deleting phone messages, the perpetrators had given false hope to the parents and police that Milly was still alive. These despicable acts not only shocked a nation, in awe at the depths at which a newspaper could sink, it also set in motion a series of events which are still unfolding as I write. The right to privacy, a right which was so distastefully trampled upon by the *News of the World*, is something which is said to come most sharply into conflict with the right to freedom of speech and freedom of the press. In addition to the rights to freedom of speech and expression, the various conventions and protocols on human rights tend, in theory at least, to give equal weight to the individual right of privacy.[1] Yet of course in practice, the right to privacy for public figures and the general public has been an area of contestation for many years. As Tambini and Heyward (2002) note, the classic legal statement on privacy came from the United States but was based on common law decisions in the U.K. which prompted Warren and Brandeis to formulate their statement on the legal status of privacy. Warren and Brandeis outlined the development of the 'right to be left alone' (1890: 193) which has significantly contributed to the modern liberal individualist conception of privacy and as the quote above highlights, they offer an almost prophetic warning against the erosion of privacy rights. Speaking in relation to the limits of freedom of the press Warren and Brandeis argue that:

> In general, then, the matters of which the publication should be repressed may be described as those which concern the private life, habits, acts, and relations of an individual, and have no legitimate connection with his fitness for a public office which he seeks or for which he is suggested, or for any public or quasi public position which he seeks or for which he is suggested, and have no legitimate relation to or bearing upon any act done by him in a public or quasi public capacity.
>
> *Warren and Brandeis (1890: 216)*

Yet Warren and Brandeis's statement that even public figures should be protected against invasions of privacy unless it can be demonstrated that such an intrusion would relate to their ability to hold public office seems somewhat outdated today. The days when the private life of politicians and other public figures is of no concern to others unless it impinges on their abilities to perform their public duties, are long gone.[2] Sex scandals involving politicians and other public figures seem to be the main emphasis of the popular press in particular and the debate has generally centred on whether the press can demonstrate that it has put the material in the public domain as a matter of public interest. The clichéd question of whether what might be of interest to the public might also serve the public interest seems apt. Another concern however is the increasing dependence on the judiciary to rule in matters of invasions of privacy. As editor of *The Guardian* Alan Rusbridger has pointed out recently, 'there are plenty who think that, as our libel laws are cleaned up, smart lawyers are switching horses to privacy' (Rusbridger 2011). The more recent examples highlighted in this chapter and developments highlighted in the following chapter would seem to suggest he is correct.

The purpose of this chapter then is to explore the relationship between freedom of the press and privacy and examine the particular tensions that become apparent when focusing on the democratic imperative of the press. The chapter will begin by providing a brief theoretical analysis of the concept of privacy. Here it will be evident that privacy is very much a modern construct in that the private sphere, as it is understood in Britain, is very much a product of liberal political thought. As such the legal parameters of privacy have been framed in the context of notions of autonomy, respect and the separation of public and private spheres. From this brief introduction to the conceptual bases of privacy I go on to deal with privacy and the press, briefly highlighting the history of debates about privacy and press freedom and the issue of self-regulation before going on to talk about self-regulation and the Human Rights Act 1998 (HRA) which some critics argue[3] have introduced damaging privacy legislation into U.K. law 'by the back door'.

Privacy in theory

As a philosophical concept privacy is a relatively recent construction. The development of the public sphere in the eighteenth century also saw the development of the private sphere in which the clear demarcation between public and private space became one of the central organising principles of social relationships. Privacy then is very much connected liberal conception of the individual which sets out the specific realms of the human condition which relate to their autonomy and dignity as essentially private entities. Though, of course, there are competing theoretical conceptions of 'public' and 'private', the distinctions between them are increasingly being blurred (Sheller and Urry 2003). Yet as we will see, the debate about what distinguishes *public* from *private* seems to be what animates much of the discussion around press freedom and invasions of privacy. What was originally thought to be an essentially private matter for Members of Parliament – for example, MPs' expenses claims – is now open to public scrutiny, and rightly so. Though there are significant debates about the constitution of privacy, it will be helpful to begin our discussion on privacy with some general principles which attempt to set out the basis of privacy in law.

Epstein (2000) has identified two principle conceptual bases on which privacy is generally considered. The first fits broadly within the classical liberal tradition which identifies certain inalienable 'rights' of individuals, such as the right to property, the right to freedom of expression, freedom of conscience and so on, within a framework of limited government. Here the right to live autonomously without unsolicited external interference from the state or other individuals is seen as a necessary aspect of human fulfilment. Within this conception then, the right to privacy is just one of a range liberties that the classical liberal conception proscribes. The second conceptual basis is based on a conception of the 'redistributive state' and pays heed to the aforementioned rights but within this framework the state is much more active in relation to the promotion of social goods such as anti-discrimination law, 'and an extensive system of subsidies and restraints that allow for massive government redistribution of income or wealth from some groups to others' (Epstein 2000: 5). The law then divides privacy into two 'broad classes' (2000: 7) the first of which is in relation to the law of tort and deals with relations between persons unknown to each other (strangers), the second, which comes under the law of contract, deals with privacy in respect of consensual relations between parties.

Epstein notes that in the first instance, the law protecting private property already allows provision to protect privacy in that no one has the right to walk uninvited into the house of another person and take photographs or eavesdrop on conversations; in this sense the law of trespass will suffice in many circumstances.[4] However, he finishes by highlighting that in the modern context eavesdropping or spying can occur when there has been no trespass and as such the association of privacy rights to property rights starts to unfurl. For example, one might listen in to a private conversation in a restaurant or in another public space, or one may intercept an email exchange between two parties, to which the interceptor has no right of access. For Epstein, there is a *social norm* that inhibits the invasion of privacy of others.[5] The notion of privacy in these circumstances is consistent with the classical liberal or libertarian approach. The problem however is the question of what further protection for privacy should be guaranteed by law? Here Epstein provides us with two examples where the law of privacy might be extended. The first is in relation to the right of privacy in a public space. The question that Epstein asks is: 'To what extent individuals should be forced to moderate their conduct in public spaces to respect the privacy of others?' His answer is broadly again that social convention comes into force when someone's privacy is breached. Yet, of course, if a celebrity is being photographed on a public beach, do they have a right not to be photographed? As Epstein notes that: 'The matter becomes the source of intense litigation when paparazzi go to inordinate lengths to bag their quarry' (2000: 13; see also note 33). This issue is one that is central to the debate on privacy and press freedom and one that we shall return to later.

The second element, which is also central to freedom of speech and freedom of the press is related to an individual's immunity from public criticism or comment. The central question here relates to the extent that individuals should be protected from the publication of material which they would rather keep private. As Barendt (2005: 230) maintains: 'The law must balance competing rights: to personal privacy on the one hand, and on the other the right of the public to be informed about matters of concern and the freedom of the media to satisfy that concern.' Epstein (2000: 13) rightly points out that a 'society that allowed aggrieved individuals to ban unfavourable comments of others comes close to being a police state'. As such it becomes necessary to mark out the specific terrain on which a person's right to privacy can and can't be legitimately suppressed. It should be noted that that the (albeit imperfect) law of defamation should suffice if the information that is made public is not based in fact (see later). However, when the case of fact is not an issue, invasions of privacy generally rest on the test of whether or not the invasion can be regarded as being in the public interest. The matter also rests on whether or not the information was gained via illegal means. For example, the Press Complaints Commission (PCC) Editor's Code of Practice states that:

(i) The press must not seek to obtain or publish material acquired by using hidden cameras or clandestine listening devices; or by intercepting private or mobile telephone calls, messages or emails; or by the unauthorised removal of documents or photographs; or by accessing digitally-held private information without consent.

(ii) Engaging in misrepresentation or subterfuge, including by agents or intermediaries, can generally be justified only in the public interest and then only when the material cannot be obtained by other means.

Press Complaints Commission Editor's Code of Practice (2009)

As noted the aforementioned issues relate explicitly to the principles of the law of tort in which the assertion of privacy rights relate to the inalienable status of a person as an individual and the rights he or she has to live their lives without intrusion or public disclosure.

Privacy in law can also be understood in relation to breach of confidence in which the press may reveal 'information which it knows, or should have a appreciated is personal or confidential' (Barendt 2005: 232). So-called 'kiss and tell' stories in which celebrities or politicians have been 'stung' by newspapers exposing their sexual proclivities are common. Increasingly however, there have been attempts to prevent such disclosure by recourse to breach of confidence in which there is an implicit recognition that private acts between consenting adults are just that and should not be subject to public exposure. The most recent notable example of this concerns Max Mosley's 2007 action against the *News of the World*. When photographs of former FIA (Fédération Internationale de l'Automobile) president Max Mosley appeared in the *News of the World* participating in a sado-masochistic 'Nazi-style' orgy with five prostitutes, the newspaper claimed public interest given the high profile nature of the FIA boss and the fact that he is the son of 1930s fascist leader Oswald Mosley. Mosley successfully sued the newspaper for £60,000 over breach of his privacy and for claiming that he was engaged in Nazi themed role-play. The judge Mr. Justice Eady argued that there was 'no public interest or other justification for the clandestine recording, for the publication of the resulting information and still photographs, or for the placing of the video extracts on the *News of the World* website' and that there was 'no evidence that the gathering […] was intended to be an enactment of Nazi behaviour or adoption of any of its attitudes'. The Judge also noted that there was an 'old fashioned breach of confidence' in that one of the prostitutes, woman E, had disclosed personal information about Mosley without his consent and had therefore breached Article 8 of the European Convention on Human Rights (ECHR).[6]

Another case which involved the law of confidence occurred in 2002 and involved the model Naomi Campbell. Campbell initially sued *The Mirror* after it had published photographs of her leaving a therapy session at Narcotics Anonymous. The identity of the source was unknown to journalists 'but whom the court concluded must have been a fellow attendee of Narcotics Anonymous, or a member of Campbell's staff or entourage' (Mayes 2002: 6). The court ruled that the newspaper had breached the law of confidence by disclosing the details of Campbell's drug therapy and had also contravened the Data Protection Act 1998 as 'it had collected personal data on Campbell after a concealed photographer took surreptitious photographs of her' (Mayes 2002: 6). Following an appeal by *The Mirror*, the case against the newspaper was overturned with the judges noting that 'it was in the public interest that readers knew the truth about the model who had lied about her drug use' (Cozens and Milmo 2002).

One of the central concerns for freedom of speech campaigners about recent privacy cases is that legal judgements are being made by high court judges who often do not agree on the correct interpretation of the law. As Mayes suggests: 'The Campbell case shows that judges have differing views about what counts as speech that is in the public interest. This means that whether judges will allow publication or not is always a grey area, subject to their own views.' However, Frost (2010: 391–92) maintains that 'hardly any of the landmark cases do anything more than firm up the law of confidence'. Moreover, the incorporation of the ECHR into United Kingdom law by the Human Rights Act 1998 has provided alternative avenues through which celebrities and public figures can assert their privacy rights at the expense of freedom of the press.

In conceptual terms, privacy need not necessarily be solely concerned with the protection of individual rights against the state or public exposure. Robert Post (1989) has maintained that the common law tort of invasion of privacy in United States law not only protects the interests of individuals but also maintains the wider interests of the community. This is done within a broader context of what he calls 'rules of civility'. In this sense privacy is not only understood in relation to the protection of individual private interests, but also within a wider social framework which guarantees the interests of the community as well. Post identifies the specific realms within which such a tort operates. First, he notes that individuals 'are constitutive of human autonomy' and should therefore be protected from the unwanted invasion of their private space (1989: 1008). This should also be balanced with the recognition that public accountability of, for example, public officials who are charged with carrying out tasks on behalf of the public and should therefore be open to scrutiny. He notes 'The claims of public officials to a "private" information preserve are simply overridden by the more general demands of the public for political accountability' (1989: 997). In other words, individuals who put themselves in the public eye have in some sense given up the same rights to privacy that the general public enjoy. They may, of course, enjoy a private life; however, the public nature of their job or social position militates against a *full* protection of their privacy rights. As we will see, this is something that has caused and continues to cause significant debate and argument. Post, however, is critical of this largely instrumental conception of privacy. Instead he exposes the 'social and communal character of privacy' (1989: 1009) and maintains that privacy is also 'part of a set of civility rules that govern the degree of distance or familiarity that is appropriate for different kinds of relationships, helping people to assert their own and respect others' dignity' (Boling 1996: 33). In this sense Post's interpretation of privacy is based on a conception of the ways in which individuals relate to one another and 'comprise an important part of the obligations that members of a community owe to each other' (Post 1989: 985).

Privacy and the press

In 1948 the Committee on the Law of Defamation 'asserted that "there are great difficulties in formulating" a law to restrain invasions of privacy while not at the same time restraining "the due reporting of matters which are of public interest"' (O'Malley and Soley 2000: 54). The point being that the balancing of press freedom with the right to privacy is one that is difficult to achieve given the press's obligation to act as watchdog for the public. Public figures, particularly politicians, by nature of their decision to enter public life, have to forego some entitlement to privacy that ordinary citizens see as essential.

The extent of the sacrifice, however, is one that generates significant debate. For example, do the sexual proclivities of politicians really have anything to do with the public so long as they are doing their job? Or has the press an obligation to poke around into the private lives of politicians and public figures in order to ensure that they are above reproach? These are difficult questions that relate to rights as specified in Article 8 and Article 10 of the ECHR respectively. If one looks to one of the most infamous scandals in recent British history – the Profumo affair, we can see that in the public exposure of Minister of War John Profumo's affair with the lover of a Soviet attaché at the height of the Cold War, the public interest was clear. Though not as politically significant as the Profumo affair, when photographs of Minister of War Anthony Lambton smoking marijuana in bed with prostitute Norma Levy were published, the controversy significantly embarrassed the Heath government. Again one could argue a public interest in that Lambton, a married Tory junior minister sleeping with prostitutes and smoking dope, is not of the highest moral standing, especially for someone in government. Sex scandals involving politicians and senior figures, it seems are fair game as they draw attention to the perceived moral failings of those whom we expect should be of greater moral standing that the rest of society. When Conservative Party Deputy Chairman Jeffrey Archer made payments to a prostitute in 1986 it led to his resignation from government and eventual imprisonment for perjury (Cloonan 1998: 67). Archer had successfully brought a libel case against the *Daily Star* newspaper in 1987 for allegations that he had slept with a prostitute; however, he was subsequently charged with perverting the course of justice and perjury when he had asked a friend to provide a false alibi during the original trial.

Self-regulation

The idea that government interference is actively regulating the press is, of course, seen as an anathema to liberal democratic notions of press freedom, and consequently successive governments have been careful to frame such inquiries as being in the public interest at large. Therefore, the notion that there should be some form of voluntary agreement among members of the press to monitor and regulate themselves should be seen as an important factor in shaping the parameters of press regulation in Britain. Despite periods of intense debate and public outrage at press standards, the industry has so far avoided statutory regulation and has managed to contrive a system of self-regulation with which to police itself. The system also allows those who feel in some way injured by the press a vehicle for redress. Though the terms and nature of such redress is an issue that remains moot.

The first detailed investigation into standards of the press standards in Britain was set up by PEP (Political and Economic Planning) and consisted of public servants, academics, members of the newspaper industry and academics which articulated concerns about standards within the newspaper industry particularly in relation to press intrusion into 'private lives and personal affairs' (O'Malley and Soley 2000: 51). Among their recommendations was the establishment of a voluntary Press Tribunal which would provide a body to which members of the public or those in the public eye could complain if they felt that they had been unfairly treated by the press. The tribunal would then investigate the complaint and if upheld, would 'use the power of publicity as a sanction' against transgressors (O'Malley and Soley 2000: 52). O'Malley and Soley (2000) suggest that there had been concerns about the Tory supporting press during the 1945 election (52 per cent as opposed to 35 per cent of the press supporting Labour) so when Labour gained its overwhelming majority in the House of Commons, it was clear that Labour MPs, some of whom were also journalists, would push for something to be done with regard the structure and orientation of the press. Following concerns highlighted by the National Union of Journalists (NUJ) which were raised formally in the house by two serving MPs that were also NUJ members that there were increasing tendencies towards monopolisation in the press, given an increasing trend towards concentration of press ownership in Britain, the Royal Commission of the Press was set up

> with the object of furthering the free expression of opinion through the Press and the greatest practicable accuracy in the presentation of news, to inquire into the control, management and ownership of the newspaper and periodical Press and the news agencies, including the financial structure and the monopolistic tendencies in control, and to make recommendations thereon.
>
> *Royal Commission on the Press (1949: 4)*

It also had the intention of looking at the 'influence of financial and advertising interests on the distortion and suppression of news' (O'Malley and Soley 2000: 53). Though the Commission asserted that the 'British Press is inferior to none in the world' (1949: 149) it did cite a number of areas of concern to which they would seek to put forward recommendations for their remedy and 'make good such deficiencies' (1949: 152).

The first deficiency was related to competition for mass circulation and the inherent tendency within such an environment to 'triviality and sensationalism' (1949: 152). In effect the blame for low standards among the press was placed squarely at the public whose appetite for such material was seen to dictate newspaper content. The Commission cited Northcliffe's dictum that 'while it is damaging for a paper not to give a reader what he wants, it is far worse to give him what he does not want' (1949: 152). In short it was a commercial decision to 'give them what they want' and as such outside the scope of government or regulatory interference. Moreover, 'proprietors had the right to safeguard their financial investments in a high risk industry' (Curran and Seaton 2010: 328). Similarly, the Commission concluded that though advertising is an important part of the newspaper industry, it had a 'negligible' effect on 'the treatment of public questions in the Press' (1949: 149). In other words though the Commission had found evidence that advertisers had 'occasionally' sought to exert influence on the press, this was not the norm. 'The public can, therefore, dismiss from its mind any misgivings that the Press of this country is mysteriously financed and controlled by hidden influences, and that it is open to the exercise of corrupt pressure from self-seeking outside sources' (1949: 149).

The Commission also cited political partisanship among the national press as 'a further weakening of the foundations of intelligent judgement in public affairs' (1949: 151). Though it argued that this was balanced out by the provincial press, and the fact that the press, as a whole, provided 'sufficient variety of political opinion', the view was that the press 'should cater for a greater variety of intellectual levels' (1949: 152) in order to fill the 'gap' between the quality and the popular press. In other words, there should be greater scope for serious and non-trivial news to be provided to those who either couldn't afford the quality press or couldn't understand it. Though it did not recommend a dramatic change in relation to ownership in the newspaper industry, it eventually recommended a General Council of the Press (O'Malley and Soley 2000: 54) which would

> [s]afeguard the freedom of the Press; to encourage the growth of a sense of public responsibility and public service amongst all engaged in the profession of journalism – that is, in the editorial production of newspapers – whether as directors, editors or other journalists; and to further the efficiency of the profession and the well being of those who practiced it.
>
> *O'Malley and Soley (2000: 55)*

Moreover, the Commission recommended that the recruitment, education and training of journalists should be a higher priority with a specific emphasis on both vocational and academic journalism education so as to ensure that journalists had a 'fuller knowledge of history and English [...] knowledge of the processes of central and local government and the courts' and 'at least a grounding in economics' (1949: 166). The General Council should also endeavour to promote a more professionalised culture among journalists along the lines of the General Medical Council and be made up of members of the press (Curran and Seaton 2010: 334).

Despite the Commission's recommendations it wasn't until 1953 that a General Council of the Press was established 'under the threat of statutory regulation' (Curran and Seaton 2010: 334) and its remit was significantly less than that which the Royal Commission had envisaged. It would, for example, have no lay members, (a key recommendation of the Royal Commission), nor would it take on board an active commitment to public service, instead favouring a more 'passive role' which involved a commitment to the much more vague notion of 'retaining the character of the British Press' (O'Malley and Soley 2000: 59). Given the relatively low horizons and limited scope of the Press Council, it was no surprise that press standards did not improve. Concerns about the lowering of journalistic standards and the seemingly ever increasing power of newspaper proprietors as concentration of ownership gathered apace in the nineteen sixties, and eventually led to two further Royal Commissions on the Press, both of which criticised the performance of the Press Council (Bingham 2007).

Self-regulation in the modern era

The Press Commissions of 1949, 1962 and 1977 sought, with only limited success to stimulate the industry into regulating itself effectively through the Press Council.[7] Even though the 1977 Commission succeeded in ensuring that a greater number of lay members, the industry was 'grudging' to say the least (Shannon 2001: 16) to the largely ineffective directives of the Council. Moreover, the fact that newspaper editors were generally to 'react with indifference, hostility or contempt to adverse adjudications'

(Robertson 1983: 4) highlighted the relative impotence of the Press Council. Continued intransigence by the newspaper industry, in part cultivated by the knowledge that it was highly unlikely that a Conservative government would seek to directly interfere in the press, coupled with a new cut-throat laissez-faire economic environment, gave a number of newspapers the confidence to push the boundaries of journalistic ethics in the 1980s. Curran and Seaton maintain:

> In the national press, this led for a time to a decline in standards of accuracy, notorious cases of chequebook journalism, more prurient intrusions into private grief not justified by the public interest, the parading of imaginary folk devils, and outbreaks of sadistic bullying of sad people.
>
> *Curran and Seaton (2010: 336)*

There was a widespread belief that the Press Council was not an effective body as journalistic standards were clearly in decline. The public were not happy with the liberties that the press seemed to be taking. As Cloonan (1998) notes during the 1980s in particular there were a relatively large number of cases in which the press had clearly overstepped the mark. These included an 'interview' in *The Sun* with widow of a Falklands War serviceman who never actually spoke to the newspaper;[8] a reporter who deceived the grandmother of a victim of the Hillsborough disaster (in which 96 people died at the Sheffield Wednesday football ground) into giving the newspaper a photograph of the victim whose parents had previously declined to provide one. Also the particularly grim practice of 'doorstepping' where journalists would seek out the family and friends of people who had been recent victims of a crime or tragedy such as those in the Yorkshire Ripper case or the Cromwell Street murders (Cloonan: 1998: 63–64). Yet Cloonan maintains that the cases that hit the headlines and caused the most outrage were the ones concerning celebrities, royalty and MPs (1998: 64). Liberal Democrat Leader Paddy Ashdown's extra-marital affair with his secretary was exposed after documents were stolen from his lawyer, while the revelation in *The Independent* that Health Minister Virginia Bottomley's first son was born when Mrs. Bottomley was an unmarried teenager caused an outcry (Cloonan 1998: 65).

The Heritage Secretary David Mellor went on record as saying that he was 'almost ashamed and embarrassed to live in the same society as journalists who wrote such stories' (Shannon 2001: 23). 'Without question, during the six years or so from 1988 there was an air of continual crisis in the three-way relationship between the press (particularly the national tabloid press), the general public and the government' (Stephenson 1998: 14). In response to such disquiet the government asked Sir David Calcutt QC to set up a Committee on Privacy and Related Matters and conduct an inquiry into press regulation and privacy (Bingham 2007: 79).[9] Though no formal tort of infringement of privacy was introduced as the definition of statutory privacy was not available, the Calcutt Report noted that 'the press should be given one final chance to demonstrate that it can put its own house in order' (Calcutt 1990: 77).[10] Yet even as the Committee was sitting, the press 'scored a spectacular own goal' (Shannon 2001: 26) when two journalists from the *Sunday Sport* accessed the hospital room of popular television actor Gordon Kaye who was severely ill following a freak accident. The journalists interviewed a semi-conscious Kaye and took photographs of him in his hospital bed. Despite attempts by Kaye to block publication of the material, he was unsuccessful given that 'there was no right of privacy recognized by common law' (Sanders 2003: 80). As Shannon notes even though the *Sport* was 'an entertainment sleaze-sheet rather than a newspaper, this was held to be a scandal too far' (2001: 26). Among the recommendations was the scrapping of the Press Council which was to be replaced by a Press Complaints Commission (PCC) which would draw up a code of practice for journalists and also adjudicate in matters where there had been complaints that journalists had not acted according to the code.[11] In the words of the new chairman of the PCC Lord McGregor it would act as 'the conscience of the industry, upholding its ethical code of practice and dealing with complaints of citizens' (Shannon 2001: 47). The PCC would be comprised of an independent chairman who was not connected to the industry and sixteen members appointed by an independent Appointments Commission, the majority of which would be drawn from the industry. It would be funded via an industry levy. The Calcutt report emphasised the difficult balancing of freedom of the press and the rights to privacy, yet because of the requirements of press scrutiny in a democratic society, privacy would be seen as a secondary consideration (Cloonan 1998: 67).

Though the press were reluctant to go along with recommendations of the Calcutt Committee there was a grudging realisation that failure to adequately be seen to regulate itself would invite tougher government control of the press. Yet the PCC was only two years old when in a review, Sir David Calcutt called for it to be scrapped as it 'was proving ineffectual' (Munro 1997: 6) and unable to manage abuses of the press. Increased concern about invasions of privacy, particularly against the royals[12] had led the heritage secretary David Mellor who had previously been highly critical of the press to ask Calcutt to conduct the review.[13] The review concluded that the PCC should be replaced by statutory control as the press seemed unable to police itself. Moreover, the Kaye case and the Princess Eugenie[14] case demonstrated the press's contempt for the PCC (Cloonan 1998: 74). Calcutt recommended that new offences for intrusion onto property become law and that the government 'give further consideration to the introduction of a privacy tort in order to establish a general legal right to privacy' (Cloonan 1998: 68). This was rejected by the government which again seemed to want to placate the press in the run up to a general election.[15]

Following the death of Princess Diana in a car crash in Paris in 1997, her brother, Earl Spencer, suggested that her death had been directly caused by pursuing paparazzi, and that the newspaper industry 'had her blood on its hands'. The industry panicked as Shannon (2001: 271) suggests: '[T]he intensity of the guilty panic in newsrooms all over the country almost amounted to a collective confession: the industry standing over the Princess's corpse with a bloodstained knife in its hand.'[16] Yet again it seemed that the press was to come under scrutiny for overstepping the mark of responsible journalism. Though the response of the PCC was to further tighten its guidelines on intrusion, it again seemed that a satisfying resolution could be achieved as 'the PCC was unable in the 1990s to set workable boundaries between the public interest and the rights to privacy, especially where the commercial interests of proprietors were at stake' (O'Malley and Soley 2000: 170).

Human Rights Act 1998

In 1997 the New Labour government entered government with a landslide majority. Among its manifesto pledges was a commitment to incorporating the European Convention on Human Rights into U.K. law and the introduction of freedom of information legislation. The subsequent Human Rights Act of 1998[17] tied the U.K. to the ECHR and guaranteed human rights protection within U.K. law. Given that the U.K. does not have a written constitution which guarantees freedom of speech or the right to privacy, the Human Rights Act enables the right to privacy (ECHR Article 8) and the right to freedom of expression (ECHR Article 10) to be enshrined into U.K. law.[18] One of the first cases to apparently signify a shift towards a tort of privacy was *Douglas v Hello!* (2001) in which the actress Catherine Zeta-Jones and her husband Michael Douglas attempted to bring an injunction against *Hello!* magazine which would have prevented the magazine from publishing pictures of their wedding. However, given that the couple had already sold the picture rights to their wedding to another celebrity magazine, the issue of privacy was only perceived as a secondary consideration after copyright violation and breach of confidence (Tambini and Heyward 2002). Another case involving breach of confidence was the *A v B and C* case (2002) in which 'the court granted an injunction to restrain a tabloid newspaper from publishing its "kiss and tell stories" concerning the adulterous affairs of a professional footballer' (Crone *et al* 2002: 282). The case was subsequently overturned by Lord Woolf CJ who maintained that 'while public figures are entitled to a private life, they should recognize that even trivial facts relating to them are of great interest to the public' (Barendt 2005: 233).

Nevertheless writing in 2002, Crone *et al* (2002: 282) suggest that cases such as *Douglas v Hello!* (and the initial ruling in the *A v B and C* case) 'illustrate an important shift in favour of protection of privacy resulting from the HRA'. This shift was noted by the editor of the *Daily Mail* Paul Dacre in his speech to the Society of Editors in 2008, when he argued that the Judge in the Mosley case – Mr. Justice Eady – was undermining freedom of the press in Britain by the imposition of a privacy law via the 'back door'. Dacre argued that the Human Rights Act had enabled the judge to undermine press freedom 'with a stroke of his pen' as it was now a single judge that could determine who had the right to freedom of expression and who did not (Dacre 2008). Dacre's self-appointed guardianship of freedom of the press, however, should be viewed with some scepticism (Toynbee 2008) as we know that since the mid-nineteenth century, the profit motive has been newspapers' primary concern and it is usually within this context that 'freedom of the press' or 'freedom of speech' is invoked.

None more so than the popular press's obsession with prurience and titillation which raises concerns among some who suggest that privacy law should be used to protect privacy and it need not threaten freedom of speech. For example, Eric Barendt (2002) suggests that the system of self-regulation of the press has hitherto proved ineffective in protecting privacy. Mover given that privacy is a fundamental human right, it is deserving of protection in Parliament rather than some self-regulatory body. It is simply too important. Rejecting the notion that privacy legislation would amount to a threat to press freedom, Barendt suggests that:

> Film stars, footballers and other celebrities, have rights to privacy, just as much as the ordinary citizen. We do not have a right to read about their sexual affairs or other aspects of their private life. Arguably, we do not even have such a right with regard to politicians or public officials, unless there is some obvious connection between their private conduct and the discharge of their responsibilities.
>
> *Barendt (2002: 20)*

Moreover, newspapers and journalists would benefit from clearer guidance on matters pertaining to a privacy law. For example, the scope of privacy could be clarified,[19] as could the guidelines pertaining to the publication of photographs without consent.[20] A public interest defence would also enable news organisations to override privacy law 'in instances falling outside the proscribed categories' (Barendt 2002: 19).[21] Also a public domain defence would be available if the published material is already in the public domain. Finally Barendt suggests that privacy law would enable remedies to be sought in which the level of damages could be awarded. Significantly he also suggests that publication could be proscribed if infringement of privacy rights is at issue.

Yet former PCC chairman Lord Wakeham has argued that that the system of self-regulation is the best system with which to monitor and regulate the press. Moreover, the original principles which have informed the HRA stem from an era in which the threats to human liberty and rights were more pronounced and significant. When the ECHR was originally drawn up in the 1950s it was 'as a response both to the barbarism of Nazi Germany and the Second World War and to the rise of Communism in the Eastern Europe' (Wakeham 2002: 27). As such the convention is primarily framed in relation to abuses by non-democratic states against the individual and is therefore not applicable to the British context. Wakeham's concern about the incorporation of the ECHR into U.K. law via the Human Rights Act is that rather than enhancing freedom of expression, it actually stifles it as it places arbitrary power to curb freedom of expression in the hands of the courts. Moreover, it would largely be those who had the wealth to take matters to the courts that would benefit. The PCC does not charge those who bring complaints against newspapers for invasions of privacy. This according to Wakeham leads to another issue. The knowledge that newspaper editors have that it would be highly unlikely that 'ordinary people' have the financial wherewithal to take the press to court, the more likely they are to risk invading someone's privacy. Finally, Wakeham suggests that such privacy law would 'establish a powerful arsenal for individuals – usually for the wrong reason – that a newspaper did not scrutinize them. Injunctions would be effortlessly deployed against newspapers undertaking legitimate investigative journalism' (2002: 26). Self-regulation, he argues, is perfectly placed to protect of freedom of the press as any statutory sanction undermines the democratic imperative of a free media. Yet the seemingly age-old debate about self-regulation rages on, despite the apparent impact of the HRA on privacy rights.

At the time of writing, Labour Peer Lord Puttnam chided the PCC for its continued inability to control the press, adding that politicians are reluctant to face up to newspapers and news organisations for fear of reprisal by their newspapers. He suggests that:

> For their part politicians and the civil servants who support them feel trapped in the malevolent glare of a media culture whose primary purpose is to undermine rather than underpin public confidence. The national – or is it international – obsession with the trivial is increasingly making the intelligent exercise of public life all but impossible.
>
> *Puttnam cited by Halliday (2010a)*

Puttnam's complaints come in the wake of particularly bad couple of years for Murdoch press in particular. Not only had the *News of the World* lost the Mosely case, the newspaper became involved in a controversy which would ultimately see its demise.

The *News of the World* phone hacking scandal, or 'Hackgate' as it has come to be known, began when the newspaper's royal correspondent Clive Goodman and private investigator Glenn Mulcaire were given custodial sentences after they admitted hacking into phone messages of staff in the royal household. Fresh allegations of phone hacking emerged from the *Guardian* newspaper in 2009 when it reported that the company that owned *News of the World* – News Group Newspapers – paid out more than £1 million in damages and costs in relation to privacy cases which were brought by Gordon Taylor, chief executive of the Professional Footballers' Association (PFA), and two legal advisors. Furthermore a string of celebrities and public figures were being paid out by the Rupert Murdoch owned company in light of the phone hacking allegations.

The controversy also penetrated the walls of No. 10, which caused considerable embarrassment for Prime Minister David Cameron. Despite attempting to distance himself from the controversy, the Prime Minister's chief of communications and former editor of the *News of the World*, Andy Coulson resigned from his role following mounting pressure concerning his role in, and knowledge of, what has been described by MPs as telephone hacking on an 'industrial scale' (Leigh *et al* 2010).

Yet the shocking exposure by the *Guardian* newspaper of the Dowler hacking proved to be the final straw, as public outrage prompted a wave of arrests of senior executives at News International including former editor of the *News of the World* and the *Sun* Rebekah Brooks and Coulson. Prior to the Dowler story the Metropolitan police had effectively called a halt to its investigations. The subsequent revelation that police officers were routinely paid for information by journalists led to condemnation by politicians and the public and pointed to complicity by members of the police force in the criminal activity of *News of the World* employees. The PCC, which had previously found no evidence of systematic illegal activity at the newspaper and even stated in its 2009 report that the stories produced by the *Guardian* had little substance, was shown to be the toothless tiger it clearly is. Its Chair Barroness Buscombe resigned soon after, with the fate of the PCC now looking more precarious than ever.

And so it continues. As Snoddy (1992: 18) in his study of press freedom and standards maintains: '[T]he 400 year history of the press shows […] how little new there is in the present controversies about newspaper behaviour.' Though Snoddy made this observation in the early 1990s, his claim retains its validity in the present day as: 'Every modern complaint or call for legislation can be matched by stories form the past' (Snoddy 1992: 18). The history of the debate about press regulation in Britain has followed an increasingly familiar pattern which has ebbed and flowed between calls for greater restraint and even statutory control – usually from government, to moments of temporary contrition on the part of the press, with the threat of firmer legislation ever present. Recent demands for tighter controls over intrusion of privacy continue to keep alive that seemingly ever-present tussle. Yet the introduction of the Human Rights Act has changed the balance of the debate as judges in Britain now have the power to decide on what is considered a matter for the public interest and what is to be kept private, something that is of concern to advocates of press freedom and freedom of speech. Such concern seems to resonate in the wake of the PCC's continued inability to promote press accountability, with *The Guardian* editor Alan Rusbridger suggesting that the credibility of the PCC was 'clinging by its fingertips' (Martinson 2010). In light of its handling of the *News of the World* scandal, it looks as if its time has finally come. The Leveson inquiry into the relationship between Parliament, the police and the media, set up by PM David Cameron in the wake of the 'Hackgate' affair, will examine again the regulation of the press.

Before the extent of the *News of the World* scandal started to be revealed in the summer of 2011, the report by the Culture, Media and Sport Committee on Press Standards, Privacy and Libel, published in 2010 was particularly scathing in its criticisms of the PCC arguing that it was 'toothless' in comparison to other regulators. Among its recommendations it suggested that the PPC should be able to impose a significant financial penalty on newspapers that have made a serious breach of the PCC code of conduct. The report noted that there was a 'widespread view that its inability to impose any kind of penalty when a breach of the Code does occur significantly reduces its authority and credibility' (HC 362-I: 130). It was criticised for not doing enough to support the parents of Madeleine McCann who were subject to the 'pack' mentality of the press in relation to its reporting of the McCann case,[22] with 'competitive and commercial factors [contributing] to abysmal standards in the gathering and publishing of news about the McCann case' (HC 362-I: 139).

The rise of the 'super-injunction'

In the wake of public concern about the perceived rise in the number of so-called super-injunctions, the Neuberger Report commissioned in 2010 is purportedly an attempt to move towards a workable system in law which facilitates a balance between the principle of open justice and freedom of expression with individuals' rights to confidentiality and privacy. In short a super-injunction is in effect a gagging order which prevents the media from revealing the existence of an injunction against public disclosure.

Super-injunctions have gained some notoriety in recent years though the first to generate controversy was the one was brought by law firm Carter-Ruck acting on behalf of Trafigura, a company specialising in oil and mineral trading. The super-injunction was an attempted to prevent *The Guardian* newspaper from reporting a Parliamentary question by Paul Farrelly MP concerning the alleged dumping of toxic waste by the firm. This gagging order was in direct contravention of the Parliamentary Papers Act of 1840 (section 3), which guarantees that 'any extract from or abstract of' a 'report, paper, votes, or proceedings' of Parliament is immune from civil and criminal liability if published in good faith and 'without malice'. Moreover, the right of the press to report matters in parliament is also codified in statute in Schedule 1 of the Defamation Act 1996. This confers 'qualified privilege', which is again subject to the tests of the report being 'fair and accurate, and published without malice' and generally in the public interest (HoC Reports HC 362-I: 32). Yet the Neuberger Report has sounded a warning to MPs and the press suggesting that Parliamentary Privilege should not be abused by MPs who should respect their privileges.

In January 2010 the High Court imposed a super-injunction[23] on the British press to stop them from reporting that the then England football captain John Terry had had an affair with the former girlfriend, Vanessa Perroncel, of one of his team mates, Wayne Bridge. Though the gagging order was later dropped, Roy Greenslade has argued that the super-injunction poses a significant threat to freedom of speech with the balance of power increasingly tipping against newspapers and media organisations who may be forced to continually defend their right to publish (2009a). John Kampfner (2009) has also noted that: 'A combination of zealous law firms, pliant and sometimes ignorant judges, cash-strapped news organisations and a public that is encouraged to think the worst of the media has produced a situation where strong, investigative journalism is in jeopardy.' Though the super-injunction brought by Terry was eventually overturned the fact that there are legal recourses to silence the press available to those with the financial resources to do so, should be a matter of concern.

In its attempt to clarify the issue in the wake of the Trafigura and John Terry cases, the Neuberger Report suggested that the principle of open justice, though not absolute '[t]he principle of open justice is an essential aspect of our constitutional settlement' (Master of the Rolls 2011, 1.36). In other words, where secrecy is ordered the reasons for secrecy should be explained as far as possible and journalists, where possible, will be allowed into the courts to enable them to understand why the interim injunction or super-injunction has been served, though of course the journalists will not be allowed to disclose information about the original injunction. This, of course, is intended to reaffirm the importance of open justice. The committee also maintained that super-injunctions and other injunctions would be short term and 'only be granted when they are strictly necessary' (Master of the Rolls 2011, v).

However, with regard online content and invasions of privacy, the law at the moment seems to suggest according to Neuberger that even if information is available on the web via social networking sites this is by no means the same degree an invasion of privacy than that of a national newspaper. Yet of course this highlights a legal inconsistency with regard the print media unable to tell a story which is freely available via social networking sites such as Twitter (BBC 2011a).

Conclusion

There is no doubt that the system of press self-regulation in Britain has favoured the industry as it has been unable to constrain the more pernicious activities of the press as it takes liberties with peoples' reputations and lives with little sanction. As the Campaign for Press and Broadcasting Freedom (CPBF) have long maintained, it is the inability of the Press Council and subsequently the Press Complaints Commission to 'develop a system of penalties that will make its judgements meaningful' that has been the fundamental weakness of the system of self-regulation.[24] Yet when thinking about privacy in relation to intrusion from the press we must remember to pay attention to the wider political and social context within which these debates take place as this can often illuminate areas that might well remain obscured. We know, of course, that the press is an industry and one that has obligations to its shareholders and patrons; we also know that scandal sells. Moreover, as we have seen the function of the press is not solely political. 'Freedom of the press', for the popular press in particular essentially concerns the freedom to trivialise, sensationalise and to gossip monger as the market dictates. As Harrison (2006: 117) points out 'freedom of expression is not limited to worthy or serious publication, but applies equally to the freedom to publish or show trivia'. One could argue that this type of coverage of celebrity scandal and prurient titillation is giving the audience what it wants. This may be true to some degree; however, we should also be mindful that the press operate on a number of levels (Gripsrud 2000; Conboy 2006) with sensation and prurience providing entertainment *and* a sense of moral righteousness with which it attempts to tap into the mood of its readership. The 'distinctive tabloid idiom [...] blends sensation and a calculated disrespect and suspicion of authority, particularly political authority within an overall concentration on the broadest appeal of contemporary popular culture' (Conboy 2006: 114). As such the ways in which the popular press in particular centre on exposing the moral failings of public figures can also act to cement common sense views about right and wrong or as a 'way to produce some minimal sort of community, an elementary sense of shared conditions and shared agenda that support the égalité central to the ideals of bourgeois democracy' (Gripsrud 2000: 299).

More critically, we must also be mindful of the specific moral contexts that the popular press in particular operate within. Demands for tighter controls on the press can often resonate with a particular type of moralistic paternalism which views prurience and salaciousness in the press as pandering to the baser instincts of the audience. Of course, such claims are sometimes made to cover up the moral failings of those who make such calls, but often they may also be representative of a particularly bullish form of elitist paternalism which laments the passing of a moral golden age. Similarly, the moral voice of the press should not be ignored as the press is often a channel through which moral outrage and public anger is expressed, another aspect of censorship and control. As Nicholas Garnham notes:

> Here we find an internalization of social control, its personalization, individuation, and in a sense privatization caused by the increased publicness of social interactions. It is precisely these self disciplining effects of public display that Foucault and his followers attack, using the metaphor of the Benthamite Panopticon as epitomizing modernity, in the name of a difference whose source and place of refuge they then seek in the privacy of a body which lies outside both discourse and politics.
>
> *Garnham (2000: 189)*

While completing the manuscript for this book Sky Sports football pundit Andy Gray was sacked from his job because of remarks made about women in football and for making suggestive comments to a female colleague. The offending comments and remarks were made off-air and never meant for public consumption. However distasteful and arcane Gray's original comments were, the fact remains that they were still made in private, yet the debate about whether or not he should have been sacked seem to have ignored this fact. It seems it is now legitimate for private conversations between individuals to be open to public scrutiny; as such this expansion of the realms of what is deemed in the public interest seems to have placed significant pressure on an individual's rights to privacy.

In the modern era the press has always been a space where moral indignation is expressed as well as one which performs a moral function of control; excoriating moral turpitude while at the same time engaging in salacious titillation for commercial gain (Conboy 2006). Historically and conceptually, as we have seen, the key argument about freedom of the press and the rights to privacy have been played out in terms of attaining an appropriate balance between the two rights. Indeed this is how many of the charters on human rights frame privacy and freedom of expression. Tessa Mayes, however, suggests that such a balancing act 'effectively means that there is no such thing as a right to free speech – or, indeed, a right to privacy' (2002: 2). Mayes maintains that the original conception of privacy relates to the protection against intrusion from the state and its agencies, yet the way in which privacy is increasingly being defined shifts the emphasis away from the state and towards individuals, with the state acting as arbiter of justice. She points out, citing a report from Privacy International, this is in the context of increasing legislation which undermines privacy from the state. The legislation includes:

> The Crime and Disorder Act (1998), which allows for information sharing and data matching among public bodies; The Regulation of Investigatory Powers Act (2000) (RIP), which allows any public authority designated by the Home

Secretary to access communications data without a warrant; and The Anti-Terrorism, Crime and Security Act (2001), which allows the Secretary of State to issue a code of practice to retain communications data held by communications providers to protect national security.

Mayes (2002: 32)

At the same time that the state is developing legislation which threatens individual privacy, the emphasis on protecting against invasions of privacy from other individuals is increasing. In addition to shifting the focus away from the state invasions of privacy, the particular shift in emphasis of privacy towards the individual exposes a significant cultural preoccupation with personal injury, hurt or offence. In other words invasions of privacy are now couched in terms of psychological harm or offence done to the person whose privacy has been 'invaded'. However, echoing John Stuart Mill, Mayes suggests that such speech can only be countered by more free speech, not tighter controls against it. Mayes also relates such a preoccupation to the 'confessional culture' in contemporary society which is centred on the personalisation of politics and the atomisation of social life within a culture of low expectations (see Furedi 2005). Yet of course for those caught up in the *News of the World* scandal, particularly those who have no interest in public life, those whose circumstances have made them targets for such vindictive and callous acts, their privacy and dignity have been affronted. How this scandal will ultimately impact on press freedom and privacy remains to be seen.

7

LIBEL AND THE PUBLIC INTEREST

English libel law imposes unnecessary and disproportionate restrictions on free speech, sending a chilling effect through the publishing and journalism sectors in the U.K. This effect now reaches around the world, because of so-called 'libel tourism', where foreign cases are heard in London, widely known as a 'town named sue'. The law was designed to serve the rich and powerful, and does not reflect the interests of a modern democratic society.

Glanville and Heawood, *English PEN & Index on Censorship (2009: 2)*

Introduction

As the quote from a report by English PEN & Index on Censorship maintains, in England defamation law remains one of the key obstacles to freedom of the press as it has the capacity to constrain public debate and 'chill' freedom of speech. It is particularly relevant to the focus of this book as it relates to one of the key functions of journalism, namely to scrutinise power and ensure that representative democracy functions according to its central tenets. Yet libel law in England has been, and continues to be, generally the preserve of the rich and powerful, often to protect them from public scrutiny and so to hold them to account. The purpose of this chapter then is to explore defamation as a legal concept which places great pressure on freedom of speech and freedom of expression and which impacts on the ability of journalism to perform one of its primary public functions. The chapter will proceed by exploring the notion of a right to reputation which underpins defamation law. From this I will go on to focus on defamation in the English context and explore some of the key concepts and judgements relating to defamation. It will also be necessary for me to explore the impact of the Human Rights Act 1998 (HRA) on libel law and the English approach to libel which is in severe need of significant reform. Finally I will briefly examine the U.S. system in order to emphasise the distinction between English and United States defamation law.

Defamation in principle

In general terms defamation might be understood as any publication, broadcast, or other public communication which tends to undermine the reputation of a person or persons in the eyes of the public. Barendt *et al* (1996: 3), drawing on legal precedent, maintain that: 'A defamatory publication is one which tends to "lower the claimant in the estimation of right-thinking members of society generally".' The claimant is the person who sues seeking to gain financial 'damages' for what was stated about him/her. The law concerning defamation is notoriously complex and it is beyond the scope of this chapter to venture too far down this particular avenue of enquiry.[1] Moreover, providing an exhaustive list and overview of key libel cases would not add to the key arguments of this book. Suffice it to say that it is necessary to discuss in general terms the relationship between defamation and press freedom given that severe punishments that can be handed out by judges in libel cases can act to chill freedom of speech and freedom of expression as well as freedom of the press.

Right to reputation

The right to reputation is stated clearly in the Universal Declaration of Human Rights in Article 12 which states: 'No one shall be subjected to arbitrary interference with his privacy, family, home or correspondence, nor to attacks upon his honour and reputation. Everyone has the right to the protection of the law against such interference or attacks' (UDHR 1948). Though the European Convention for the protection of Human Rights does not carry such specific protection, it does under Article 10 which, of course, relates to freedom of expression, state that such freedom comes with responsibilities and restrictions which protect, among other things, 'the reputation rights of others' (ECHR 2010; Rogers 2010a). Eric Barendt, in his major work in freedom of speech, highlights the fact that the 'right to reputation' has been around for much longer than the right to freedom of speech and expression, even receiving protection under Roman law (2005: 198). Post (1986: 699) also notes the historical significance of a good reputation highlighting that the Bible and William Shakespeare, valued 'a good name' above money and financial gain. As such in historical terms the conception of reputation as honour can be described as 'a form of reputation in which an individual personally identifies with the normative characteristics of a particular social role and in return personally receives from others the regard the estimation that society accords to that role' (Post 1986: 699–700). In other words an honourable reputation is a form of social credit which is bestowed on an individual or body (corporate or public) by members of the society. Before the establishment of the civil law of libel the traditional means by which a person could redress the balance when libelled was via the duel (Robertson and Nicol 2008). However, Milo (2008: 17) states that reputation is in fact a very difficult concept to define given that 'what reputation protects is not "character", which is what a person really is; reputation is what he [and presumably she] seems to be'. As such reputation is in the eye of the beholder and 'dependent upon the external views of a community' (Milo 2008: 17). Robert Post (1986)[2] provides a nuanced elaboration of the principle of reputation as 'three distinct concepts' which 'corresponds to an implicit and discrete image of the good and well-ordered society' (1986: 693). The first concept relates to reputation as property. This concept, as Post suggests,

> underlies our image of the merchant who works hard to become known as creditworthy or of the carpenter who strives to achieve a name for quality workmanship. Such a reputation is capable of being earned, in the sense that it can be acquired as a result of an individual's efforts and labour.
>
> *Post (1986: 693)*

In other words reputation as property is said to correspond to the notion that 'individuals are connected to one another through the institution of the market' (Milo 2008: 27) and as such defamation in this context is said to constitute an unwarranted assault on a person's rights within the market to cultivate his or her good name based on their labour or commercial energies. Therefore, 'the purpose of the law of defamation is to protect individuals within the market by ensuring that their reputation is not wrongfully deprived of its proper market value' (Post 1986: 695).

The second way in which reputation has been theorised by Post is in relation to reputation as honour. In contrast to reputation as property, individuals, as Post (1986: 700) observes do 'not earn or create [...] honor through effort or labor; he claims a right to it by virtue of the status with which society endows his social role' (sic). Aside from the obvious gender specific exclusions which, of course, tell us much about the status of women in the historical development of legal concepts, the notion of honour may be understood in relation to the social consensus which is applied to the specific social status of individuals. The most obvious historical example might be in relation to public criticisms of an office or person of state such as the monarch. The offence of seditious libel therefore held that speech and expression which was deemed to lower the estimation in the minds of the public the office or person (see also Chapter 2). The law pertaining to seditious libel covered any publication which sought to:

> bring hatred or contempt to the person of his Majesty [...] or the Government and the constitution of the United Kingdom [...] or either houses of Parliament, or to excite his Majesty's subjects to attempt alteration of any matter in Church of State as by law established by any other than lawful means [...].
>
> *60 Geo. 3 and 1 Geo. 4 c. 8, (1819)[3]*

Reputation as an aspect of dignity is the third concept which relates to defamation. Here Post formulates his notion of the 'rules of civility' (see also Chapter 6) where individuals are conceptualised within a broader social framework in which the interests of the community as well as the individual are fore-grounded. As Milo observes the 'dignity rationale for reputation is based upon the relationship between the private and public aspects of the self […] reputation has internal and external dimensions that are integral to personality' (2008: 33). So it is a person's internal sense of validation which is at stake as such validation takes place within the wider social sphere. As Milo points out Post here is informed in his analysis by Erving Goffman who was prominent in the symbolic interactionist school of sociological theory. Goffman argued that identity is formed in part via and through our social rituals and interactions with others as others reinforce one's sense of self within the community. Post suggests that 'our own sense of intrinsic self-worth, stored in the deepest recesses of our "private personality," is perpetually dependent upon the ceremonial observance by those around us of rules of deference and demeanour' (1986: 710). As such 'defamation can be conceived as a method by which society polices breaches of its rules of deference and demeanour, thereby protecting the dignity of its members' (1986: 710). In other words reputation in this context is related to a person's sense of self-worth which is in part validated via his or her relationship with the community. Moreover, there is a societal interest in ensuring that these boundaries are adhered to as they reflect the rules of civility. Simply put, if a person is libelled then not only will their standing in the community be tarnished, but also their own sense of self worth will be negatively affected and the broader rules of civility will be undermined (Milo 2008). Though Post's theorisation of reputation is not without problems it does offer a useful way in to thinking about libel law and its central concern: that being the scope of the offence of libel with respect a person's rights to reputation. However, if we look at how defamation law has been applied, we will see that it is generally those wealthy and powerful enough to seek redress through the courts who tend to make use of it. From a freedom of speech and freedom of the press perspective it is the practice of defamation law which has done much to chill freedom of speech and it is with regard defamation law in practice that we now turn.

Defamation in practice

In England lawyers representing newspapers in particular tend to be all too familiar with English libel law yet though there are too many examples to cite in this chapter, I do hope to sketch out and highlight the key features and problems with defamation in respect of freedom of speech. It is my intention here, therefore, to highlight the complex and problematic nature of libel law in England and the specific features which impact on freedom of speech and freedom of the press. As noted extensively throughout this book, one of the key functions of journalism is to hold those in power to account yet English defamation laws make it relatively easy for those in positions of power and influence to stifle criticism and discourage legitimate investigations into their affairs. As Robertson and Nicol note absolute privilege is provided to among others, MPs speaking in Parliament or on select committees; lawyers, judges and witnesses in court; Ombudsman's reports; ministers of the Crown, as well as officers in the armed forces in some contexts (2007: 156–57). The chief reason why absolute privilege is required in these contexts is because in the process of making policy and law, and in the administering of justice, 'persons with a public duty to speak out might be threatened with vexatious actions for libel or slander' (Robertson and Nicol 2008: 156).

Though absolute privilege extends to Members of Parliament politicians can waive their rights to absolute privilege in order to pursue a libel action through the courts. Although absolute privilege means that MPs cannot be sued for what they say in Parliamentary proceedings, they can sue others for what is written or said outside of Parliament. This was the case when former barrister and Member of Parliament for Tatton Neil Hamilton began libel proceedings against *The Guardian* over allegations that he had received financial and other rewards in exchange for asking questions in the House of Commons. However, on the eve of the court proceedings Hamilton dropped the action after the newspaper presented evidence to Hamilton's lawyers which included statements claiming that Hamilton 'regularly called for envelopes stuffed with £50 notes in return for parliamentary lobbying' (Hencke *et al* 1996). Another Conservative MP and former Chief Secretary to the Treasury Jonathan Aitken was also involved in a libel action against *The Guardian* and Granada Television's *World in Action* programme concerning allegations that he had had abused his parliamentary privilege and lobbied British arms manufacturers on behalf of Prince Mohammed of Saudi Arabia. In the run up to the trial Aitken set himself up as a defender of truth and intent on 'cut[ing] out the cancer of bent and twisted journalism in our country with the simple sword of truth and the trusty shield of fair play'.[4] After the libel trial had collapsed charges were brought against Aitken for perjury. He was found guilty and served eighteen months in gaol. Of course, the aforementioned cases, and the eventual outcome of the Jeffry Archer case (see Chapter 6), demonstrate the power of responsible journalism in exposing corruption and wrongdoing. It is worth noting, however, that media organisations opting to defend themselves against defamation cases can still lose out even if their defence is a success. As it stands the law does not allow them to recoup all their costs automatically. Moreover, many organisations may choose to settle out of court rather than risk the financial burden of going to court.

Popular newspapers and celebrity magazines, of course, make money from selling stories about celebrities and the lives of the rich and famous so it is no surprise that from time to time they trouble the courts with defamation and privacy claims against them (see Chapter 6). However, politicians and celebrities are not the only group of people who have sought to pursue claims for damages in court. For example, a recent case involved The British Chiropractic Associate (BCA), which eventually dropped an action it brought against the science writer Simon Singh. Singh, in a comment piece in *The Guardian* newspaper, suggested that chiropractic treatments claiming to help treat children with conditions such as asthma, ear infections and sleeping problems were 'bogus' (Singh 2008). Though the court initially found with the claimant, the BCA eventually dropped the case after the Court of Appeal ruled against the original ruling. The court ruled that Dr. Singh's comment piece was protected as fair comment (see later). The ruling stated that it was not for the courts, as some form of 'Orwellian ministry of truth', to try to disentangle fact from fiction (Gibb 2010).

Moreover, the ruling noted that the litigation 'has almost certainly had a chilling effect on public debate'[5] – something for which libel reform campaigners have been arguing for years. However, defamation suits against academics are particularly worrying as they not only have implications for freedom of speech and expression but also for freedom of academic inquiry. As science writer Ben Goldacre (2010) has suggested 'mutual criticism is vital in science' as it is in all academic enquiry and the recent trend in academics being targeted by defamation suits, rather than being subject to peer review, is a very worrying trend.

As we have seen the most high profile libel cases tend to be those where a public figure seeks redress following revelations or accusations about their conduct in the media. However, media organisations are not immune from turning to the libel laws themselves. In 2000 the radical left-wing publication *LM* (formerly *Living Marxism*) was forced to close down following unsuccessful attempts to defend itself in a libel action brought by ITN and two of its journalists, Penny Marshal and Ian Williams. The case against *LM* centred on the 1997 publication of an article in the magazine written by independent journalist Thomas Deichmann. The article, entitled 'The Picture that Fooled the World', claimed that news footage and copy taken by ITN in 1992 of Bosnian Muslim refugees at a camp at Trnopolje in Bosnia incorrectly gave the impression that those at the camp were victims of a modern-day Holocaust. In particular the photograph of Fitrec Alic, emaciated and apparently caged behind a barbed wire fence, was akin to those images taken by Margaret Bourke-White at Buchenwald (Campbell 2002a and 2002b)[6] and other similar images from Auschwitz, Dachau and Bergen-Belsen following their liberation in 1945. Though Deichmann acknowledges that Williams and Marshall never used the term 'concentration camp', the article implied that the images were contrived in order to imply that the Serbs were moral equivalents of the Nazis and that the barbed-wire fence in the footage was surrounding the news crews and not those at the camp. Deichmann noted that 'whatever the British news team's intentions may have been, their pictures were seen around the world as the first hard evidence of concentration camps in Bosnia' (Deichmann 1997: 26). McLaughlin suggests that 'although the ITN reporters expressed concerns privately about such an effect, they made no attempt to set the record straight about the exact circumstances of their film report' (2002: 180). There is no doubt that the images were powerful and certainly conjured up memories of the Holocaust and the debate about the particularities of the case as well as the wider interpretation of events during and following the break up of Yugoslavia continues (see Campbell 2002a and 2002b, 2009). However, as we have seen the particularities of English libel law meant that the burden of proof during the trial was on the defendants in that they had to prove that the claimants had contrived to create such an impression. A burden of proof that was impossible to establish, giving the jury no option but to find in favour of the claimants.

Public interest defence

As we saw in Chapter 6, often the basis on which journalists declare their right to publish stories about individuals rests on the notion of the public interest.

However, defining the realms of what constitutes public interest is not as straightforward as it might be. We should in the first instance, of course, dispense with the notion that stories in public interest are those stories which interest the public. Of course, this definition has been used by newspaper proprietors to defend intrusions into the private lives of public figures for generations. Despite the vulgar sentiments a satisfactory definition of public interest is as yet unforthcoming with numerous definitions and statements failing to provide a full-blooded definition. For example, the Editors Code of Practice published by the Press Complaints Commission states that the public interest 'includes, but is not confined to':

> Detecting or exposing crime or serious impropriety
> Protecting public health and safety
> Preventing the public from being misled by an action or statement of an individual or organisation
>
> *PCC (Code of Practice)*

However, as a report on English libel law by English PEN & Index on Censorship (Glanville and Heawood 2009) has stated there is 'no robust public interest defence in English libel law' the authors of the report goes on to maintain that 'a stronger public interest defence [should] extend to journalists and writers who may not appear obvious candidates for a Reynolds defence' (2009: 9). They argue that freedom of expression would be significantly enhanced if the public interest defence was strengthened.

Defamation in English law

As we have seen the development of defamation law in England emerges from the perceived requirement to protect the reputation of individuals in the face of misleading or contemptuous information. Unlike privacy, where an injunction can be brought to prevent publication or broadcast, libel law only comes into effect once the purported defamatory remarks or claims have been made public. Defamation law has been conceived therefore to 'provide the legal means to vindicate the wrongs to reputation leading to both civil actions and criminal penalties'[7] (Fenwick and Phillipson 2006: 1043). However, unlike all other areas of English jurisprudence the defendant in a libel action has to either prove the truth of their allegations, prove publication constitutes fair comment[8] or is protected by absolute or qualified privilege. In other words they are presumed guilty and have to prove their innocence to avoid liability (Glanville and Heawood 2009).

In England the right to be tried by jury in libel 'dates back to Fox's Libel Act 1792, when libel proceedings were criminal rather than civil, before that time a judge would decide on the outcome of the case'.[9] However, as Robertson and Nicol (2007) suggest the refashioning of libel law in the nineteenth and twentieth centuries significantly reflected the class system in England. They note:

The idea that large sums of money must be awarded to compensate people for words which 'tend to lower them in the estimation of right-thinking members of society' directly derives from an age when social, political and legal life was lived in gentlemen's clubs in Pall Mall. ...

Robertson and Nicol (2007: 96)

The characteristics therefore of English libel law can be seen to be overwhelmingly geared towards protecting the reputations and therefore interests of people with some power and authority. As such, libel laws tend to have little significance to what might be termed 'ordinary folk' instead, they are overwhelmingly orientated towards the protection of privilege and power. As I have maintained for journalists and the media more generally one of the central problems with English libel law has been its tendency to chill freedom of speech and expression. Though there is no prior restraint, this is not to say that libel law does not have a negative effect on freedom of speech and freedom of the press in that the threat of a libel action might well undermine freedom of expression. As Greenslade (2010a) succinctly points out, noting journalists' dislike of libel laws: 'Some of us feel it inhibits our freedom to write what we think the public should know.' The implications of such a chill on investigative reporting are obvious in that journalists may be discouraged from venturing into territory which places them and their organisation under serious threat from prosecution. However, the courts have arguably gone some way in recognising the important role of journalism, particularly in relation to scrutinising the powerful, and have developed protective legal measures that are intended to lessen the chill on freedom of the press.

Qualified privilege

The key development in this 'warming' of freedom of speech is the principle of qualified privilege which 'provides in certain circumstances, a second line of defence to disseminators of libellous material who cannot satisfy the defence of justification, *i.e.* to prove the truth of what they have published' (Loveland 1998: 637). In other words the defence of qualified privilege is intended to allow for honest mistakes to be made where no malice is evident in the pursuit of providing information which is deemed to be in the public interest. As Loveland suggests:

Qualified privilege absolves the disseminator from liability for publishing false and defamatory material unless the plaintiff proves that the publication was actuated by 'malice'. [...] To avail herself of the defence, the publisher must establish that she was under a duty (either moral or legal) to pass the information concerned to a given audience and that the audience had a reciprocal interests in receiving it.

Loveland (1998: 637).

It is obvious that the principle of qualified privilege is particularly important in that it allows journalists to conduct investigations which are deemed to be of such importance and significance to the public interest that they may be protected from prosecution. In the United States, as we will see later, the use of qualified privilege in respect of political libels has been established for some years; however, in the U.K. the position is less clear cut as Fenwick and Phillipson argue it was not until the late 1990s that the law in England developed 'any special protection from defamation law for misstatements of fact published to the general public by the media' (2006: 1076). Arguably, the two most important recent developments which have sought to give journalists more protection from defamation suits, other than the Human Rights Act 1998, are the cases of *Reynolds v Times Newspapers* (1999) and *Jameel v. Wall Street Journal* (2006).

In 1994 *The Sunday Times* alleged that the Irish Prime Minister Albert Reynolds had misled the Irish parliament in relation to a cover up of child sexual abuse in the Catholic Church in Ireland. Though Reynolds was in one respect successful when he sued the paper, as the jury found that *The Sunday Times* had 'acted unreasonably' in its report of the affair, his victory was pyrrhic with the court only awarding Reynolds one penny in damages. The minimal nature of the damages can be seen as a vindication of the notion that in matters of genuine public interest journalists and news organisations should be protected from actions even if they publish inaccurate information in good faith. Though, as Barendt (2005: 219) notes, 'both appellate courts ruled that the publication of the particular article was not covered by privilege', the principle of qualified privilege was seen as important in protecting journalists from action in this instance. As such *The Sunday Times* was vindicated as the judge 'endorsed the specifically investigative role of public 'watchdog" which has since been perceived as a "major extension of qualified privilege giving serious investigative journalism a very great deal of legal protection"' (Horrie 2008: 117). Reynolds is seen as a landmark case because of its contribution to the development of a 'new category of qualified privilege encompassing the publication, to the public at large, of "political information", that is information, opinion, and arguments concerning government and political matters affecting the people of the UK' (Fenwick and Phillipson 2006: 1077). The Lords' statement noted that:

> Liability arises only if the writer knew the statement was not true or if he made the statement recklessly, not caring whether it was true or false, or if he was actuated by personal spite or some other improper motive.[10]

As Robertson and Nicol (2007: 98) note, however, the Lords' view regarding Reynolds was in part shaped by decisions in Australia and New Zealand,[11] which held that 'reasonably researched allegations should be published about powerful public figures, which would be "privileged" from libel actions even if they subsequently turned out to be untrue' (see also Kenyon 2009). As such Reynolds was important in the development of the public interest defence against libel actions. It is important to stress, however, that though 'political speech is an important example of protected material, Reynolds privilege is defined by a test of public interest' (Kenyon

2009: 298) as the Lords' viewed that providing specific protection for political speech alone did not provide sufficient protection for reputation (Barendt 2005).

Significant though the Reynolds case was, the final judgement in *Jameel v The Wall Street Journal* has arguably reinforced the principle of qualified privilege in supporting responsible journalism (Reuters Institute 2009: 53). *The Wall Street Journal* was taken to court following article on the surveillance of bank accounts of high profile Saudis suspected of funding terrorist organisations by the U.S. and Saudi Arabia. The action was brought by Mohammed Yousef Jameel who had been named in the article via a hyperlink. Though the jury found that the article was defamatory, the judgement was overturned by the House of Lords on the grounds that the principle of serious journalism should be encouraged and the newspaper had originally been denied a Reynolds defence on very narrow grounds' (Glanville and Heawood 2009: 17). As Glanville and Heawood notes 'Jameel is a significant case, as it demonstrated and codified the liberalising effect of Reynolds when applied correctly' (Glanville and Heawood 2009: 17). A 2009 report by the Reuters Institute for the Study of Journalism highlighted the appeal ruling in which the House of Lords suggested that the indicative factors which should be taken into account[12] in libel cases outlined in the Reynolds judgement had 'been interpreted too strictly in the past. They should be seen as pointers rather than hurdles to be overcome' (2009: 54). It seems therefore that in respect of Jameel the Law Lords recognised the difficulties confronting serious and responsible journalism and the realisation that when the public interest is at stake journalists should be protected from defamation suits. However, journalists are not protected if they have not sought to verify their allegations or put them to the claimant prior to publication (Barendt 2005). This was the decision by Eady J. in the *Galloway v Telegraph Group Ltd.* action in which *The Daily Telegraph* published articles which purported to show evidence that George Galloway had received secret payments from the Iraqi regime and had benefitted from Iraq's oil for food programme. *The Telegraph* based its allegations on documentation, purportedly found in burned out government offices in Baghdad which implicated Galloway. In his judgement Mr. Justice Eady noted that *The Telegraph* had not sought to verify the authenticity of the documentation and were therefore not covered by privilege. Moreover, the court criticised the tone of the report and that Mr. Galloway was not given a proper chance to respond to the allegations. Galloway received £150,000 damages.

Though the decision in Jameel significantly strengthened Reynolds and the principle of qualified privilege (see Fenwick and Phillipson 2006) English PEN & Index on Censorship (Glanville and Heawood 2009) argue that freedom of expression is still significantly chilled by English libel laws. They cite a 2008 report by the United Nations Human Rights Committee which suggested that 'the practical application of the law of libel has served to discourage critical media reporting on matters of serious public interest' (cited in 2009: 6). Moreover, the report suggests that the law in England may in fact be in 'breach' of the right to freedom of expression as expressed in Article 19 of the International Covenant on Civil and Political Rights (ibid.: 6). Of course, the continued potency of English defamation laws is reflected by the fact that English courts still offer scope for successful prosecutions for libel. So called 'libel-tourism', the practice whereby wealthy pursuers of defamation claims opt to use English courts so as to give them greater chance of securing a successful outcome, has received renewed attention in recent years. For example, Russian businessmen Boris Berezovsky and Nikolai Glouchkov brought an action against *Forbes Magazine*, which claimed that the businessmen were criminals and had associations with the criminal underworld in Moscow (House of Lords Judgements – Judgments – *Berezovsky v Michaels and Others*; *Glouchkov v Michaels and Others*). Though the trial judge remarked that the case should be heard in Russia or the United States he was subsequently overruled by the House of Lords. However, it seems that some countries are taking steps to safeguard their journalists and academics from English defamation law. For example, in 2010 the Obama administration passed the 'Securing the Protection of our Enduring and Established Constitutional Heritage Act' which sought to protect U.S. journalists, authors and academics from the English defamation actions (Greenslade 2010b).

Libel tourism has been made possible in England largely because of a ruling in the case *Duke of Brunswick v Harmer* in 1849. The case relates to a precedent set following the Duke of Brunswick's success in his attempts to sue the *Weekly Dispatch* for defamation seventeen years after it had published the article defaming him. The long-term effect of the ruling is that an action can be brought against each individual publication, the so-called multiple publication rule. However, in March 2010 following an initial consultation (Ministry of Justice 2009) the Ministry of Justice issued a response document (Ministry of Justice 2010) which highlighted how the internet in particular has exposed significant flaws in the rule and suggested that a single publication rule be introduced with the courts being left to decide if extension is required. The government is also engaged in a consultation exercise regarding responsibility for publication on the internet and particularly whether the law should be changed and clarified to give greater protection to secondary publishers such as internet service providers, online discussion forums (Ministry of Justice 2011: 6). It is clear then that new technology presents new problems for the law regarding defamation and privacy, as the Reuters Institute has pointed out (RISJ 2009), journalism, particularly in its more prurient forms, makes much use of online content. Citing the Amanda Knox case[13] the report notes that 'many journalists are taking advantage of the wealth of private information that is being exposed via the Internet [...] to find material for their own stories, with little discussion of the ethics of doing so' (RISJ 2009: 34).

Impact of the Human Rights Act 1998

As we have seen in Chapters 5 and 6 the Human Rights Act 1998 has had a significant impact on U.K. media law as it has meant that courts and other public bodies are bound[14] to the requirements of the European Convention on Human Rights (ECHR). With regards defamation and privacy cases, Milo (2008: 5) notes that the courts, as public authorities, 'must act compatibly with the Convention rights that are incorporated into the HRA'. In other words the courts as public bodies are bound in principle to develop common law which is based on ECHR requirements. With regards the media this has most significance in respect of Articles 8 and 10. Yet as Fenwick and Phillipson note the HRA does not 'incorporate the rights into U.K. law – rather […] it gives the rights particular effects in particular contexts' (see Fenwick and Phillipson 2006: 125). Moreover, the authors note that the HRA does not bind private bodies such as newspapers and broadcasters to rights set out in the Convention (ibid: 125). The result is that though under the provision, public bodies have to formulate judgements or legislation which is not incompatible with a Convention right, in respect of defamation, as Barendt (2005: 225) notes in English courts, are 'still inclined to ask whether there are good reasons for the freedom to prevail over reputation rights, rather than whether the need to protect the latter justifies infringement of freedom of expression'. However, as Rogers (2010a) points out the European Court of Human Rights has recently demonstrated that a person's reputation can also be protected under Article 8 which is concerned with privacy. What this means that in certain circumstances when a person's private life has been judged to have been invaded, their reputation may also suffer as a consequence of that exposure. Rogers cites the judgement in *Pfeifer v Austria* (2009) 48 EHRR 8 at [35] which states that:

> The Court considers that a person's reputation, even if that person is criticised in the context of a public debate, forms part of his or her personal identity and psychological integrity and therefore also falls within the scope of his or her 'private life'. Article 8 therefore applies.
>
> *Cited Rogers (2010a)*

As we can see therefore a person's reputation is in fact increasingly being seen as coming under the protection of Article 8 under the European Court of Human Rights. Another way in which privacy law and libel law are becoming increasingly difficult to separate, particularly in the European context, and increasingly in the U.K. context (Rogers 2010b).

Defamation in U.S. law

As we have seen the United States allows special protection for freedom of speech and expression which is constitutionally guaranteed. However, the right to reputation does not receive such constitutional protection. Instead the U.S. courts have produced a response to defamation which leans heavily towards free speech protection over and above the right to reputation, a power which the U.S. Supreme Court has essentially devolved to individual states. Historically, as Barendt (2005: 199) points out, until a number of landmark rulings the U.S. Supreme Court viewed 'an attack on an individual's reputation did not contribute to public discussion, but was rather to be equated with an assault'. As such:

> the victim of a defamatory statement was entitled to recover unless the defendant could prove the truth of his statement – and sometimes his good motives as well – or establish that he had a privilege to publish the statement in question and had not abused that privilege.
>
> *Anderson (1975 cited Barendt 2009: 215)*

However, following the ruling in *New York Times Co. v Sullivan* (1964)[15] the U.S. Supreme Court, citing the First and Fourteenth Amendment, held that public officials could not sue for libel relating to their office 'unless he proves that the statement was made with "actual malice" ... or with reckless disregard of whether it was false or not' (*New York Times Co. v Sullivan* 1964). The case was brought against the newspaper by an elected Alabama official who cited an advertisement in the newspaper which carried false statements about police action against civil rights marchers. The claimant was named in the advertisement as he oversaw the police department as part of his duties as a public official. What is significant about this case is summed up by Stone and Williams (2009) who note that the U.S. Supreme Court recognised that the

> requirement that a defendant prove the truth of otherwise defamatory statements would sometimes deter speakers (most importantly journalists and publishers) from publishing statements that they thought were true, but which they were not sure they could prove to be true.
>
> *Stone and Williams (2009: 276)*

As such the judgement makes the provision that false defamatory statements made by defendants should be protected even if damage to reputation had occurred (ibid.). In this sense therefore the court ruled that free speech rights, as long as they are expressed without malice, take priority over the rights to reputation. This, of course, is in stark contrast to the defamation law in England as though common law has slowly moved towards a more balanced approach to defamation, it still places far too much emphasis on the value of reputation at the expense of freedom of expression. The *New York Times* case also stresses the significance of qualified privilege, which, although applied differently in different states, has been 'built on a common rationale – namely that the law should recognise that the electorate's interests in the circulation of political information was sufficiently important to require some adjustment to be made to the basic rules of English libel law ... ' (Loveland 1998: 639).

As Trager and Dickerson note:

> The general rule adopted in the United States is that a citizen will be liable for defamation of a public official only if it is determined that the defendant knew the information was false and disseminated it anyway [...] or was extremely reckless in how the information was gathered and disseminated it without regard to whether the information was true or not.
>
> *(Trager and Dickerson 1999: 185).*

Though U.S. defamation law has a slightly different approach to the status of public officials and figures and ordinary citizens as Barendt (2005) has pointed out defamation claims are not considered a significant threat to freedom of the press in the United States with relatively few trials finding in favour of the plaintiffs. However, though it seems that freedom of expression and freedom of the press are prioritised, it should be noted that following *Sullivan* there may be implications for journalism ethics.

As Watson points out, the principle of 'truth telling' for journalism in journalism ethics is fundamental, yet because of *Sullivan* and other subsequent decisions (2002) the core journalistic value of telling the truth seems to have been placed lower down the moral and legal hierarchy. He notes that '[a]lthough the *Sullivan* ruling is generally hailed by journalists as a triumph of free-speech rights, care must be taken to tally the cost to a most highly prized ethical principle' (Watson, 2002: 17).

Conclusion

So damaging to the interests of freedom of expression are English libel laws that a number of attempts to reform them have been mooted. English PEN[16] & Index on Censorship[17] are lobbying for a radical shake up of the libel laws in England with measures such as the claimant having to demonstrate damage and falsehood instead of the defendant having to prove their innocence; a cap on damages of £10,000; the introduction of a single publication rule; strict criteria in relation to the pursuance of foreign suits; tribunals to replace full trials; a stronger public interest defence; an expansion of the definition of fair comment; a cap on the cost of bringing an action so that those who may not have had the financial resources to bring an action will not be prohibited because of their financial status; an exemption of liability in online interactive fora, and the exemption of large and medium-sized corporate bodies from libel law unless malicious falsehood can be proved (Glanville and Heawood 2009: 2). In their report on the impact of libel laws on freedom of expression, English PEN & Index on Censorship conclude English libel law has a negative impact on freedom of expression both in the UK and around the world' (Glanville and Heawood 2009: 2). There is much to commend in the report's recommendations as there is no doubt that the English libel law is in need of desperate reformation. Irresponsible journalism, which is in itself is a threat to freedom of the press, should be brought to task, while at the same time protecting the public interests and the public's right to know. Moreover, the libel laws need reformation so as to limit their exploitation by the wealthy and powerful and create a level legal context in which libel claims can be made by all if they feel that they have been misrepresented by the press.

At the time of writing a draft Defamation Bill is being drawn up by the British coalition government which will seek to 'better protect freedom of speech and expression in the media and the research sector, and to cut down on "libel tourism"' (Sweney 2010). Amongst the proposals are a new requirement that a statement must have caused substantial harm in order for it to be defamatory; a new statutory defence of responsible publication on matters of public interest which is effectively a statutory defence on Reynolds principles; a statutory defence of truth and honest opinion which would replace 'fair comment'; updating and extending the circumstances in which the defence of qualified or absolute privilege can be used; the introduction of a single publication rule; action to address libel tourism and the removal of the presumption in favour of a trial by jury (Ministry of Justice 2011). Clearly these are significant reforms, yet it remains to be seen whether or not they will provide greater scope for the protection of responsible journalism.

8

SECURITY AND INSECURITY

The United States is fighting this war in part to preserve democracy and freedom, neither of which can truly be achieved without an informed public. We need to keep the information flowing and work with each other to sort out what's true and what's not ... there may be other instances in the next few months in which good judgement should inspire editors to hold back on information that could put the nation's troops or civilians in danger. But editors, not government, must be the arbiters of what's fit to print. For a free society that's fighting to retain its freedom and procure it for others around the world, no other alternative is acceptable.

Baltimore Sun cited by Graber (2003: 41)

Introduction

The expectation that during times of war the freedoms enjoyed by press in peacetime can no longer be guaranteed surely makes sense. Censorship, secrecy, misinformation and media management are expected when national security or the national interest is at stake. Of course, it would be reckless and irresponsible to allow journalists the scope to divulge sensitive information to our enemies. Once a nation is at war the relationship between security and liberty becomes strained. For journalists and news media, censorship and control, whether self-imposed or not, is just part of the deal when the stakes are so high. However, an important question concerns the extent and legitimacy of attempts to undermine freedom of speech, and other liberties, during times of national emergency and the balance (or not) that is achieved when covering such important issues. The quote above from the *Baltimore Sun* emphasises the importance of editorial responsibility in times of crisis and warns against government intrusion in journalism. It also highlights the apparent tension between security and liberty when journalists report on war and conflict. This chapter then explores this evident strain between security and liberty and focuses on these tensions with regard journalism, censorship and control during times of war and when dealing with terrorism.

The chapter will begin by outlining the notion of national security and national interest which tend to be the main justifications for curbing civil liberties. We will also examine the Official Secrets Act and the D-A Notice system. From here we go on to discuss terrorism and the various domestic policy responses that have been put in place in recent years to combat terrorism before going on to examine the 'troubles' in Northern Ireland and the specific issues that governments had in managing media coverage of the conflict. The chapter then goes on to explore the so-called 'war on terror' before looking in more detail at the media and its relationship with and to terrorism. We then go on to analyse war and the media, first by briefly examining the historical development of war journalism and factors that have shaped it, then by looking at a number of examples where Cold War insecurities led to a crack down on freedom of speech and freedom of the press. The chapter concludes by analysing censorship and modern warfare, looking particularly at the operationalisation of the war on terror in Iraq and Afghanistan.

National security and national interest

Because of their commitment to the democratic imperative, governments in liberal democracies generally don't like to be associated with the term 'censorship'. It paints them as illiberal, secretive, and undermines the idea that in a democracy there should be a free flow of information and ideas. During times of crisis or national emergency, the liberties and freedoms that societies enjoy, come under pressure for their own protection in the long term, or so it is claimed. As we will see, liberal democratic states do formally censor and censorship, when it rears its head either formally or informally, is usually in the name of national security or the national interest as Hocking maintains.

> The interests of 'national security' have long been seen as generating critical tensions for values that are fundamental to the political and legal systems of contemporary liberal democracies. Every expansion in security has been accompanied by the claim that certain needs – the need for secrecy, for protection of sources, the urgency of conviction, for instance – require a less than strict observance of what would otherwise be seen as untouchable, indeed elemental democratic, political and civil rights.
>
> *Hocking (2004: 335)*

Similarly, as Simons and Strovsky (2006: 193) suggest, the problem of 'acting in the so-called national interest is that sometimes the national interest is not in the public interest'. The authors go on to cite former U.S. Secretary of Defense Donald Rumsfeld's reference to Churchill's claim that 'sometimes the truth is so precious it must be accompanied by a bodyguard of lies' (2006: 193). Defining national security is not easy, and, as a justification of state censorship necessarily so. The fluid nature of the concept of national security enables states to adapt to particular events and circumstances; too static a concept would be excessively restrictive and not allow states the scope with which to defend their authority.

As a concept 'national security' has historically been linked to the notion of military security in which a state's armed forces and the intelligence services operate to protect the national interests from foreign or domestic threat. Mary Kaldor (2001: 140) has suggested that the term 'national security' is historically related to the 'external defence of national borders' and as such can be seen in this context as the protection of national sovereignty against external aggression. Following the Second World War, the rise of great ideological contestations between liberal capitalism in the 'West' and Soviet communism in the 'East' helped shape national security polices of states intent on protecting their national security even beyond their national borders. 'Hot' wars in Latin America and Indo-China during the second half of the twentieth century gave expression to this ideological contestation as the Cold War provided the ideological context of many of these conflicts of national liberation in which 'bloc security' was very much a component of national security within the context of what Kaldor calls 'old wars' (Kaldor 2001). However, since the end of the Soviet era and the expansion and development of globalisation, where the concept of the nation state has been superseded by the emergence of a global civil society (Kaldor 2003), the concept of national security has become somewhat amorphous. Protecting 'national security' today goes far beyond military and strategic imperatives and has to be seen in the context of the so-called 'war on terror' which is framed in terms of overseas as well as domestic security initiatives.

State control

As we saw in Chapter 2, the development of freedom of the press was one that saw formal government controls over print gradually diminish over time. As O'Malley and Soley (2000: 1) suggest: [The] idea that the state should not control the press was the product of a long historical development and became a central part of the way people, within and without the industry, have understood the relationship between the press and the people.' Yet, of course, the state does have the statutory power to curb freedom of speech and censor the press and power is usually invoked in respect to specific legal sanctions, the most significant of which is the Official Secrets Act.

Official Secrets Act

The Official Secrets Act (OSA) was first introduced in Britain in 1889 and was replaced by the act of 1911. As O'Malley and Soley (2000: 48) suggests the legislation was introduced during a period of increased tension between Britain and Germany and was intended to prevent both domestic and defence-related 'leaks' to unauthorised recipients. The thinking behind the OSA is that civil servants and government employees undertake a commitment not to disclose official, particularly defence-related information to a third party as such information could pose a threat to national security (see Hooper 1987). Following a series of high profile cases in the 1980s the Act was amended so as to ensure that a 'public interest defence' would not be available to signatories of the OSA. The view was that in signing the Act, individuals who worked for the intelligence services were giving up their rights to freedom of speech, even if they considered that they were acting in the public interests in doing so. The case involving former MI6 operative David Shayler highlights particular tensions in respect of such issues, tensions that also alert us to the conflicting demands of the OSA (1989) and the HRA (2000). Shayler was charged under section 1(1) and section 4(1) of the OSA 1989 in relation to allegations he made about MI6's involvement in a plot to assassinate Libyan leader Colonel Gaddafi and other alleged illegal activities of MI6 (Fenwick and Phillipson 2006). In attempting to defend himself Shayler argued that section 1(1) of the OSA was incompatible with Article 10 of the HRA. However, this view was rejected by the judge who suggested that Shayler could have disclosed his concerns about alleged illegal activity within the service to an authorised body. The judge therefore dismissed the contention that the two pieces of legislation were incompatible. As Fenwick and Phillipson (2006: 947) maintain, the OSA can also be used in conjunction with other pieces of legislation to prevent media exposure of security service activities. Most notably: 'Sections 1 and 4(3) work in conjunction with the provisions of the Security Services Act 1989 to prevent almost all media scrutiny of the operation of the security services.'

There is no doubt that secrecy in relation to the work of the security services is important. However, it does not automatically follow that they should not be democratically accountable to the public. At the time of writing the British security services are embroiled in controversy surrounding their alleged collusion in the torture of suspected terrorists. Though the terms of an inquiry into the torture allegations are in the process of being drawn up, the government is under increasing pressure to force MI5 produce the internal guidance given to security officers in relation to the questioning of terrorist suspects. However, in view of the specific protection given to the security services, it remains unclear whether full democratic accountability can ever be achieved.

D-Notice system

The D-Notice system is another mechanism whereby the government can prevent the media from putting information into the public domain. First established in Britain in 1912, Sadler notes that the D-Notice system is 'an arrangement between the government and the media whereby the media agrees not to publish certain government information which is sensitive on the grounds of being a threat to national security' (Sadler 2001: 1). The system today is known as the Defence Advisory Notice System which is managed by the Defence, Press and Broadcasting Advisory Committee (DPBAC), which is made up of government and media members who oversee a voluntary code that provides guidance to the British media on the publication or broadcasting of national security information. The objective is to prevent inadvertent public disclosure of information that would compromise UK military and intelligence operations and methods, or put at risk the safety of those involved in such operations, or lead to attacks that would damage the critical national infrastructure and/or endanger lives.

DPBAC (2010)

The DA-Notices provide general and specific guidance to the media on matters it sees as warranting special protection. The system emphasises the obligation that editors and producers have in protecting and maintaining national security. As noted the composition of the DPBAC is made up of representatives from specific government departments[1] and from sections of the media;[2] this mix is intended to ensure that a proportionate balance exists between the interests of national security and the interests of the news and wider media. The system is managed by a secretary and deputy secretary who are usually senior service personnel and it is their role to effectively acts as an 'independent broker' (Sadler 2001: 59) between government and the media. Sadler (2001: 61) suggests in the absence of any significant controversy about the workings of the DA Notice system, one may conclude that the system is a success. However, she also notes that this perception is 'largely due to the public relations skills of the secretary' (2001: 61) who is at pains to emphasise their neutrality. Despite this balancing act appearing to work in public, Sadler suggests that both sides of the system are keen to emphasise their own particular version of the public interest in ways that further their particular interests (see Sadler 2001).

Terrorism

Margaret Thatcher's famous dictum that the media should not give terrorists the 'oxygen of publicity' served as a warning to journalists that they should not give terrorists and their sympathisers a public platform. Her government's subsequent decision to implement a broadcast ban on Sinn Fein, a lawful political party, along with other illegal paramilitary organisations, demonstrated the power of the state to instigate a strategy of censorship over sections of the media. Since the attacks on the World Trade Center and the Pentagon in September 2001 terrorism has coloured both domestic policy and international affairs to significant effect. Within an international context, of course, we have witnessed the deployment of U.K. and U.S. forces in Iraq and Afghanistan in the so-called 'war on terror' at significant human and financial cost. The transformation of terrorism from an essentially domestic issue to one that is now a global problem has meant that terrorism has been identified as one of the most important international issues facing liberal democratic societies today.

Policy responses

On a domestic front in the U.K. the Terrorism Act of 2006 was introduced with the intention to curb the circulation of materials which are deemed to 'encourage' terrorism as well as seeking to ban material that could be deemed of use to the commission and exercise of terrorism. In the United States, the Patriot Act of 2001 was introduced with a view to 'Uniting and Strengthening America by Providing Tools Required to Intercept and Obstruct Terrorism' (United States Department of the Treasury 2001). Both pieces of legislation have sought to provide scope for the prosecution of persons suspected of inciting, encouraging, glorifying, or commissioning terrorism, with the internet in particular becoming a focal point. Campaign group Liberty has suggested that the creation of new offences under legislation such as the Terrorism Act 2006 'represent a serious incursion on free speech, criminalising careless talk and banning non-violent political organizations' (Liberty 2006). Along with the Terrorism Act 2000, the British State has been able to add to its armoury of powers in the name of combating terrorism at home. Such powers include detention without charge extended from fourteen to twenty-eight days, the curbing of protest rights, the extension of powers of the intelligence services to undertake surveillance operations, and the criminalisation of certain forms of speech.[3]

In the United States the Patriot Act has given the FBI and other federal agencies extended power, principally in the form of national security letters, to collect information from internet service providers, financial institutions and credit companies without judicial approval (American Civil Liberties Union 2005). In 2007 the FBI was found to have acted 'improperly' and at times 'illegally' when using the Patriot Act to covertly gather information about people in the U.S. (*The Guardian* 2007). A piece in the *New York Times* in 2007 reported that civil rights groups and academic organisations are claiming that 'the government is increasingly using secret evidence under new anti-terrorism laws to prevent certain critics from entering the United States', thereby limiting freedom of speech (*New York Times* 2007). It seems then that the U.K. and U.S. governments are potentially undermining democratic freedoms in the name of protecting those same freedoms in the 'fight against terrorism'. Yet this is nothing new as the following discussion on the media and the troubles in Northern Ireland highlights.

The media and the 'troubles' in Northern Ireland

Media coverage of Northern Ireland during the height of the conflict in the 1980s and 1990s highlights the delicate and complex nature of the relationship between the news media's commitment to serve the public sphere, and the state's ambition to fight terrorism on all fronts (Schlesinger 1983).

Though the British Prime Minister Margaret Thatcher famously pronounced that terrorists should be denied the 'oxygen of publicity', it was Labour Northern Ireland Secretary, Roy Mason, who publicly stated in 1976 that the BBC would suffer if it did not stop 'encouraging terrorists' in their coverage of Northern Ireland (Wilby 2006). Mrs. Thatcher's government was determined to strengthen its attempts to clampdown on what it perceived was sympathetic media coverage of terrorism, particularly from the BBC who had broadcast a number of interviews with members of illegal paramilitary organisations in recent years (Walker 1992: 142). Unfortunately for the BBC things were about to get much worse.

After receiving an anonymous tip-off 'that they would see something of considerable interest' (Bolton 1990: 64), a BBC *Panorama* team travelled from Dublin to the village of Carrickmore, County Tyrone. Soon after their arrival they came across a number of armed hooded men apparently conducting random vehicle checks in the village. Cameraman Paul Berriff obtained roughly ten minutes of footage of the men apparently in control of the village in broad daylight. Clearly this was a publicity stunt by the IRA who were hoping to use the BBC to cause embarrassment to the authorities in the Northern Ireland by demonstrating that they could take effective control of a village at will. Even though there was no reason to suggest the BBC was ever going to broadcast the footage, when news of the filming reached Downing Street, Margaret Thatcher was said to 'incandescent' (Bolton 1990: 76) as this seemed to be another example of the BBC associating with terrorists. It could not continue, the BBC must 'put their house in order' argued the Prime Minister at Prime Minister's Questions (Schlesinger 1983: 127; Bolton 1990: 79).

Fleet street also piled the pressure on the BBC with headlines such as 'Betraying Journalism', 'Field day for IRA thugs' and even one from the *Daily Express* suggesting that the BBC were 'Close to Treason' (Bolton 1990: 80). The programme's editor Roger Bolton was sacked and though he was later reinstated, the incident demonstrates how sensitive (supposedly independent from government) BBC management can be to government pressure, particularly in relation to coverage of paramilitaries. The Attorney-General suggested at the time that the BBC was in contravention of Section 18 of the Prevention of Terrorism Act in that it 'failed to inform the security forces until long after the trail was cold' (Walker 1992: 142). Yet, of course, had the journalists immediately informed the security services of the activities of the IRA that day, they would have effectively been seen as agents of the state and collaborators placing themselves and their colleagues in significant danger, not to mention undermining their journalistic commitment to objectivity and balance.[4]

Another incident that provoked the ire of the Thatcher government was the BBC's *Real Lives* 'At the Edge of the Union' programme, in which Sinn Fein's Martin McGuiness was interviewed. The programme had not even been broadcast when the Home Secretary wrote to the BBC's board of governors and suggested that they postponed the programme 'in the wake of a speech by Mrs. Thatcher in Washington lambasting those who gave terrorists the "oxygen of publicity"' (Lee 1990: 110). The BBC's board of governors subsequently postponed transmission of the programme citing procedural non-compliance and lack of balance as its core rationale (Walker 1992: 268).

What seemed like the final straw for the government was Thames Television's *This Week* which produced a programme called 'Death on the Rock'. The programme examined the killing of three unarmed republican paramilitaries by members of the elite SAS regiment in Gibraltar in 1988. The programme raised questions about the circumstances surrounding the shootings, which the government had argued were in self-defence as the three were planning to detonate car bomb during a changing of the guard ceremony on the rock. However, eyewitness accounts broadcast in the programme cast doubt on the official story. Contrary to the government's version of events, a number of eye witnesses suggested that two of the individuals who were shot had their hands in the air as if to surrender and were not given any opportunity to give themselves up peacefully, while a third member of the group was killed moments later after fleeing the scene. The official line was that the security forces were worried about the possibility that the terrorists might detonate the car bomb remotely. Yet a retired army bomb expert interviewed in the programme challenged this view. Moreover, the programme makers seemed to suggest that British and Spanish security forces had ample opportunity to arrest the suspects as they tracked the team in Spain thereby negating the risk of an explosion.

'Death on the Rock' was criticised by large sections of the British press for casting doubt on the British version of events and implying that the British were operating a shoot-to-kill policy on Gibraltar. The *Daily Mail* headline was 'Fury over SAS "Trial by TV"' while *The Sun*'s editorial was 'headed Blood on Screen – Thames' cheap telly scoop is just IRA propaganda' (Bolton 1990: 236). One witness in particular, Carmen Proetta, came under a sustained attack from *The Sun* and *The Sunday Times* which claimed that Proetta, dubbed the 'tart of gib', was involved in drugs and prostitution. As Roger Bolton (1990: 240) points out the Tory supporting members of the press 'alleged that she and her husband were anti-British'. Not only was it the programme makers and contributors who came under pressure as a result of 'Death on the Rock', but also *New York Times* journalist Jo Thomas was put under pressure not to cover the story and was encouraged to drop it altogether by a 'high-ranking' British official and some of her American colleagues. She declined and was subsequently removed as London correspondent for the *New York Times* (Irvin 1992).[5]

The furore around 'Death on the Rock' and the Thatcher government's resolve to deny terrorists and their supporters the 'oxygen of publicity' that it argued they sought and were being given by the media, meant that they would pursue a policy of direct censorship of media coverage of terrorists. In 1988, Home Secretary Douglas Hurd 'issued a notice under section 29(3) of the Broadcasting Act 1981 and Clause 13(4) of the BBC Licence and Agreement, restricting interviews with eleven Irish organizations' (Miller 1990: 34). In practice the ban was a farce. Though the words of Sinn Fein members or supporters could not be heard viewers could see them speak on screen and read subtitles of what they were saying. Broadcasters also used actors to voice-over the images of speaking individuals.

Even though the media ban was seen as something of a joke the intention of denying Sinn Fein and their supporters a public platform in the media seemed to be working. As Miller (1995) suggests, television appearances by members of Sinn Fein declined following the introduction of the ban. Though the BBC and the Independent Broadcasting Authority (IBA) were anxious about the ban, no attempt was made to take the government on (Miller 1995). *The Guardian*'s deputy editor Jonathon Fenby accepted that one of the main reasons that the newspaper did not attempt to challenge the ban was the perceived 'apathy' and weariness of the Northern Ireland situation and its unfathomable complexity (Finlay 1991). Though there is much to be said for Fenby's analysis of the situation, it should also be noted that there was also widespread contempt among the media for an organisation like Sinn Fein which was after all the political wing of the IRA. Such disdain led some journalists and newspapers to intensify its efforts to silence Sinn Fein and vilify those that were against the ban and portray them as IRA sympathisers (see Miller 1995). Only the National Union of Journalists and a number of independent journalists sought to have the ban lifted in the High Court (Horgan 2002). The ban was eventually lifted in 1994 following the IRA's first ceasefire though it was not reinstated when the ceasefire ended a year later.

What is striking are the claims made by Miller in relation to the media buckling under government pressure to deny a legitimate political party such as Sinn Fein air-time with media organisations and newspapers receiving flak if they did not toe the line. Moreover, it could be argued that the legislation used to silence Sinn Fein and their supporters essentially created a chilling effect which led new organisations and journalists to self-censor so as not to venture on to problematic ground which could have had repercussions for them individually and for their organisations. What is particularly worrying, however, are the attempts to undermine investigative journalism by journalists and news organisations themselves, as in the case of *The Sun* and *Sunday Times* attacks on the makers and contributors of 'Death on the Rock'. Flak, it seems, is not just the preserve of the political elite but can also stem from news organisations that support the government line.

The 'war on terror'

In his 'State of the Union Address' on 20 January 2002, U.S. President George W. Bush delivered his now famous 'axis of evil' speech in which he set out, in broad strokes, his plan for taking up the fight against 'evil regimes' who seek to destroy the principles of democracy and freedom. With reference to Iraq, Iran and North Korea, Bush was alerting the world that America would seek revenge against those that committed the attacks on 11 September 2001 (9/11) and would not tolerate states that, in its view, supported terrorism. Kellner (2004) suggests that in its framing of the highly complex dynamics of international politics, the Bush administration, with significant help form the U.S. media, has aided the neo-conservative agenda following 9/11. With its characterisation of the so-called civilised world (by default the Western democratic states with the U.S. at the helm) coming under attack from uncivilised barbarians, the U.S. generated the context for the so-called 'clash of civilizations'. According to this view, America leads the way in the battle between the forces of darkness and the forces of good. Kellner argues that such a view played on the extensive media coverage of the attacks on 9/11 and exploited people's fears and anxieties about a new age of global terrorism. He suggests that rather than 'critically debating' the issues facing America, the U.S. corporate media went a long way in setting out the context for the attack on Iraq in 2003 and 'established a binary dualism between Islamic terrorism and civilisation, and largely circulated war fever and retaliatory feelings and discourses that called for and supported a form of military intervention' (Kellner 2004: 145). Ultimately, by not engaging critically with the view that the terrorists who brought down the twin towers were supported by Saddam Hussein, or at least had a significant relationship with him, the media effectively helped Bush to muster support for military action against Iraq.

Russia's 'war on terror'

The United States and the U.K. are not the only states that have waged 'war on terror'. Russia's 'war on terror', following the apartment bombings in the Russian cities of Moscow, Buynaksk and Volgodonk in 1999, heralded the 'Doctrine of Information Security' which, though not a legal document, set out the view that the Russian Federation would be re-evaluating its relationship with the media in the light of perceived threats from international terrorism. With the new 'doctrine' came the expectation that the media would fulfil its patriotic duty and not undermine the national security of the Russian Federation. Simons and Strovsky (2006) have argued that it has been both the historically significant political and cultural legacy of Russia's particular circumstances – harsh control over media under the Tsars and the Soviets – that has led to journalists ingraining the practice of self-censorship, particularly in relation to its 'war on terror' to be so pervasive. They note that media coverage of the Moscow theatre siege in particular raised a number of issues surrounding publicising the aims of the terrorists, protecting the security services and protecting the hostages and their families (2006: 203).

However, following media coverage of the siege President Vladimir Putin tried (and failed) to push through new media control legislation which would have imposed tighter controls over the media coverage of terrorism. Subsequently, the 'Convention on Counter-Terrorism' suggested voluntary 'rules of conduct' (Simons and Strovsky 2006: 205) for journalists and news media in order to provide responsible coverage of terrorism. The tenor of the language about media responsibility in relation to its coverage of terrorism significantly has contributed to a culture of self-censorship among journalists (Simons and Strovsky 2006). Similarly, television coverage of the Beslan School siege was widely criticised as providing inaccurate information (see Haraszti 2004) with television channels coming under fire for misrepresenting or ignoring the facts and journalists suffered physical attacks at the hands of a number of local residents who were despondent and angry at the media's coverage of the hostage crisis (Haraszti 2004).

Analysing media and terrorism

Defining terrorism

There has been a vast amount of debate about the definition of terrorism (Schmid 2004; Weinberg, Pedahzur and Hirsch-Hoefler 2004). For example, Walter Laqueur's seminal analysis of terrorism suggests that 'terrorism is the use or the threat of the use of violence, a method of combat, or a strategy to achieve certain targets' (cited in Tuman 2003: 6). Terrorists' use of violence 'aims to induce a state of violence in the victim' and 'does not conform to humanitarian rules'. Laqueur's analysis implies that terrorists are external to the state and systematically illegally direct their energies against the state and its interests (Tuman 2003: 6). Yet Annamarie Olivero suggests that states themselves are capable of acts of terrorism as the phrase itself 'contains its own rhetoric, which has been transformed throughout history by different states' (cited by Tuman 2003: 6). In other words the capacity to define terrorists as such largely rests with the state and the media which have the power to distinguish between legitimate and illegitimate acts of violence (Tuman 2003). The use of the terms 'terrorism' and 'anti-terrorism' are anything but value-neutral (Hocking 1992; see also Townshend 2002: 3–6). Yet Raphael Cohen-Almagor (2006: 186) suggests that there is no grey area when it comes to terrorism, arguing that: 'Terrorism is conceived as inhuman, insensitive to human life, cruel, and arbitrary. To remain morally neutral and objective toward terrorism and to sympathize with terrorist acts is to betray ethics and morality.'

Definitional issues aside, our sense that terrorism has become something different since 9/11 is one that is certainly pervasive (Curtis 2004). With 'old style' terrorism one at least knew that the perpetrators of terrorism had identifiable motives or rationales, even if they were considered outside the mainstream of political spectrum. Today, however, we arguably live in an era in which acts of terrorism and the terrorists themselves are seen in an altogether different light which defies any sense of rational or logic. In the post-9/11 world acts of terrorism are widely perceived simply as nihilistic and evil. Unlike its predecessors, modern day terrorism, it seems, has no rationale or motive beyond the destruction of Western civilisation and its values and the instillation of fear and chaos among the population. Yet as Townshend (2002: 9) asserts, following 9/11 there was 'a marked reluctance' by officials and those in the media 'to accept the fairly well-established view that Osama bin Laden's primary *casus belli* against the USA was the defilement of Saudi Arabia by the presence of US troops'. Indeed, as we shall see, it is in respect of this lack of attention given to serious analysis of the historical and political context behind acts of terror that proves dangerous, particularly in relation to threats against civil liberties.

Though terrorism seems to have been a constant feature of democratic societies in the late twentieth century (see Schlesinger 1983), only since 9/11 does our perception of terrorism's threat seem to have exponentially grown. In attempting to understand why this is the case, it is worth examining the relationship between terrorism and the news media more closely.

News media and terrorism

Coverage of terrorism presents news media organisation with a range of particular problems. News organisations generally have a political obligation, a set of professional values, as well as commercial incentives to cover acts of political violence and terrorism. During times of national crisis, however, the media can be placed under pressure to conform to, or resonate with overtly patriotic values which might undermine balanced reporting of events. Following the attacks on 9/11, Condoleeza Rice (the U.S. National Security Advisor), asked national television executives to stop broadcasting tapes of Osama Bin Laden as she argued that the tapes could contain 'coded messages' to terrorists (Graber 2003: 36). Similarly, Al-Jazeera has been criticised by the U.S. for releasing video and audio tapes of Osama Bin Laden which it argues are providing a platform for terrorism and airing 'anti-American views' (Committee to Protect Journalists 2001).

It is clearly a difficult job that media organisations have in relation to attempting to strike a balance between providing coverage that informs the audience of the important issues and emphasises the impact and context of terrorism and at the same time ensuring that they need to protect themselves against the possibility of being seen to be exploited by the authorities or terrorists. Publicity is seen as a key weapon in their armoury, as William Catton Jr. argues 'Terrorist activity is basically a form of theatre. Terrorists play to an audience. Without the mass media they would seldom be able to reach audiences as large as those from which they now gain attention' (cited by Gerrits 1992: 30). Cohen-Almagor's analysis reflects this perspective when he cites a number of examples in which he suggests that irresponsible media reporting of terrorism not only provided sensational coverage for the terrorists but also cost lives of some of those involved.[6] 'When people are forced into alarming situations, the media should accept the instructions of the authorities' and report responsibly and with news organisations and editors 'thinking about the consequences of reporting' (Cohen-Almagor 2006: 209). Moreover, competition for exclusives can be a powerful factor in journalistic recklessness, particularly in relation to the more dramatic events, yet this can be at the expense of glorifying terrorist activity or endangering lives. This, of course, is a difficult balance. During the Beslan School siege in 2004 it was reported that terrorists watching Russian news coverage of the siege were angered by the 'distorted information' being provided by the media. The response of the terrorists, according to one journalist who interviewed a hostage, was to deny the hostages, many of them children, access to tap water (see Haraszti 2004).

Another problem for media organisations in their coverage of terrorism relates to issues of taste and respect for the dead and injured. News media reporting such as that of the siege of the Dubrovka Theatre in Moscow in 2002[7] and Beslan[8] showed images of the dead and wounded. In the case of Beslan, of course, many of these were children (BBC 2005). Similarly, the coverage of the terror attacks on 9/11 was similarly graphic with the image of the 'falling man' providing one of the most resonant images of many of the events of that day (Perivolaris 2010). Cohen-Almagor remains critical of media coverage which he argues exploits the images of death and destruction for commercial gain. The broadcast media in particular 'exploited the suffering of people who were trapped and subsequently died inside the struck towers, playing again and again the emotional mayhem of people who were trying to cope amidst overwhelming horror, disbelief, fear and terror'. (Cohen-Almagor 2006: 200). Sanders (2003: 99) suggests that showing scenes of intense suffering can become akin to 'visual pornography' especially if there is no moral engagement by journalists.

This analysis seems to reflect the notion that acts of terrorism are 'media events' which is something that Nacos (2002) has explored. She suggests that the relationship between the media and terrorist organisations are essentially 'symbiotic' – with the two entities effectively needing each other. She suggests that: 'All told, the mainstream media and terrorists are not bedfellows, they are more like partners in a marriage of convenience. […] it serves the self-interest of the corporate media and, unwittingly, the very scheme of mass mediated terrorism' (Nacos 2002: 99; see also Tuman 2003). Here the relationship is characterised as one in which terrorists and the media need each other – with the terrorists requiring media coverage to spread their message and cause panic and chaos in the streets, with the media using the coverage in order to secure a competitive advantage over their rivals.

There is no doubt that coverage of terrorism presents news media with a difficult set of problems. However, the characterisation of a symbiotic relationship between media and terrorism may be one that simplifies a more complex set of dynamics. This is the view of Irvin (1992) who has suggested that the media/terrorism symbiosis model tends to ignore the essentially dynamic relationship between terrorism and the media. Based on her research interviews with a number of convicted terrorists as to their views of the media, she concludes that from their perspective 'selective media coverage can impede, as well as advance, the aims of insurgent "terrorism"' with media coverage been seen by terrorist groups as 'at best, reluctant allies and, at worst, hostile and powerful enemies' (1992: 83–84).

Another criticism of the 'symbiosis' model is that it does not explore the extent to which the media itself might, in its coverage of terrorism, serve to 'block' the means through which a social and political settlement could occur which would then negate the stimulus for acts of terrorism. In other words such a model does not explore the roots and of terrorism from within its analytical framework nor the power relations inherent within that framework (Hocking 1992).

Terrorism, media and fear

As we have seen, the generation of fear is something that is part of the *raison-d'être* of terrorism. Huddy *et al* (2003: 256) suggests that 'the media play a crucial role in framing and amplifying the effects of terrorism'. The argument here is that acts of terrorism are designed to generate fear and anxiety in society, however, the authors maintain that terrorists target the promotion of fear in order to negotiate with governments and ultimately attempt to undermine the very fabric of the political system or society they oppose. The authors argue that we need to think about this anxiety in terms of its effect on government policies and on how the media engage with government in this respect. Increased airport security (including the appearance of tanks at airports); the proposed introduction of I.D. cards; harsher immigration controls; the appearance of barricades around Westminster and at airports, all add to our sense that our society is under threat. The research concludes by noting that following the attacks on 9/11 'Americans' dominant reaction […] was not one of fear'. Rather it was one of apprehension about future attacks which actually 'galvanized support for government anti-terrorist policy' (Huddy *et al* 2003: 274). As Altheide (2002: 196) has noted: 'Fear destroys justice. A just society can never come from fear.' Moreover, 'the fear industry promotes fear by offering solutions that attack the objects of fear. Promises of safety, restitution, and so forth are exchanged for justice' Altheide (2002: 196).

In the television series *The Power of Nightmares* Adam Curtis takes up this theme of fear and applies it to the idea that fear in Western societies can be a powerful tool for those in power or those wishing to obtain power. Curtis argues that since the collapse of the Soviet System and the 'victory of liberalism', those in the military machine and whom one might call 'hawks' or neo-conservatives have effectively invented a new and terrible invisible enemy with which to justify military spending and with it the assertion of U.S. global military dominance. The argument the hawks use is that if we don't protect ourselves, then we face the prospect of our society as we know it being totally destroyed, in much the same way as society was under threat in the 1950s and 1980s from the Soviet red menace. Curtis argues that we are being scared into believing that we should trust our leaders, because they are best placed to protect us and our interests. The fact that we can't see our enemies (like we could see the old enemies the Soviet Union) makes us even more prone to suspicion and anxiety. Our leaders tell us that terrorism is the biggest threat to our way of life and that the whole fabric of our society is under threat if we don't respond appropriately. Curtis argues that the threat is overblown and used to justify the ambitions of the 'hawks' in the pentagon as well as secure powerful elite interests.[9]

As horrifying and traumatic as they were, the attacks on 9/11 did not of course bring down Western civilization. Though the threat of terrorism remains, the likelihood that our society will be radically altered or brought to its knees by such acts seems unlikely. Yet the rhetoric of fear remains. This is the view of Mick Hume in *The Times* (2004) who emphasises the point about the magnification of fears of terrorism when he talks of the media coverage of the Beslan massacre and the events of 9/11. He says that: 'Terrible though these events and images are, how could they paralyse a state of 150 million Russians by killing 350? Or traumatise a nation of 300 million Americans by killing 3,000?' He suggests that, of course, they can because media coverage of such atrocities encourage people to internalise the exaggerated threat and that our leaders and the media, particularly the tabloid press, and even many of those who opposed military action in Iraq, make it easy for the likes of Bin Laden to scare us to death. Moreover, Hammond (2007) suggests that despite the bullish responses from the hawks in Washington D.C. following the attacks on 9/11 the political class and the media itself operate within a culture of low expectations and limited horizons. He suggests that the overriding emphasis on risk and fear following the attacks betrayed a significant lack of confidence among political elites in the West about how to deal with the threat of terrorism and a lack of faith in politics itself. The media too reflected this malaise by mirroring elite anxiety as well as scepticism about the war on terror itself. In the face of any alternative set of meaningful values with which to develop a confident political agenda, the default setting of political elites and the media is one of caution and risk aversion.

War

As we have already noted, there has always been a tension between the journalists' need to access a story and the state's requirement to ensure that its security and strategic interests are not compromised in any way. War, of course, is 'politics by other means' as was once famously remarked (Kaldor 1999: 17) as such wars provide fertile ground for news journalists eager to get the exclusive. Yet, of course, the issue of reporting war is controversial with journalists and news organisations facing difficult questions concerning balance, objectivity, control and bias as well as the suitability and benefit of showing images of death and destruction. Though possibly a more fundamental issue is at stake when journalists cover war and conflict as Philip Knightly (2003) suggests, the first casualty, once war breaks out, is not human, rather it is truth itself. For some journalists and news organisations, the truth may not be a priority, as former CBS anchorman Dan Rather suggested in an interview on CNN's *Larry King Live* in 2003. When questioned about the differences between Arab and U.S. media in their coverage of Iraq he famously stated:

> Look, I'm an American. I never tried to kid anybody that I'm some kind of internationalist or something. And when my country is at war, I want my country to win, whatever the definition of 'win' may be. Now I can't and don't argue that is coverage without prejudice. About that I am prejudiced.
>
> *Rather cited by Solomon (2004: 157)*

Of course, Rather is not suggesting that he would advocate dishonesty or lying,[10] he is suggesting that his patriotic allegiances override his journalistic commitment to accuracy, fairness and balance. However, such advocacy can, of course, impact on audience access to balanced reporting of war and conflict as Solomon (2004: 157) has pointed out, referring to FAIRs study[11] of on-camera sources used at the start of the Iraq war, noting that: 'Once the war began, the major network studios were virtually off-limits to vehement American opponents of the war.' Of course, a patriotic media is nothing new, from images of Prime Minister Margaret Thatcher sitting in a Challenger Tank in 1988 (Nunn 2003), Tony Blair in the cockpit of a Harrier Jump Jet in 1999 (Hammond 2000) to George W. Bush's 'Top Gun' moment in 2003 (Thussu 2009: 123)[12] the mainstream media, and tabloid press in particular[13] has always been able to demonstrate its commitment to supporting the nation's troops in battle. As Hallin and Gitlin note 'the primary role of the media in wartime in the Anglo–American world has long been to maintain the ties of sentiment between the soldiers in the field and the home front' (cited by Carruthers 2000: 6). During the Falklands conflict there was an air of competition among most newspapers in relation to which newspaper could appear the most patriotic (Greenslade 2004). Yet not all journalists and news organisations are comfortable toeing the government line and stand out as examples of independent and critical journalism.

John Pilger has lamented the conformity of conventional war coverage, particularly in relation to alleged Israeli atrocities in Gaza in 2007. Pilger likened journalists to passive onlookers unable to take responsibility for their lack of action and critical scrutiny in the name of 'even-handedness'. Controversially Pilger compared Western journalists to the women who looked 'silently from the side' while trains were packed with Jews heading towards the death camps of Dachau and Bergen Belsen

(2007). The implication being that because the women did not speak out they were in some ways complicit in the Holocaust. In other words he is suggesting that news journalism in its coverage of war, by conforming to established journalistic norms (norms which are inherently biased towards Western imperialism) is complicit in the death and destruction that they survey.[14] Journalists have also, of course, received 'flak' from government and the military over unpatriotic reporting. Alastair Campbell's famous jabbing finger, as he sat in a Commons Foreign Affairs Committee, pointed explicitly to the failures of the BBC over the report from Andrew Gilligan which claimed that an unnamed source had suggested that the government had 'sexed up' some of the evidence leading to the invasion of Iraq in 2003. Campbell continued to attack the BBC in his appearance at the Iraq Inquiry in 2010 stating that the 'subsequent controversy was, frankly caused by an utterly dishonest piece of journalism. That's the fact' (Iraq Inquiry 2010: 17).

Reporting war

Though there is a longstanding belief that in times of war the military and the media have opposing agendas, McLaughlin (2002: 71) suggests that in the period from Crimea to Korea there was a rapprochement 'with the military moving away from the chauvinistic assumption that the journalist has no business in the war zone'. The extent to which this rapprochement has converged is the source of much controversy.

Historically the war correspondent has been perceived as a job that is glamorous, yet a job with inherent dangers. Stories of war reporters braving the battlefields, dodging bullets and bombs in order to get a true account of the war are the stuff of journalistic folklore. The most famous war correspondent was William Howard Russell who is best known for his coverage of the Crimean war for *The Times*. Russell is widely seen as *the* war correspondent, someone who 'stuck to his principles of reporting everything he knew to be true without fear or favour. He would report the blunders and disasters of war as well as the incompetence of generals and strategists' (McLauglin 2002: 20). Russell's dispatches from the front exposed 'the chaotic nature of military administration in the Crimea' (Hudson and Stanier 1997: 19) as well as the poor and dejected state of the troops. This drew criticism from the commander of the British troops in Crimea Lord Raglan who suggested that Russell's dispatches were providing the enemy with important information and 'involved serious breaches of security' (Knightly 2003: 11). Russell was not the only journalist to report on the Crimean war. Edwin Lawrence Godkin wrote for the *London Daily News* and like Russell, also provided controversial coverage of the Crimea. Both were highly critical of military blunders and incompetent leadership as well as the terrible conditions suffered by the troops (McLaughlin 2002: 50), though war itself was never questioned.

This critical journalism meant that some measure of control was required by governments to prevent valuable information being passed to the enemy in the reports, or to prevent the undermining of the war effort. So in February 1856 the Commander in Chief at the Crimean front prohibited all correspondents from reporting 'military details of value to the enemy on pain of removal from the front' (McLaughlin 2002: 51). However, as Knightly argues, though the order was only passed after the war was over it had an impact on how later war and conflict would be reported (cited by McLaughlin 2002: 51).

The period from the end of the American Civil War (1861–65) to the First World War (1914–18) has widely been seen as the 'golden age of war reporting' (Knightly 2003). We see stories of heroic journalists risking life and limb reporting conflicts around the globe to send back to the readers back home. Such accounts would neatly fit into any 'boy's own adventure story' as war reporting was becoming increasingly popular with the public.[15] Knightly (2003) has suggested that a number of factors are relevant during this 'golden age'. First, the popular press was 'on the rise' with newspapers desperate for competitive advantage over their rivals. The telegraph too enabled reporters to send their dispatches from the front lines, dispatches that would be in print within days rather than months as before. Finally, Knightly (2003: 44) suggests that military censorship was not as effective or as efficient as we might expect today, as such journalists could take liberties with the truth and 'write virtually what they liked'. The effect was that the job of the war correspondent became as much a part of the coverage as the war itself with correspondents often portraying themselves as the heroic seeker of truth, an image that resonates in contemporary popular culture.[16] This is not to say that journalists did not suffer the hardship and trauma of war as journalists would often enter the battlefield themselves or take enormous risks to ensure that their dispatches reached home.

Given the liberties that many journalists and war correspondents were taking in their coverage, freedoms that could both cost lives and victory in battle, censorship and control of journalists seemed to be the only option. As Lasswell noted in his study of propaganda during the Great War: 'There is no question but that government management of opinion is an unescapable corollary of large-scale modern war' (cited by Carruthers 2000: 54). Carruthers argues that: '[T]he roles allotted to mass media and state techniques for regulating the flow of news and shaping its presentation in the First World War prefigure those of the Second' with Nation States hoping 'that their media would provide both a positive projection of war aims while crystallizing public animosity towards the enemy' (Carruthers 2000: 55–57).

For the most part the British government's wish came true, though with some skirmishes on the way. Even before the war, moves were made to ensure that control of the press would be easier than during previous military campaigns, even though the Department of Information[17] was not established until 1917 (Carruthers 2000: 61).[18] When war began, as Carruthers (2000) suggests, two important mechanisms of control were established: first, in August 1914 the Press Bureau was created with a view to managing and controlling the flow of information through telegraph wires. The second were measures included in the Defence of the Realm Act (DORA), which would prohibit information that might be beneficial to the enemy. The measures provided for under DORA were so wide-ranging and vague they effectively encouraged journalists and editors to self-censor as any infringement would mean harsh consequences for those that were found in contravention of the measures

(Carruthers 2000). This system of self-regulating censorship effectively removed the cloak of officialdom from view and gave the impression that journalists and editors were, for the most part, acting responsibly.

In May 1915 the military finally granted 'permanent, pooled accreditation to five war correspondents'. These journalists would be under the protection of the military but their reports would be strictly censored and controlled. Farrar (1998) suggests that this process effectively created a class of journalists 'who conformed to the conspiracy and lies of propaganda' rather than reporting of the war truthfully and accurately. In other words, they became part of the military establishment (cited by McLaughlin 2002: 60) and as such, according to this perspective, gave up any obligation to truthfulness and balance.

The Second World War saw journalists having to return to a system of controls and accreditation put in place by the Ministry of Information which would ensure that reporters could not undermine the war effort by passing useful information to the enemy (McLaughlin 2002). The idea that journalists might undermine the war effort was also felt at home with the government banning the communist newspapers *The Week* and *Daily Worker*, both of which criticised the war as an imperialist adventure (Curran and Seaton 2010: 56).

Vietnam and beyond

Since the end of the Second World War in 1945 until the Persian Gulf War in 1991, British and U.S. military forces have been engaged in numerous covert and overt interventions in Africa, South and Central America, the Middle East, North and South East Asia which have all seen U.S. and U.K. forces deployed in the name of securing strategic interest or 'liberating' oppressed peoples. However, it is the legacy of the U.S. war in Vietnam from the early 1960s until 1975 that has come to dominate conventional thinking about the military's relationship with the media ever since (Carruthers 2000). Media coverage of Vietnam was like no other, as Carruthers suggests:

> Unlike correspondents in the Second World War or Korea, American reporters had unparalleled freedom, even military assistance, to roam South Vietnam; they were helicoptered, more or less on demand, to destinations of their choice, where they could freely interview military personnel and accompany them into action.
>
> *Carruthers (2000: 120)*

With journalists able to gain access to the conflict with relative ease they were able to provide, in vivid detail, pictures of the death and destruction that were, in many peoples' eyes to undermine public support for the war in the U.S. (Hallin 1989). American families had almost daily television coverage of the conflict in their own homes (Carruthers 2000) where they were repeatedly reminded of the horror of war, and as the war dragged on, the seeming futility of its commission. Some of the images shown on television have since become embedded in Western consciousness about the brutalising effects of war, especially on its innocent victims.[19] The widespread coverage of the war, particularly on television, has been criticised from a range of perspectives, not least because of the way in which the medium itself limits understanding and focuses on the dramatic and the sensational. Hudson and Stanier (1997: 115) argue that with regard the chaos and confusion of the Vietnam War 'it is too much to expect the media, and particularly television, to produce balanced, sane and sensible reports on which sensible objectives judgements can be made by the public'. Moreover, 'television predominantly played on negative themes – death and destruction – and its images lent themselves to anti-war interpretation alone' (Carruthers 2000: 115). It could be argued therefore that the sentiment that the war in Vietnam was futile stemmed from the chaos and confusion as well as the 'negative' images of the war available to the American people.

Critics also argue that an overly critical culture, particularly among the younger journalists, fostered a type of confrontational and overtly negative type of coverage in which the historical deference shown to the military by journalists was no longer evident (Carruthers 2000). The so-called 'five o'clock' follies' – daily press briefings to journalists in Saigon which were 'hasty, fragmentary, inevitably inaccurate field reports' were given little credence by journalists (Braestrup cited by McLaughlin 2002: 75), did not add to correspondents' respect for military briefers and may have contributed to a more critical analysis among some reporters. Moreover, it has been suggested that the way in which journalists reported the Tet Offensive led to the widespread belief that American involvement in Vietnam was doomed and that journalists' disposition towards the U.S. military was overwhelmingly hostile.[20] Hallin (1989: 212–13) suggests that following the Tet Offensive public opinion did act as a constraint on U.S. policy in Vietnam and prove decisive. However, despite the conventional view that the military and the journalists on the ground had oppositional aims – the former to keep 'tactical blunders', 'strategic errors' and 'military setbacks' away from the press, the latter to expose them to the American public, the relations between journalists and the military were often very good (McLaughlin 2002: 78). Critics of the conventional view suggest that rather than the media losing the war in Vietnam, it was the political and military objectives, their operationalisation, along with poor planning and execution that should be blamed for declining lack of public support during the campaign (Hallin 1989).

The media's relationship with the military during the Falklands conflict was in marked contrast to that during the Vietnam War. A system of direct control and censorship of media reporting would ensure that coverage of the war conformed largely to the directives of the British government. McLaughlin (2002: 79) suggests that during the Falklands War military censorship operated on three levels. First, because of the logistical problems of filing reports back from the remote South Atlantic journalists were reliant on naval communications to get their stories back home with 'unfavourable reports and pictures [taking] days to find their way to the newsroom, by which time they were stale and useless as news'. Second, the briefing system in operation early on in the conflict, which denied journalists the opportunity to ask questions, ensured that reports would conform to the official line. The tone and style of delivery of Ian McDonald, the MOD civil servant given responsibility for delivering the briefings, reflected the austere and cold relationship between journalists and the MOD during the conflict. Third, McLaughlin suggests that a culture of self-censorship by journalists helped to ensure that if the government line was not adhered to, it certainly reflected across the media as journalists were reminded of their obligations not to undermine national security or compromise the safety of British troops. He notes that 'journalists would seek informal guidance by telephone or meeting about whether to include certain information', as such journalists took it upon themselves to gain clearance (McLaughlin 2002: 80). The daily briefings from McDonald and the limited access to alternative sources of information, a poor communication infrastructure for those reporting from the islands, coupled with a system of off the record briefings to journalists, some of which were directly intended to misinform,[21] all led to widespread frustration among many journalists reporting the conflict (see Morrison and Tumber 1988).

However, the government didn't have it all its own way. Harris (1983) suggests 'the enemy within' proved troublesome for Churchill in the Second World War and for Eden during Suez. In the course of the Falklands crisis this relationship did not change. During the BBC's *Nationwide* programme in which members of the public were invited to put questions to the Prime Minister, Mrs. Thatcher came up against a formidable opponent in Diana Gould, a geography teacher from Gloucestershire. Mrs. Gould asked Mrs. Thatcher why she gave the order to torpedo the Argentine cruiser the *General Belgrano* when it was clearly sailing away from the islands and was outside the British exclusion zone. The Prime Minister's response was that it was not sailing away from the Islands and posed a threat to British service personnel. This was challenged again and again by Gould, much to the obvious annoyance of Thatcher.[22] Similarly, when the British recaptured South Georgia from the Argentineans, Margaret Thatcher emerged from No. 10 and proudly announced that she had some good news for the press.[23] 'Are we going to declare war on Argentina? What happens next, Prime Minister?' asked the assembled press. Thatcher responded indignantly: 'Just rejoice at that news and congratulate our forces and the Marines.' Such an obvious lack of respect for what had been achieved clearly annoyed the Prime Minister. When the broadcast was shown on the BBC's *Newsnight* programme, the BBC was roundly criticised by the government and Conservative supporting sections of Fleet Street (Harris 1983: 75).

Morrison and Tumber (1988) suggest that the attacks on the media, and the BBC in particular during its coverage of the Falklands conflict, represented more than a government's desire to keep the media online and attack 'patriotic disloyalty' (1988: 349). They suggest that the attacks on the BBC 'exposed [...] the dislike of certain social groups which traditionally have been either brokers of ideas or formed the receptive cultural fabric for their creative expression' (Morrison and Tumber 1988: 351). In other words the attacks were part of a wider ideological and cultural conflict between the 'liberal intelligentsia' – or the so-called 'chattering classes' (represented here by the BBC) and the New Right.[24] The contestation for the appropriate framing of the Falklands conflict was only one aspect of the wider battle for political and cultural resonance.

Cold War insecurities

The Thatcher era of government from 1979 to 1991 provide us with a number of historical examples of government clashes with the news media in the name of national security and the national interest during the period of the Second Cold War (see Halliday 1986). The first major scandal involved Foreign and Commonwealth Office (FCO) clerical worker Sarah Tisdall who passed confidential memoranda, from the then Defence secretary Michael Heseltine to Prime Minister Margaret Thatcher, to *The Guardian* newspaper in 1983. The memo concerned the date of the arrival of American Cruise Missiles at Greenham Common Airbase in Berkshire and plans by Heseltine to keep their arrival quiet. The government sued *The Guardian* newspaper and forced it to hand over the documents thus exposing Tisdall as the source of the leak (Greenslade 2009a).[25] Tisdall was charged with 'communicating classified information' to an unauthorised person contrary to Section 2 of the Official Secrets Act 1911' (Jefferson 1984: 197) and pleaded guilty to the charge. As Jefferson (1984: 196–99) has suggested, contrary to government claims, national security was not at issue here as the arrival of the missiles was widely known to be imminent at the time of the publication of the memoranda in 1983; rather the prosecution of Ms. Tisdall under the Official Secrets Act was more about 'reducing public debate on the arrival of nuclear weapons' and with the Defence Secretary's desire assert government authority over the Campaign for Nuclear Disarmament and the peace protestors at Greenham Common.

A similar case involved Ministry of Defence (MOD) civil servant Clive Ponting who leaked an internal MOD document concerning the sinking of the Argentinean cruiser the *General Belgrano* in 1982 to Labour MP Tam Dalyell. As with Tisdall, Ponting was charged under Section 2 of the Official Secrets Act, with 'disclosing "official information" without authority to an unauthorized person', though unlike Tisdall, Ponting pleaded not guilty. As he points out (Ponting 1985), the case was not about the issue of national security as the government had admitted during the committal proceedings, rather it was about exposing the fact that government ministers had misled Parliament and the British public in relation to the circumstances surrounding the sinking of the *Belgrano*. The trial lasted two weeks and though the judges' summing up encouraged the jury to convict, the jury found in his favour and acquitted him. Ponting's defence was centred around the argument that he was not acting out of spite or for political gain, rather he was acting in the public interest and the jury believed his testimony.

The following year investigative journalist Duncan Campbell recorded a programme for the BBC as part of its *Secret Society* series; the programme centred on project Zircon, which was a secret operation to develop a spy satellite for deployment as part of Britain's nuclear defence strategy. There was no intention for the programme makers to disclose the specifics of the technology being used, only to 'identify its broad purpose, its cost, and the concealment of its existence and cost from parliament' (Thornton 1987: 4). During production it became clear to the programme makers that they were dealing with a significant story and the BBC sought consultation from the government. The government ordered the BBC not to broadcast the programme suggesting that the programme posed a threat to national security and later sacked the Director General of the BBC Alasdair Milne.[26] As a result, Campbell decided to publish his findings in the magazine the *New Statesman*. Campbell's main findings were that the funding of the project was obtained without approval from the House and, even more embarrassing for the government, it exposed Britain's total dependence on the United States system of satellites as part of its nuclear defence strategy. The government's purported anxiety about publication of the material led to raids on both the BBC and the offices of the *New Statesman* (even though the government had known about the programme). Thornton (1987: 11) has suggested that the action against Campbell, the *New Statesman* and the BBC constituted a 'campaign to intimidate the press' and an attempt to challenge the broader 'right of the press to publish without government interference'.

Though the Zircon affair became somewhat an embarrassment for the government, a bigger furore was about to erupt that would cause it even more humiliation to the government. This was sparked by events on the other side of the world in Australia with the publication of the book *Spycatcher*, written by retired former MI5 operative Peter Wright. The book dealt with two key issues that were considered sensitive to issues of national security. First was the accusation that the security services had conspired with the CIA to destabilise the Wilson government during his second term of office (1974–76). The second was the claim that the former head of the organisation Roger Hollis was working as a Soviet double agent – the so-called 'fifth man'. Speaking in a debate in the House of Commons in 1986 Labour MP Gerald Kaufman suggested that the government's decision to attempt to ban the book was 'bogus' as there had been other similar examples[27] of sensitive material released into the public domain that had not been subject to prosecution by the government.[28] Despite this the government attempted to stop publication of the book in the U.K. and in Australia, the latter with only short-lived success. It seems that attempts to ban publication of the book were made because the government was concerned that the book posed a significant threat to British national security at a time of heightened Cold War tensions and there was a point of principle about former secret services personnel profiting from their memoirs. Attorney-General Sir Patrick Mayhew argued in the House suggesting that: 'The "Spycatcher" proceedings are civil proceedings instituted by the Government as a result of a collective decision in pursuance of their policy to uphold the duty of confidentiality owed to the Crown by former members of the security services.'[29] The government also subjected *The Guardian* and *Observer* newspapers to gagging orders preventing them from publishing extracts. As I have noted elsewhere[30] citing Burnet and Thomas (1989) the *Spycatcher* case was much more than an attempt to uphold a principle of confidentiality owed to the Crown. Rather it became part of a strategy through which panic about national security could be used to further the ideological ambitions of the Thatcher project and 'the British government's right to disseminate its own version of reality. It was about the government's monopoly on "truth"' (Burnet and Thomas 1989: 212).

Censorship and modern warfare

Redefining war and conflict

Since the first Iraq war in 1991 Britain has been involved in air strikes against Iraq in 1998, the Kosovo conflict in 1999, Sierra Leone in 2000, air strikes and attacks on the Taliban in Afghanistan from 2002 to the present and of course the Iraq war in 2003 (see Kampfner 2004). Hammond (2000: 367) has argued that in the NATO air strikes on Kosovo in 1999 we saw 'the culmination of a number of [...] trends in conflict reporting,' the most significant of which is the shift in thinking about the rationale for war or military intervention.[31] Western military deployment is now in the name of humanitarianism, to save lives, liberate the oppressed or protect democracy. Hammond suggests that this shift can be traced to the changing nature of the relationship between the military and the news media where the media are now perceived in 'non-military' terms – 'as peacekeepers, humanitarians, aid workers and childminders' (Hammond 2000: 374). This shift in emphasis has had some important implications for journalism and its coverage of war and conflict. Significant among these is the advent of so-called 'journalism of attachment'. This phenomenon is most closely associated with former BBC journalist Martin Bell who suggested that the journalism of attachment is 'journalism that cares as well as knows; that is aware of its responsibilities; that will not stand neutrally between good and evil, right and wrong, the victim and the oppressor (Bell 1998: 16). Via the journalism of attachment it becomes permissible and legitimate for journalists to abandon objective reporting in favour of articulating a clear moral dimension in their coverage. Hammond suggests that not only can such reporting obscure the truth and accuracy of reporting, but also it can act to justify further intervention by accepting states' simplistic and Manichean rationale for war (Hammond 2000: 377).

Not only are modern-day wars fought on so-called humanitarian grounds, but also, increasingly, military deployments are made in the name of 'pre-emptive action' – the idea that military interventions are necessary in order to prevent states from acts of aggression or supporting terrorism. As we know this was the original rationale for invading Iraq in 2003, yet this shifted once it became clear that there were no weapons of mass destruction (WMDs) after all. At the time of writing British soldiers are still fighting a war in Afghanistan against the Taliban in the context of the wider 'War on Terror' against Al-Qaeda and other radical Islamist organisations (Foreign Affairs Committee Eight Report 2009).

Naming and framing

The capacity to frame the parameters of debate within a war context is something that has led Keeble (1997) to argue that the naming of a conflict as a 'war' (the example he uses is Gulf War I) effectively silences or rules out other readings or explanations for conflict within the media. Keeble is scathing in his attack on the media and he suggests that they blindly went along with the official framing of the conflict in the Gulf as a 'war' fought more or less on conventional terms. This he argues was in fact a myth. A 'war' implies a level of balance in military capacity and capability; this was not the case in 'Gulf War I'. Rather, Keeble asserts that what took place in the Gulf in 1991 was a 'series of massacres' of Iraqi conscripts which were framed as warfare in order to make military intervention more acceptable to the public. However, Keeble is not arguing that in reporting the conflict as a war, the media were complicit in some sort of conspiracy with the government and the military, rather, the propaganda that was reproduced by the media arose via an 'ideology of news reporting that incorporates a set of routines, constraint, expectations – and myths' (Keeble 1997: 200). Censorship here then is not state or even self-imposed, rather it comes about through the dynamics of the relationship between officials and journalists and the historically salient routines and practices associated with journalism. The framing of events in certain ways that conform to the official line can be seen therefore as even more effective than outright traditional censorship and can shape the parameters of reference and debate.

The power to frame war and conflict in certain ways is not just confined to governments and the military. The media itself has the capacity to frame conflict and war in ways that conform to certain cultural explanations and narratives. For example, the media coverage of the massacres in Rwanda in 1994, particularly early on, demonstrates the power of even quality media to simplify conflict in a way that can reinforce stereotypes of conflict in Africa (see Myers *et al* 1996; see also Carruthers 2004). In his study of television audience understanding of conflict and disaster Greg Philo (2002) suggested that the quest for greater audiences encourages news organisations to focus on sensational coverage of conflict and disaster – violence, trauma, drama and so on, at the expense of fuller contextualised coverage of events in the developing world. Unfortunately for Philo this also has the effect of generating unhelpful stereotypes of and 'negative attitudes towards the developing world' (2002: 185). It is therefore this lack of context that shapes the nature of the coverage. Even if explanations are offered they are generally simplistic and do not add to the audiences' deeper understanding of events. The possible reasons for this emphasis on the relatively simplistic and sensational coverage of war, conflict and disaster relates to larger issues around the commercial imperatives of news organisations and the drive for a greater market share, as well as a historically powerful set of cultural dispositions towards the people of the developing world that all too readily dismisses their circumstances as emerging from long standing ethnic rivalries or geographical accident (Myers *et al* 1996).

Media management

Hammond (2000) also makes the important point that modern day media management of warfare has been transformed in recent years with a highly professionalised media strategy in place well before any bullets are fired or bombs dropped. This increasingly professionalised approach to managing the media in the U.K. during Kosovo was primarily down to New Labour Director of Communications Alastair

Campbell running the media operation and employing many of the tactics that had served Tony Blair so well before and after the election of New Labour in 1997. During the Iraq war in 2003, Miller highlights the changes within the machinery of the British state itself and the formation of various departments such as Civil Contingencies Secretariat and its News Co-ordination Centre which works with other state agencies with a view to improving the U.K.'s 'resilience to disruptive challenge' all with an eye to ensuring sympathetic media coverage (Miller 2004: 85). In the United States the Office of Global Communications was set up to manage the Coalition Information Centres, originally formed in the wake of the military interventions in Afghanistan and Kosovo and which sought to ensure a consistent line between the U.S. and the U.K. Miller suggests that in the wake of responses to 9/11 such co-ordinated efforts by the U.S. and the U.K. demonstrate that the two have 'systematically overhauled their propaganda operations' (Miller 2004: 95) in ways that go far beyond any previous propaganda effort by either country (see Miller 2004: 80–99).

If we look at Iraq in 2003 one of the most famous images to emerge from the war was the iconic toppling of the statue of Saddam Hussein in Firdos Square in Baghdad. Television pictures and photographs beamed across the planet showed crowds of cheering Iraqis celebrating the fall of the tyrant Saddam with 'BBC reporters [enthusing] that it was a momentous event [and] a vindication of the strategy of the coalition' (Hammond 2007: 68). However, photographs later released showed that the square was in fact sparsely populated and ringed in by U.S. tanks (Exoo 2010: 113). The military later admitted that it staged the toppling of the statue in Firdos Square as part of its 'psy-ops' strategy (Exoo 2010: 113). Yet as Zelizer (2004b: 117) suggests, such photographs are powerful as they are an important symbolic representation of revolution. More generally, 'it is the photograph's symbolic or connotative force – its ability to contextualize the discrete details of a setting in a broader frame – that facilitates the durability and memorability of a news image' (Zelizer 2004b: 130). In other words such images can provide a potent force in framing distinctive events.

New media and war

Another thing to note about news media coverage of contemporary warfare is that, of course, within the context of established news organisations, coverage is extensive and operates across a range of media providing up-to-the-minute coverage and ongoing analysis and debate. However, as Berenger (2006: 23) states 'much of what the world learned about the 2003 war in Iraq was learned from non-traditional news sources, often before the mainstream media reported the stories'. Weblogs, email, digitisation of images and video and mobile communications technology have all enabled the dispersal and diffusion of information and discussion about war and conflict in ways that completely undermine the traditional news cycle (Berenger 2006). For example, the photographs of abuse and torture of Iraqi prisoners at Abu Ghraib that were exposed to the world by the CBS programme 60 Minutes 2 and in *The New Yorker* magazine,[32] were originally posted online by guards at the prison (Berenger 2006: 23).[33]

Pictures and video of the beheadings of Ken Bigley, Nick Berg and Kim Sun-il by insurgent groups in Iraq are widely accessible online on websites and weblogs and 'recent studies suggest that almost a quarter of online users have seen graphic war images not available from the mainstream media' (Johnson and Kaye 2006: 316 citing Fallows and Rainie 2004). Of course, such images would not be permissible on the mainstream media yet online they are freely available to view and in the case of Iraqi resistance and insurgency, were intended to both intimidate and propagandise (see Al Marashi 2006). As we saw in Chapter 3, the internet's destabilisation of traditional news processes is something that the news industry, academics and media commentators are still working through and attempting to come to terms with. Yet it is clear that the mainstream news media both make use of online media as a resource as well as a space for dissemination of news content. Such proliferation of media also provide opportunities for the public to gain alternative perspectives on war and conflict with the Qatari-owned Al Jazeera offering an alternative view of the conflicts in Iraq and Afghanistan which according to Bodi (2004) resulted the news organisation being targeted by the U.S. military.

The technology also allows news media organisations to provide both dramatic yet 'safe' depictions of conflict and the more dramatic and sensational the footage the better (Thussu 2009). The suggestion is that the intense competition and rivalry among global news media organisations generates what Thussu terms 'infotainment' – superficial amounts of information with maximum amounts of drama. The major advances in satellite digital communications technologies, coupled with relatively small cost of high-tech camera equipment, have enabled journalists to report, sometimes live from the battlefield, bringing even greater pressure on news organisations to get the most dramatic coverage. Yet for the most part, the images display lack any context or critical examination. They speak for themselves, with the viewers left to make sense of the events unfolding before their eyes. Hoskins also suggests that live or near live television reporting diminishes the reality of warfare and removes any sense that there is suffering and death behind the video wall images of rocket launches and graphical representations of enemy casualties, while the anchors chat with studio pundits about the range of a certain type of missile or the thickness of armour on an RPV.

> The Iraq war involved the prioritising of image-dissemination over news gathering and time over content. Effective analysis and understanding were substituted with the self-evidency of immediate images as the thresholds for what was included as news is lowered. Commentator prompts reveal the utter emptiness of much of the live coverage, with 'let's listen in' or 'let's watch and see what's going down' directing audiences to adopt reality TV modes of consumption.
>
> *Hoskins cited by Cottle (2006: 94)*

Embedding

Given the perceived failures of military-media relations since Vietnam and the problems associated with managing the media in wartime since Vietnam, a more sophisticated arrangement was required. Learning from their experiences of the pool system during the first Gulf War, the U.S. military devised a system of embedding which would enable reporters to have a sense of what it was actually like experiencing conflict at first hand with reporters even undergoing specific military training at Pentagon media 'boot camp'.[34] More than 900 embedded journalists lived, ate and slept in the same conditions as the service personnel deployed to Iraq. This allowed them to provide their news editors with first hand accounts of the conflict. Marlantes (2003) suggests that the embedding programme

> gave many reporters a first-hand understanding of how the military conducts warfare, and, many say, a greater respect for service members. Similarly, the troops and commanding officers in the field had a chance to observe the dedication and professionalism of journalists – and see them in a more sympathetic light.
>
> *Marlantes (2003)*

However, critics have suggested that the access and level of protection given to embedded reporters was at the expense of journalistic independence. The Committee to Protect Journalists (2004) suggested that the 'close quarters shared by journalists and troops inevitably blunted reporters' critical edge'. Other criticisms of the system, however, have been more scathing. According to Miller (2004) the embedding system, in tandem with Centcom – the United States Central Command in Doha – enabled the U.S. led military to stage a significant propaganda exercise in the name of international security and the war on terror. Miller suggests that the embedded system in 2003 ensured that journalists who opted into the system 'agreed to give up most of their autonomy in exchange for access to the fighting on military terms' (2004: 89). This involved signing a contract drawn up by the Pentagon in which 'The media employee further agrees to follow Government regulations. The media employee acknowledges that failure to follow any direction, order, regulation, or ground rule may result in the termination of the media employee's participation in the embedding process' (U.S. Department of Defense 2003).

Former Pentagon spokeswoman Victoria Clarke disagrees that in being embedded with the military journalists are compromising their independence. 'War is war, and it's bad and it's ugly and people get hurt and people die. I don't think you can manage it in any way. I think the best thing you can do is demonstrate as much of the truth as possible' (Marquis 2003). Yet reports from inside Iraq from Western correspondents all concluded their reports with the 'health warning' that the reports had been made under the conditions imposed by the Iraqi military. Thus suggesting that the picture that they were presenting to the public back home was subject to censorship. Though this was undoubtedly the case, similar health warnings were generally not forthcoming from embedded journalists – the implication being, therefore, that our enemies censor; we do not. Yet, of course, a reading of the Pentagon contract suggests otherwise.

Another side effect of the embedding system was the 'credentializing' effect it created among reporters, with embedded reporters being considered 'official journalists' by the military whereas 'unilaterals' were often treated as pests' (Shafer 2003). This lack of credibility has been seen in some quarters as outright disregard for the safety of independent or unilateral journalists. Certainly operating as a journalist in a war zone without military protection is a risky business, but for Knightly (2003: 100) unilateral journalists reporting the war in Iraq were operating in what was to become 'the most dangerous […] ever' with the majority of journalist deaths being caused as a result of allied firepower – so-called 'friendly fire'. The warnings (Tumber and Palmer 2004: 40) given to news organisations by the Pentagon and the British government about the potential dangers of reporters not being embedded with the military seemed prophetic. The Committee to Protect Journalists (CPJ) reported in 2004 that the Pentagon had repeatedly warned journalists that their safety could not be guaranteed and 'urged them to avoid the country' (CPJ: 2004). Another CPJ special report on journalists and media workers killed in Iraq suggests fifteen journalists and media workers were killed by U.S. forces between March 2003 and August 2005 (CPJ: 2006a).

The actual targeting of journalists and news media organisations in conflict situations is nothing new. In Afghanistan in 2001 Al-Jazeera and BBC news studios in Kabul were hit by U.S. missiles (Gopsill 2004: 251–52) and in Belgrade in 1999 Serbian state television station RTS was deliberately destroyed by allied bombing (Hammond 2000: 367–68). However, the apparent blatant disregard for unilateral journalists in Iraq, demonstrated by so many casualties, could be seen as an act of aggression against non-embedded journalists. Soon after the start of the war in March 2003 ITN reporter Terry Lloyd, Lebanese interpreter Hussein Othman, and cameramen Daniel Demoustier and Fred Nerac came under fire from U.S. Marines, even though their vehicles were clearly marked as press vehicles (CPJ 2003). Lloyd was killed, and Othman and Nerac were declared missing, later acknowledged dead. A subsequent inquest into the death of Lloyd found that he had been unlawfully killed by a bullet to the head while travelling in a minibus which had come to the aid of the injured. The inquest reported that there was 'overwhelming' evidence that Lloyd was killed by a bullet from a U.S. gun (CPJ 2006b).

Clearly the safer option for journalists was to be embedded with the military, as this would provide greater security, it would also allow journalists to get an insight into the daily routines and lives of the troops. Miller (2003) has suggested that this proximity allows reporters to identify with the soldiers and provide a portrait of the war that is up close and personal at the expense of objectivity and dissent against the military perspective. To explore the claims that embedded reporting necessarily leads to a skewed picture of events, Justin Lewis and colleagues at Cardiff University (Lewis *et al* 2006) undertook a study of embedded journalism during the Iraq war. Rather than blindly regurgitating the propaganda line, their research suggests that the embedding process enabled journalists to gain unprecedented access to the front line with reporters able to provide instantaneous coverage of events without military mediation. Moreover, the reports from embedded journalists were perceived to be more balanced than some accounts, particularly of studio based anchors back home (2006: 190). The research concludes that the majority of the embedded journalists did not succumb to overt propaganda in the way that critics such as Miller suggest.

Rather it was the way in which many journalists related to the embedding process that provides the key to understanding its success from the point of view of the military. The embedding process was part of a public relations strategy which sought to disrupt the 'normal' working patterns of journalists as little as possible. The success of the military embedding process was largely due to its ability to replicate the sorts of relationships that journalists deal with during their day-to-day business of being journalists – with their sources and on their beats. In other words the embedding process was part of a much wider public relations enterprise in which the issue of overt censorship never entered the equation. To paraphrase the authors of the research, for journalists it was 'business as usual'. Given that the Pentagon viewed the embedding system as a success, it could be suggested that the process demonstrated a significant PR victory for the U.S. and U.K. military.

One of the main reporting restrictions that Lewis *et al* identified was largely imposed by themselves and related to graphic coverage of death and the horrors of war (Lewis *et al* 2006: 101). Such self-censorship is in significant contrast to the coverage provided by news organisations such as Al-Jazeera and the various news websites which did not avoid showing graphic pictures of dead Iraqi civilians and coalition troops, much to the ire of the U.K. authorities. Herman (2004: 181) argues that such coverage undermined the notion that this war was a 'high-tech' enterprise using precision laser guided weaponry with the military 'going to great pains to avoid civilian sites'. Petley (2004a: 170) suggests that the flak from Defence Secretary Geoff Hoon and from newspapers like Rupert Murdoch's *Sun*, act as further elements of 'pressure on broadcasters to censor themselves'. He continues to point out a paradox in contemporary war reporting when he suggests that:

> [W]hilst modern media technology has the potential to permit us to see more details of warfare than ever before, and whilst fictional representations of warfare, and of violent acts in general, have become ever bloodier and more explicit, non-fictional ones (at least in the British and US mainstream media) have become increasingly restrained and sanitized.
>
> *Petley (2004a: 164)*

However, sanitisation itself is not necessarily a symptom of pro-war bias. Even the most harrowing images of death and destruction do not stimulate a default anti-war response as Petley rightly points out. Rather it is the wider context of the images which people are (or not) viewing that makes all the difference. As news organisations tend to focus on the dramatic and sensational (with or without the harrowing images) the question of *why* these people have been killed in this way is largely avoided. This is the question that highlights a significant failure of media in reporting war and conflict. Ultimately, as Cottle (2006: 95) suggests, 'crude forms of military censorship could become increasingly irrelevant because they become largely redundant given the media's own proclivity towards the dramatic, visual and immediate'. The 'bigger picture' just does not enter into the frame because it has no place in the coverage of modern warfare.

Conclusion

During times of national and international emergency freedom of speech and freedom of the press often come under intense pressure in order to safeguard the national interest. During times of war, this pressure is arguably at its most acute. The protection of 'the national interest' be it in the security of borders, strategic or economic interests at home and overseas, or even the public and their way of life, tends to override some civil liberties which might be suspended in such times of emergency. Following terrorist attacks in particular the normal rules of reporting seem to be put on hold as security considerations are seen to usurp free speech and press freedom rights. Yet as (Hocking 2005) argues:

> [T]he abrogation of rights and legal protections had already become so pronounced that the United Nations Commission on Human Rights expressed deep concern over what it called a 'reckless approach towards human life and liberty', which would ultimately undermine any counter-terrorism measures that were implemented.
>
> *Hocking (2005: 319)*

However, as Graber (2003: 27) has observed: '[P]ress freedom is particularly vital in crisis periods because decisions made at the time are apt to produce profound consequences for the nation and its people.' Moreover, the more unencumbered the news media is in theory, the more it should allow for greater public scrutiny and debate at times of national trauma.

> Rather than seeing national security and democracy as being in perpetual friction (as if each exists somehow independently yet in tension with the other), political and civil rights and a robust democratic process are the key elements in the maintenance of national security itself.
>
> *Hocking (2004: 336)*

In other words Hocking is suggesting that the tension between security and safety on the one hand and civil liberties and the proper functioning of democratic institutions on the other, is one that ignores the importance of civil liberties and particularly a free press as a fundamental component of democratic life. During periods of national crisis and war, as we have seen, freedom of speech is placed under severe pressure by an assertion that national security and the defence of democracy actually involves undermining the very values that the state wishes to protect. Yet, as Graber notes, when the time comes for sober reflection on those limits on freedom of speech, the limits always turn out to be an overreaction (Graber 2003).

9

OWNERSHIP

The greatest difficulty in preserving free communications in a technical society arises from the concentration of power within the instruments of communication.

Hutchins Commission (1947: 104)

Introduction

The idea that the market is best placed to provide a diverse and rich media environment is by far the most dominant view in Europe and North America. The free market facilitates freedom of the press and the free market of ideas as it is necessarily unconstrained by government control in the name of the democratic imperative. However, as we have seen the media operates within a range of regulatory frameworks which act to both monitor and control its output and to ensure that the best interests of the public are met. Though the liberal market orientated 'light touch' from government approach is favoured, controls and constraints are seen as essential as to ensure diversity and quality of service as well as ensuring that the media do not overstep the mark in relation to taste, decency and offence. Harrison (2006: 81) suggests that in the news media environment in Europe and the United States 'policy makers and legislators have traditionally attempted to ensure that a range of news providers coexist to provide a diverse variety of news'. This has been primarily achieved via the implementation of policy which places 'restrictions on the concentration of news media ownership' (Harrison 2006: 81) in order to ensure that there is sufficient choice within the news media marketplace and to protect against the concentration of ownership. Yet despite the existence of such controls, the market remains dominant and is the driving force behind news media in advanced liberal democracies such as the U.K. and U.S.

The chapter begins by briefly examining the growth of news as a corporate entity. Here it focuses on the rise of the so-called 'press baron' in which particular styles of content adapted to market needs and the drive for circulation resulted in increased concentration of ownership. Given increasing concerns about the impact of newspaper concentration of ownership I go on to examine the Hutchins Commission report in the United States which was an attempt at striking a balance between the commercial imperatives of the market and the imperatives of democracy. As we will see, the summary of the Commission report identifies the particular value of the public service ethos within the context of a free market. I then go on to examine the political economy of media ownership and specifically the concept of market censorship which is exemplified in the media empires of Rupert Murdoch and Silvio Berlusconi, before going on to explore the work of Herman and Chomsky (2008) and Robert McChesney (2000; 2003).

Press freedom and the market imperative

The issue of private ownership of the news media is one of the key problems with regard debates about freedom of the press. It is a problem that has caused confusion and consternation in legal and philosophical terms in relation to both the function of the news media and the extent to which these functions are protected in law. As we saw in Chapter 2, the commercial expansion of the newspaper press during the Victorian era changed the central dynamic of the press as one that shifted from an essentially democratic imperative to that of a commercial or market imperative. Assertions that freedom of the press was now an absolute necessity, following the repeal of the stamp tax, paid lip service to the democratic imperative despite the overriding commercial drive of the newspaper industry. The press was and continues to be a commercial entity and this is its overriding *modus operandi*.

The era of the press baron

The spectre of the 'press baron' assuming control over the content and the political slant of newspapers is a powerful and resonant cultural trope which acts as a potent reminder of the early commercial imperatives of the news media in Britain and the United States and the extent to which owners can use newspapers as vehicles for self aggrandisement and power. *Citizen Kane* may well be a work of fiction, but of course Orson Wells based his film of the life and times of newspaper proprietor Charles Foster Kane on newspaper tycoon William Randolph Hearst. Hearst famously sought to control every aspect of his newspaper empire in his long-running rivalry with Joseph Pulitzer in the drive for market leadership.

Similarly in Britain, the rise of British press barons such as Lords Northcliffe, Rothermere and Beaverbrook reflect the potential of the press in achieving significant influence and power. Newspaper owners and proprietors have a reputation for ruthlessly stamping out dissent within their organisations and for ensuring that their world view is sympathetically endorsed in the pages of their newspapers. As Temple (2008: 34) points out 'press barons were ruthless and their own personal and business interests dominated their papers' coverage of political and economic issues'. Once the commercial constraints of the duties on newspapers, advertising and paper were removed in the nineteenth century, owners of newspapers such as Northcliffe, Rothermere and Beaverbrook were relatively free to develop their newspaper enterprises as they wished and it is with regard to this that control of the content of newspapers raises problems for freedom of speech and freedom of the press. Murdock and Golding (1978: 130) note that 'the inter-war period saw a mushrooming of national newspaper circulations' and a relative decline in the local press. They continue:

> In the years between 1921 and 1937, no less than 30 daily and Sunday newspapers disappeared through closures and amalgamations. By weeding out some of the smaller concerns, this thinning of the ranks reinforced the market dominance of the leading five companies;[1] and during this period they increased their control of titles from 15% to 43%.
>
> *Murdock and Golding (1978: 135)*

Concentrated levels of ownership made sense as Conboy (2010: 58) suggests as proprietors could combine their production and distribution operations much more efficiently. Moreover, the industrialisation of the press (Chalaby 1998) enabled proprietors to expand not just their capacity but also their influence. Former editor of the *Daily Mirror* Roy Greenslade (2004: 3) suggests: 'Newspapers themselves were not neutral spectators. They not only had an interest in how things might work out; they had a view about how they would prefer them to do so.' In other words 'press barons attempted to use their publishing power to propagandize to large readerships and assumed that they exercised an absolute measure of power over the opinions of both ordinary readers and leading politicians' (Conboy 2010: 59).

During the early years of the twentieth century, newspapers such as the *Daily News, Pall Mall Gazette, Morning Post* and *Daily Chronicle* had close ties with the Conservatives and the Liberals, ensuring the close connection between politics and the press (Curran and Seaton 2003: 50). However, the growth of the newspaper industry necessitated significantly more investment than its supporters in the political establishment could afford and eventually became free from political patronage as it became solely dependent on advertising revenue (Curran and Seaton 2003). The independently wealthy press barons of the early twentieth century such as Rothermere and Beaverbrook were now free to exert political influence in the pages of their newspapers and also within the corridors of power, as both gained positions in government. Yet as Curran and Seaton (2003: 49) suggest press barons such as Rothermere and Beaverbrook were unique in using their newspapers for political gain in the sense that 'they sought to use their papers, not as levers of power within the political parties, but as instruments of power against the political parties'. For example, Rothermere and Beaverbrook's formation of the United Empire Party (UEP) demonstrated both the contempt they had for the political establishment and the extent of their ambition, with the UEP established primarily to protect trade within the Empire and to undermine the Conservative leader Stanley Baldwin (Temple 2008: 35). Rothermere's publication of the infamous 'Zinoviev letter' in the

Daily Mail, which implicated the Left and the British Labour Party in a Soviet-inspired revolutionary uprising, was another effort to shape the political landscape, primarily by attempting to undermine the credibility of the Labour Party. Though the letter was a fake and made little impact as most working-class voters at that time did not read a daily newspaper (Curran and Seaton 2003: 52), this event demonstrates the extent to which the right-leaning press barons attempted to influence the political colour of Britain during the 1920s and 1930s; a practice that has continued throughout the twentieth century with the growth of media moguls such as Robert Maxwell and Rupert Murdoch. The *Daily Mail*'s flirtation with fascism in the 1930s under the close control of Rothermere (Temple 2008), with headlines overwhelming supportive of Oswald Mosley's British Union of Fascists,[2] highlights if nothing else the supreme confidence of press barons such as Rothermere.

In the 1920s and 1930s, newspaper circulation grew significantly due in no small part to the increasingly populist style and content of the press. Though this was effectively a continuation of trends set in place during the late 1870s and 1880s with developments in 'New Journalism' by journalists such as George Newnes and William T. Stead (Collier 2006), Northcliffe's innovations, particularly with regard to appealing to a hitherto largely ignored demographic – women – proved almost revolutionary. Northcliffe's

> greatest individual contribution was probably the realization that women consisted a vast, largely untapped market for daily newspapers; his publications responded to this vacuum with such innovations as serial fiction, advice columns on domestic economy and child rearing, and coverage of fashion, including clip-out dress patterns and illustrations by skilled commercial artists.
>
> *Collier (2006: 13)*

Yet such innovations led to charges of populism and of lowering the tone of the press (Collier 2006). With their increasing emphasis on crime stories which provided sensational and often lurid accounts of murders and robberies and the emergence of so-called human interest stories appealing to everyday folk, the daily newspapers under the leadership of the Northcliffe, Beaverbrook and Rothermere transformed the press in Britain. Yet, of course, it was their success in relation to the way in which they were able to draw a close association between their commercial freedoms and democratic freedoms that has impacted on how the notion of press freedom has come to be understood. For the press barons, 'any state intervention in the affairs of the press was inherently tyrannical and a violation of centuries of hard-won press reform' (Hampton 2004: 132). In other words the owners of the press were 'able to claim that their own economic interests were synonymous with the more generalized freedom of the press' (Conboy 2010: 62) and any attacks on these freedoms were attacks on all freedoms.

Mark Hampton (2004) has suggested that the New Journalism of the later Victorian era witnessed the beginnings of a shift in the role and function of journalism from an educational ideal, in which the press was viewed in relation to its capacity to enlighten and inform the public, to one where the press is seen as assuming a representational role. This representational function of the press essentially encapsulates the idea that the press is concerned less with preaching to its readership and more with reflecting its interests given the commercial incentives to reach a larger audice.

> The Press Barons' market ideology effectively co-opted the representative ideal that had become so pervasive in the three decades before World War I. By claiming to give the people the newspapers they wanted, proprietors could cast themselves as the voice of democracy, in contrast to the paternalistic or snobbish defenders of an educational press.
>
> *Hampton (2004: 132)*

Of course these claims continue to resonate in contemporary defences of 'press freedom' yet this is not to say that there were not attempts during the twentieth century to re-evaluate the function and purpose of the press as concerns about its overwhelming commercial imperative were voiced. As Bingham (2007: 80) has suggested 'public criticism of the press clearly fluctuated across the twentieth century, and only at certain periods did the problem of regulation rise to the top of the political agenda'.[3] Hampton (2004: 139) contends that the interwar period in which concentration of ownership has been critiqued 'can only be understood in the context of the continuing attachment to the doctrine of liberty of the press' which echoed well beyond the repeal of the 'taxes on knowledge' in 1855. The period of the nineteen thirties in particular was a period in which the state was increasingly seen as posing a threat to press freedom, particularly from the Left (Hampton 2004).

The Hutchins Commission

In the United States similar debates concerning the role and function of the press and the power of media ownership in potentially undermining the public sphere stimulated the establishment of the Hutchins Commission on Freedom of the Press in 1947 which produced its report entitled *A Free and Responsible Press*. The question that prompted the report was 'is freedom of the press in danger' to which the authors responded with an emphatic 'yes'. The Commission suggested that threats to press freedom stemmed from three relatively recent developments within the media more generally. First was the recognition that while the press had expanded and developed as an 'instrument of mass communication' it has, at the same time, 'decreased the proportion of people who can express their opinions and ideas through the press' (Hutchins Commission 1947: 1). Second, it noted that the press industry has not been successful in catering to the needs of American society; and third, as such, regulation and control were a threat in curbing the excesses of the news media. In other words, the Hutchins Commission was expressing wider social concerns, as well as those from within the industry itself, about the ability of the press to fulfil its liberal democratic functions given increased concentration of ownership and the continuing ascendency of the market imperative. If the press did not heed the warnings then the press itself would be at fault for any regulation that would curb its practices rather than any threat from government. As Nerone (1995: 92) suggests it was 'misuse of press power and freedom [that] would necessitate regulation'. One of the central claims that the Hutchins Commission made was that the press, even in the context of a market driven capitalist democracy, has a responsibility to the public and the communities in which it operates to provide a responsible public service. The report noted that:

> An over-all social responsibility for the quality of press service to the citizen cannot be escaped; the community cannot wholly delegate to any other agency the ultimate responsibility for a function in which its own existence as a free society may be at stake.
>
> *Hutchins Commission (1947: 126)*

In other words the press has a moral obligation to serve the community as it is the press's relationship *with* and *to* the community that animates the notion of a free society. The theory of 'social responsibility' of the press therefore emphasises the essential characteristics of the relationship between freedom of speech for the individual and freedom of the press as it is via press freedom, with the press acting in the interests of society more generally, so that the two correspond in theory and practice. Self-regulation was required because of the necessity to remain outside government interference, yet it should also clearly demonstrate its commitment to public service. In 1956 Theodore Paterson sought to expand and develop the notion of social responsibility in his chapter in *Four Theories of the Press*[4] and emphasise the positive and negative components of press freedom[5] which also related to the press's public obligations. Speaking of the Hutchins Commission report, Paterson notes that:

> The Commission is concerned not just about freedom of those who own the media; it is also concerned about citizens who possess merely negative freedom of expression. Freedom of the press, the Commission argues, is a somewhat empty right for the person who lacks access to the mass media. His freedom, too, must be implemented − by a press which carries viewpoints similar to his own; by media operated by government or nonprofit agencies to provide him with the required services which the commercial press does not provide.
>
> *Paterson (1956: 94)*

Again we can discern the nexus, in theory at least, between freedom of speech for the individual and freedom of the press. The social responsibility theory of the press sought to combine both negative and positive theory of liberty; negative in the protection of the press from government interference, but positive in the sense that it viewed some government intervention or initiative necessary so as to create the circumstances for a representative and responsible press with a steadfast civic dimension. This seemingly contradictory assertion that on the one hand government intervention should be countenanced, yet on the other it should be resisted, demonstrates the difficult terrain that the Commission was trying to negotiate, as Nerone (1995) has pointed out. Yet ultimately the Commission sought to outline the context in which government should enable the press to serve its civic function, 'the nature of the press's freedom is ultimately in serving the public, […]. The press has no moral right not to serve the public' (Nerone 1995: 95–96). This public service imperative is, as we have seen, something that was central to the inception of the BBC and which has come under sustained pressure especially since the era of deregulation in the 1980s and 1990s and it is to this era that we now turn.

The political economy of ownership

Market censorship

Julian Petley has argued that the 1980s and 1990s witnessed a period of deregulation which set in motion a set of processes which have undermined any public service dynamic that the media had. Moreover such impulses remain powerful within the rhetoric of media freedom but actually constrain choice and undermine the democratic imperative. One of the key arguments that Petley and others make is that the de-regulation of the media (what he calls re-regulation) actively leads to the concentration of ownership. Market censorship, then, relates not only to the idea that media control not just determines the content to a large extent (which is bad enough in itself) but also that the market actually re-invents the concept of media freedom to serve its own purposes. In making this point Petley focuses his ire at the media empires of Rupert Murdoch and Silvio Berlusconi.

Berlusconi made his initial fortune in the building trade; however, during the 1980s, in the era of deregulation, he established not one but three commercial television networks: Canale 5; Rete 4 and Italia 1. This effectively gave him a monopoly of the commercial networks which was under the control of the umbrella company Mediaset. The bulk of the programming on Berlusconi's channels was unapologetically populist and commercial and targeted at the largest possible audience. Petley argues that with his form of populist commercialism he was able to shift the emphasis of his main competitor – the state owned RAI – away from any public service remit and helped generate a media context in which 'produced a deeply conformist, repetitive and uncritically consumer-orientated television system' (2009: 153). Petley goes on to examine how Berlusconi then developed his political career by exploiting weaknesses in the discredited mainstream political parties and formed the *Forza Italia* (Come on Italy!) party which had been empowered by a political alliance with the proto fascist Northern League. Given the market saturation of Berlusconi's media corporations and the unapologetic way in which he has sought to publicise his political credentials, it comes as no surprise that Berlusconi's political career took off with him as Alexander Stille notes:

> Even if the principle effect of Berlusconi's TV was in creating a general cultural–political disposition that was favourable to him, his unusual access to television during the campaign cannot be dismissed as an unimportant contributing

factor. Berlusconi's campaign is simply inconceivable without his television networks. Being able to immediately reach half the households in Italy whenever he wanted is something no other candidate enjoyed.

Cited Petley (2009: 155)

So Petley's main point about Berlusconi's ownership of such a large part of Italian television is that it, of course, undermines the notion of media plurality and facilitator of genuine democratic culture. Furthermore he has also clearly exploited his media power for influence and significant political gain.

Murdoch and News Corp

Though not a new development, the concentration of newspaper ownership, which stemmed largely as result of the ideological shifts emerging during the 1960s and 1970s, has led to the assertion of a particular type of right-wing populism in the press which has sought to appeal to increasing numbers of the public in the drive for increased circulation figures, none more so, of course, than in the Murdoch press. Rupert Murdoch's first newspaper in Britain was the *News of the World* which he bought in 1969. Robert Maxwell had also wanted to buy the newspaper but Murdoch managed to appeal to the right-leaning sensibilities of the newspaper shareholders and finally gained control (Greenslade 2004). Soon after his acquisition of the *News of the World* he bought the *Sun*, again after seeing off Maxwell. Following his acquisition of the *Sun* Murdoch 'immediately began to restructure its editorial character and journalistic style to exploit the growing permissiveness of the age, with its iconic Page 3 Girl and a blend of light-hearted and entertainment led journalism designed to capture the youth market' (Conboy 2011: 54). This populist, anti-establishment, vehemently anti-European and pro-market stance was both reflected in his newspaper titles and in his approach to broadcasting. Moreover, Murdoch's well-documented approach to running his media operations reinforces the hard-line bullying image of a media tycoon bent on power. Since his acquisition of *The Sun*, *The Times* and *The Sunday Times*, and with no small help from the Conservative government in the 1980s (Barnett and Graber 2001; Petley 2009), Murdoch has continued to expand and develop his media portfolio in the U.K. and overseas. The launch of satellite broadcaster Sky TV in 1990 gave Murdoch further leverage in the U.K. media market. Initially running at a loss, in March 2011 the company's operating profit stood at £261 million pounds, up on the previous year by £12 million pounds (BSkyB 2011).[6]

Murdoch has always been careful to protect his business interests particularly in Asia and when the focus of his newspapers or television states has been too critical – whether in Malaysia, Indonesia or in particular China, Murdoch has been quick to ensure that his business interests are not compromised (Petley 2009). For example, when he acquired Star TV in 1994, which could be picked up in parts of China, he made sure that the BBC was not carried on the channel as the BBC had been critical of Chinese human rights abuses. Similarly, *The Times*'s former East Asia correspondent resigned on the grounds that 90 per cent of articles he'd submitted to the newspaper had not been published as they were critical of the Chinese authorities. In 1997 when he found out that Harper Collins (which he owned) was publishing former Governor of Hong Kong Chris Patten's memoirs, Murdoch demanded that the book be dropped as again it was less than favourable to the Chinese regime (Petley 2009).

During the summer of 2011 Rupert Murdoch's News Corporation was well into the process of attempting to gain full ownership of satellite broadcaster BSkyB despite concerns from some quarters, including the Business Secretary Vince Cable, that there were significant issues of public interest surrounding media plurality. If Murdoch's bid was a success and he acquired the remaining 61 per cent stake in BSkyB it would have meant that News Corporation would not only have been in a dominant market position with regard to ownership of newspapers, but it would have taken full ownership of the television company, with an estimated turnover of £7.5 billion. Even though the regulator Ofcom had expressed some concern (Ofcom 2010) the buyout looked highly likely with the European Commission clearing the way for News Corporation to push on with its proposed acquisition of BSkyB, stating that News Corporation's full ownership would not impede competition in the European Economic Area (EEA) or sections of it (European Commission 2010). However the public and political outcry over the revelations of the extent of the phone hacking scandal (see Chapter 6) meant that News Corporation was severely compromised and was left with little option but to withdraw the bid for the time being.

There is no doubt that concentration of ownership increases the prevalence of market censorship, yet a macro analysis of ownership has been discussed relatively little so far. It is therefore necessary to devote some attention to this, particularly with regard to the process of market censorship within news organisations in particular. For this we turn to Herman and Chomsky's propaganda model as identified in the book *Manufacturing Consent* and the work of Robert McCheseney.

Manufacturing Consent

One of the most stimulating and controversial analyses of the impact of media ownership and its impact on public debate and press freedom is that put forward by Edward Herman and Noam Chomsky (2008 [1988]) in their 'propaganda model'. Herman and Chomsky argue that the way in which the media explicitly orientates itself towards the goal of making a profit, at the expense of genuine democratic delibera- tion, betrays the news media's limitations in its provision in sustaining an arena for debate and dialogue. According to this perspective, capitalism essentially imposes a form of censorship on media organisations as they work to achieve and maintain market advantage. In their 1988 book *Manufacturing Consent*,[10] Herman and Chomsky provided one of the most striking analyses of the power of the media and its relationship it has with capitalist ideology. *Manufacturing Consent* offers 'an alternative paradigm for understanding media operations and the role which the media play in maintaining and indeed, manufacturing consent' (Scatamburlo-D'Annibale 2005: 21). Herman and Chomsky suggest that any truly objective media analysis of politics is impossible because of the way in which the media self-censor in order to protect and advance their economic position. In other words the media have a 'systematically biased world view' (Street 2001: 28) which benefits elite interests at the expense of democracy in any meaningful sense. Herman and Chomsky suggest that 'US media act to inculcate and defend the economic, social and political agenda of privileged groups that dominate the domestic society and the state' (Herman and Chomsky cited by Street 2001, 30). In other words 'capitalist news media generally function to generate support for elite policies rather than attempting to empower people to make informed decisions' (Scatamburlo-D'Annibale 2005: 22).

Herman and Chomsky argue that the propaganda model operates via a number of 'filters' which effectively work to exclude inappropriate material or items that do not conform to the prevailing ideological world-view. The first filter is economic and explicitly relates to media ownership and the reinforcement of capitalistic norms and values. The media generally and the news media in particular reflect the dominant ideology because they themselves operate within that economic framework. As such, according to this perspective, our view of the world and the information we access in order to make sense of it, is largely framed by perspectives that are supportive and sympathetic of the capitalist system and the hierarchy that it sustains. Rather than operating with regard a democratic imperative, the news media work within the confines of a commercial imperative which significantly reduces its ability to function as a safeguard of democracy. In their afterword to the 2008 edition of *Manufacturing Consent*, Herman and Chomsky stress the continuing role that dominant elites have in shaping the news agenda and its implications for democracy.

> Globalisation has continued its advance; the concentration, conglomeration and joint venture arrangements among the big firms have increased; commercialization and bottom-line considerations dominate as never before; and the competition for advertising has intensified, with the 'old media' [...] steadily losing ground to their cable, Internet, and wireless progeny [...]. These developments have resulted in more compromises on behalf of advertisers, including more friendly editorial policy, more product placements, more intrusive ads, more cautious news policy, a shrinkage in investigative reporting and a greater dependence on wire service and public relations offerings, and a reduced willingness to challenge establishment positions and party lines.
>
> *Herman and Chomsky (2008: 289)*

The second related filter is that of advertising. Herman and Chomsky argue that advertisers have the capacity to significantly shape and constrain media output. In order to compete, media organisations need to sell their readers and viewers to advertisers. This then to a large extent determines media content as advertisers will increasingly 'avoid programmes with serious complexities and disturbing controversies that interfere with the "buying mood"' (Herman and Chomsky 2008: 17). As such only certain types of content – crime, scandal, gossip, celebrity etc. will attract significant revenue from advertisers. The third filter is political and related to the ways in which dominant elites shape news and the news gathering process. Herman and Chomsky argue that the news is primarily shaped by dominant forces, usually political institutions and powerful political groups. If the media fail to reflect the elite perspective they are usually confronted with the fourth filter, that being 'flak'. Flak relates to the ways in which governments and institutions can pressure the media, either privately or publicly. Former Downing Street Director of Communications Alastair Campbell has been seen as the archetypal political elite administering flak to anyone that failed to toe the party line, what Oborne and Walters describe as 'guerrilla warfare with the media' (2004). The final filter identified by Herman and Chomsky, and one that has been significantly modified since the fall of the Berlin Wall and the collapse of Communism, is that of anti-communism. During the Cold War and right up to the fall of communism in the late 1980s a vehement anti-communist rhetoric pervaded the media which made much of defending American interests overseas in its fight against Communism. This manifested itself in positive media coverage of U.S. interventions in places like Grenada, and Panama, support for anti-communist guerrilla movements like the Contras in Nicaragua and the backing of right-wing and often highly repressive regimes in South Africa, Indonesia, Iraq and Guatemala. Any attempts to draw attention to and criticise U.S. support of such regimes were roundly condemned and usually labelled as sympathetic to communism and anti-American.

Since the fall of the Soviet Empire and the end of the threat of the so-called 'red menace' Herman and Chomsky argue that a new threat has been identified to replace the threat of Communism. This threat is in many ways much worse as it stems from both 'rogue' states and Islamic terrorism. The notion that we in the West face a constant threat from a 'dirty bomb' or terrorist atrocity such as 9/11 is being used, according to this analysis, to justify the invasion of nation states, crippling sanctions on states that do not comply with the market-orientated U.S. worldview, and excessive military spending and the curbing of civil liberties and restricting rights. Herman and Chomsky (2008: 291) argue that in relation to the wake of significant public outrage against the 2003 invasion of Iraq there was a 'massive propaganda effort on the part of the [U.S.] administration to sell the war, with fear mongering, intimidation, and an extraordinary level of deceit about the evidence and threats posed by the demonized villains'. So the filter of anti-communism which was used to whip up support for strategic alignments across the world, however unpalatable, shifted towards emphasising the threat from the 'other' and garnering support through the media of episodes such as the Iraq War in 2003 (see Scatamburlo-D'Annibale 2005) and the continuing war in Afghanistan (see Chapter 8). To summarise, these filters can be viewed as the machinery of t>he propaganda model which ensure that dissenting viewpoints and opinions do not appear on the mainstream media and the dominant ideology is reflected in the production and consumption of the news media. Market censorship in action.

Criticisms of the propaganda model

Herman and Chomsky's notion of the manufacture of consent is certainly controversial and not without its critics. The suggestion that the mass media and the news media in particular are operating a policy of effective thought control does seem somewhat excessive. Phrases like 'propaganda', 'policing minds' and 'manufacturing consent' are more reminiscent of an Orwellian characterisation of a totalitarian state than a twenty-first century democracy. Herman and Chomsky's suggestion that the masses are relatively easily controlled by elite power also seems somewhat hysterical and extremely patronising to ordinary people. Yet Herman and Chomsky reject this label as it suggests some sinister rationale executed by clandestine organisations. On the contrary they suggest their analysis is of the media as it is and can be seen to be. Rather than a conspiracy theory the Propaganda Model is a structural analysis of the media system and its workings. As Klaehn suggests, the Propaganda Model 'highlights the relationship between patterns of media behaviour and institutional imperatives' (2005: 224). The Propaganda model 'assumes self-censorship without coercion and contends that media discourse be explained in structural terms' (2005: 224).

Another criticism of Herman and Chomsky's model is that it seems to award far too much power to the media with little or no space for people to react or respond to the ways in which the news media frame issues or represent elite agendas. It could be argued that it is simply not the case that the public are taken in and swayed by the media to the extent that Herman and Chomsky suggest. The abundance of alternative and dissenting media, protest groups and widespread dissatisfaction of both politics and the media (Hay 2007) suggests that people are far more discerning than Herman and Chomsky credit. Critical media does exist and it performs an important function in holding those in power to account. However, Chomsky and his supporters would argue that dissent is built into the system. Liberal democracies succeed because they provide space for dissenting ideas and opinions which can act as a form of safety-valve for society. Yet though the space is provided for dissenting ideas, for the most part it is largely ignored. For example, millions of people around the world took to the streets in 2003 to protest against the impending invasion of Iraq, yet of course though their voice was heard and their protests seen, the U.S. and U.K. governments ignored them and even dissenting mainstream media largely fell into line once the forces were deployed (Exoo 2010). Moreover, their research is not about media effects as such, rather it is about the way in which the media is structured and how stories are chosen and reported. Of course, there are challenges to the dominant agendas, yet the overall power dynamic of the propaganda model is unaffected (Klaehn 2005). Finally, a criticism that is laid at Chomsky himself rather than the propaganda model as such is that Chomsky seems to be morally ambivalent in his analysis of regimes with questionable motives and agendas. Critics of Chomsky suggest that he is eager to point the accusing finger at the U.S. and their military interventions in the developing world, yet he seems reluctant to be equally morally outraged when atrocities are committed by say the Khmer Rouge or even groups like Al-Qaeda.[11]

McChesney and journalism

Herman and Chomsky are not the only media critics to explore the way in which the corporate nature of the news media undermines the democratic imperative, Robert McChesney (2000, 2003) has also commented on the impact on democracy, specifically with regards to the role that corporate ownership and elite control of the media has on actively undermining democracy in society. As we have seen, one of the central roles of journalism within liberal democracies is to ensure political accountability and provide information to the public with which they can judge the performance of their elected representatives. Yet within a globalised capitalist marketplace, this essential function of journalism can be seen as secondary, with its primary purpose being the generation of profit. Indeed, it is not just discursively that the 'liberal' in liberal democracy prioritises the central organisational principle of democracy. Liberal democracy is a capitalist democracy and we should not forget that news organisations operate to maximise profitability. McChesney has argued that the growth and concentration of power of media organisations has had a damaging affect on democracy particularly in the United States. He suggests that contrary to our expectations, there is a direct correlation between the wealth and amount of power media corporations have and the level of media facilitation of democratic engagement; the greater the former, the less the latter. According to McChesney, though the media positions itself as the guardian of democracy, they are really the purveyors of mass cynicism in which people are deeply untrusting of politicians and political institutions. Given that the media has expanded and grown exponentially in the last few decades we should have seen a more politically literate and engaged public, yet of course this has not been the case largely because of the denigration of journalism which has lost sight of its public service obligations in the wake of the pressure to compete in the global media arena. McChesney argues that what he calls 'hypercommercialism' determines much of the content of the media. Moreover, the values of consumerism and the virtues of the market promoted by the mainstream media serve to reinforce the dominant ideological premise that a weak political culture is fundamentally beneficial to the operation of markets. The more politically literate and socially informed the public are, the argument goes, the greater the likelihood of a challenge to the status quo. However, as long as the public have sports, entertainment and celebrity culture to keep them occupied (as Lippmann would have no doubt preferred), the less likely they are inclined to challenge media and political control.

If we look at McChesney's analysis of journalistic practice, he is similarly pessimistic. Market pressures have undermined any strong civic dimension that journalism once aspired to. Greater institutional pressure on journalists to produce more output, often with fewer resources has led to the squeezing of quality and investigative drive within journalism. Of course, there are exceptions to the rule, but by and large McChesney argues that the much of the news media is more concerned with scandal and gossip than hard political news. Moreover, he suggests that the market is off limits in terms of any critique or sustained analysis and that though the politicians may be corrupt, the economic system is beyond reproach.

In combination these trends have had the effect not only wiring pro-status quo biases directly into the professional code of conduct but also of keeping journalists blissfully unaware of the compromises with authority they make as they go about their daily rounds.

McChesney (2000: 50)

McChesney doesn't blame journalists for the state of professional journalism rather he places the blame on the commercial imperatives of the media organisations themselves. The argument remains though that because of the powerful commercial inducements within the broader media context in the United States, and to a lesser but still relevant extent in Britain, the market imperative actively undermines freedom of the press.

Conclusion

As is maintained throughout this book, it is primarily the free market rationality, masquerading as freedom of the press, which animates contemporary censorship, not some modern day Torquemada or Stalinist censor. As Curran and Seaton (2010: 370) argue 'Free market ideas have been the main driving force shaping media policy since the early 1980s', and have led to a situation in which the public service commitments of broadcasters have been eroded and exposed to the full force of the market. Such a force is increasingly having a deleterious effect on diversity among both the newspaper and broadcast sectors, with the trend towards monopoly and concentration of ownership (Keane 1991). Newspaper circulation in Britain is on a downward spiral. Claims relating to the slow demise of the newspaper industry and its causes are salient (Davies 2008). The advent of free titles such as the *Metro* seems to add to the sense that the traditional commercial model for newspaper industry is no longer viable. In the United States the picture is similar with newspaper sales figures falling and newspaper titles folding. Despite the gloom, there is some optimism that 'brand diversification' and the introduction of pay walls for online content might offer a possible escape route out of the abyss. In June 2010 Rupert Murdoch's *Times* and *Sunday Times* titles switched to a subscription based service which requires readers wishing to access the newspaper to register and pay for content. The move has come in the midst of a significant collapse in advertising revenue in the sector and the realisation that, in Rupert Murdoch's words 'Quality journalism is not cheap' (Clark 2009). The Newspaper Society, which represents local media in Britain, maintains that regional newspapers are engaging in 'brand extension' and 'portfolio publishing' in order to combat the demise of the traditional newspaper format. This seems to be with some success as it claims that 'audits show continued growth in online audiences for local media publishers' (Newspaper Society 2009). Yet, of course, such initiatives are primarily concerned with maximising profit and limiting losses. Diversification might be the buzzword, yet what is increasingly apparent is a homogenisation, particularly within the local sector (Franklin 2006). Local newspaper readership seems to be in terminal decline despite attempts to 'rebrand' and 'diversify'. As for pay walls, it is too early to tell; however, a month after Murdoch's move to pay for access, *The Guardian* reported that *The Times* lost nearly 90 per cent of its online readership since it made registration compulsory for its online readers (Halliday 2010b).

It could be argued that the invisible hand of the market is determining the fate of the sector with the likely outcome being that only the strongest are able to weather the storm. Unfortunately, the implications for diversity in the newspaper sector are worrying with even greater concentration of ownership a likely result of market forces. Though the broadcast sector, as we have seen, is to some extent shielded from the ravages of the free market, regulation in Britain is orientated towards effective communication; cultural and political diversity; economic viability and public service commitments (Feintuck and Varney 2006: 58–65) within the wider market context. The public service obligations of the BBC and of other broadcasters have historically sought to ensure that media content does not fully succumb to the market. Yet in the wake of the economic collapse brought about by financial deregulation in the banking sector and the British government's commitment to bail out the banks, the financial pressures on public service remit may become too much to bear and continue to be put under strain. Regulation of broadcasting is anything but a limitation on freedom of the news media and media freedom more generally. As Feintuck and Varney (2006) maintain regulation is necessary so as to ensure effective communication. The mantra has historically been that the market will provide, though the signs are not promising, this author hopes that such blind faith in the market will not be tested to the full.

10

CONSTITUTIVE CENSORSHIP

News, language and culture

> At any given moment there is an orthodoxy, a body of ideas which it is assumed that all right-thinking people will accept without question. It is not exactly forbidden to say this, that or the other, but it is 'not done' to say it, just as in mid-Victorian times it was 'not done' to mention trousers in the presence of a lady. Anyone who challenges the prevailing orthodoxy finds himself silenced with surprising effectiveness. A genuinely unfashionable opinion is almost never given a fair hearing, either in the popular press or in the highbrow periodicals.
>
> Orwell (1989: 99)

Introduction

This book has concerned itself with a relatively simple idea: the notion that there is both historically and philosophically a significant set of tensions between freedom of speech and the generally assumed associated freedoms of the press. Furthermore, the control or suppression of these freedoms are usually perceived as essentially external mechanisms of control via regulation. As we have seen the traditional liberal view of the development of 'free' media frames it largely in terms of a struggle first against the authoritarian control of the *ancien regime*, then as a gradual process of liberalisation as nation states moved from autocratic rule towards democratic institutions and the idea that democratic societies require a neutral state through which a free media can operate. In other words, the legal and political structures of democratic societies have developed to encompass a free media as part and parcel of the machinery of democratic societies. Freedom of speech and freedom of the press in particular, it is argued, oil the wheels of democracy and enable it to function according to its central tenets. We have seen throughout this book examples of formal controls and structural impediments which can impact on the ability of the news media to function fully in the service of its democratic imperative. However, as stressed throughout, to conceive of the modes of censorship already discussed solely in such formal and structural terms is to miss the more subtle and nuanced ways in which censorship is conceived. The quote from Orwell gives a clue regarding the direction and focus of this chapter as it attempts to focus more specifically on informal mechanisms of control and censorship, thereby further stressing the dynamic nature of censorship. Much of the focus here therefore will be on language and its significance as an aspect of censorship. Language is particularly significant to journalism as Zelizer (2004a: 111) points out: 'As journalism has progressed towards increasingly complex systems of information relay, the notion of what constitutes a journalistic language has grown as well.' As such we can discern a distinctive realm of language pertinent to journalism. This chapter examines the ways in which language functions as a means of control and censorship. This picture of language and its deployment as a component of power relationships is not simple to paint; however, we will see that informal censorship as linguistic norms and conventions should be considered within the parameters of censorship.

The chapter begins with a brief examination of news values within journalism before going on to examine French sociologist Pierre Bourdieu's conception of the journalistic field. This is particularly important in the discussion of language as he maintains that journalism, like other professions, operate within specific 'fields of cultural production' that not only shape the language and discourse within the particular field, but also account for the particular structures of power that journalism operates within. The discussion of discourse is also of significance as it contributes to an understanding of language and its relationship to power. As such the chapter moves on to examine discourse and power and frame these within other studies which have explored the particular power of discourse within the news. Following this I move on to discuss the impact of so-called political correctness or 'PC'. Often debates about PC shift into emotive language about Orwellian thought control and censorship. However, drawing on some particularly insightful literature, it is suggested that the actual debate about PC, particularly from the right, is itself an attempt to limit language and control debate within the context of specific contestations over reality. We then go on and discuss the topic of freedom of speech and religion. Of course, not a topic central to debates within journalism until the so-called Danish cartoons controversy which seemed to highlight the so-called clash of civilisations between the West and Islam. Here I will look beyond this simplistic theorisation and draw on important debates about multiculturalism and identity politics. The chapter concludes with an overview of Orwell's understanding of the power of language to structure thinking and drift into propaganda. Orwell is important here as he draws attention to the constraining power of language, particularly in relation to its power to misdirect and confuse. What is crucial here is the emphasis on language as a potent limiting force and its capacity to act to coerce and constrain through the mechanism of constitutive censorship.

Language and news values

Of course, the news that we consume is not a random collection of assorted events that journalists just happen to pull together for our benefit. News is carefully constructed within a framework of principles, norms and dispositions that are generally termed 'news values'. News values are essential tools of the trade for journalists and those that work in the news media. They are the informal 'ground rules' that journalists work with which enables them to select and write stories that are appropriate for their news organisation. These 'ground rules may not be written down or codified by news organisations, but they exist in daily practice and in knowledge gained on the job, albeit mediated by subjectivity on the part of individual journalists' (Harcup and O'Neill 2001: 261). News values are a difficult concept to grasp as specific news values may be more evident in one news organisation than in another. For example, the editorial priorities of say *The Independent* newspaper will be very different to those of *The Daily Star*. The former tend to present what might be called 'serious' or hard news with special features and comment on social affairs, international and domestic politics; while the latter's news values will tend to encourage journalists to gravitate towards stories that are more in keeping with its tabloid or more accurately 'popular' identity – a focus on sensation, gossip, celebrity and crime (Conboy 2006; Sparks and Tulloch 2000). Similarly, in the broadcast environment, the news values of say, the *Today Programme* on BBC Radio 4, which tends to focus on stories of national and international significance, will be markedly different from those of a local BBC radio station, which has a statutory obligation to strike a balance between stories of national and international significance with the concerns of its local constituencies (Harrison 2006: 178). It is also worth noting that news values can be disturbed *within* news organisations operating across a range of media. For example, the news values of *The Sun* newspaper broadly remain the same in its newspaper and its online version; however, there are modifications to its news values brought about by the ways in which online content, with its multi-faceted aspects and levels of emphasis and engagement, have the capacity to reshape the relationship between *The Sun* and its readership (see Conboy and Steel 2010).

Galtung and Ruge (1965) provided the first systematic study of news values in the print media and focused on the ways in which four news organisations select and structure foreign news stories. In their analysis of Galtung and Ruge's study, Harcup and O'Neil (2001) sought to come up with a taxonomy of news values that is more flexible, transparent and up-to-date than that of Galtung and Ruge while still ascribing a set of criteria through which journalists generally make judgements about what is and is not newsworthy. The very existence of such criteria therefore gives us a clue as to the specific scope that journalists have at their disposal in producing news and as such; this then sets informal limits on what is and is not acceptable within a given news organisation.

Clearly, the placing of news values in a given hierarchy will differ according to the overarching values of the news institution. Yet it is important to note that it is largely via news values that journalists routinely self-censor as they reflect on the newsworthiness of a story within a given institutional framework and make judgements about its suitability (Gans 1980). In addition to the formal regulatory constraints news is 'constrained by a range of organisational influences which reflect the role and remit of different news organisations and which allow different types of mediated news to emerge' (Harrison 2006: 128). Organisational cultures, routines and hierarchies, or 'habitual conventions' (Fowler 1991: 41), play an important role in shaping such frameworks and impact on the final product. News values are thus learned and absorbed by journalists within their working environment and to a large extent, help them regulate their decision making process about the sorts of stories that are appropriate and those that are not. News values are important to the discussion about journalism and freedom of speech because news values set the parameters within which a journalist will make judgements about the newsworthiness of a story. News values express both formal and informal mechanisms of control which have the capacity to shape news coverage to a very large extent. If a story does not sit within the particular news values of any given news organisation then it is likely that it will be demoted in the news hierarchy or even ignored. In other words journalists discriminate against stories that do not fit the specific editorial profile of their news organisation, and favour those stories that do.

However, it is not just the institutional dynamics and values of an organisation that determine what particular news values a news organisation will adopt; news organisations are also necessarily responsive to the expectations of their audience. As such we should also be cognisant of Bell's notion of audience design (1991) which asserts that journalists are forever aware of the demands of their viewers, listeners and readers given the commercial imperatives of the organisations for which they work. The language they use will therefore be tailored to these specific ends. As Conboy has stated in his analysis of the language of newspapers, newspapers 'have "always encapsulated what would sell to audiences and how information could best be packaged and presented to achieve this commercial end at any particular time"' (Conboy 2010: 1). This will also fit in with broader cultural expectations. For example, in relation to coverage of crime stories in say Russia, Russian television will show much more graphic images in its coverage than say in the U.K. Thus the content can also be shaped by the news organisation's preconceptions about its audience and the perceived expectations that the audience has.

Aesthetic concerns are also of crucial significance, with news organisations seeking to deliver news according to their own 'house style' or set of pre-defined stylistic and presentational guidelines (Cameron 1996). Though the news values will differ from one organisation to the next as Allan (1999: 61) has observed, there tends to exist a 'broad similarity in the "stories" being covered, and the hierarchical order in which they have been organized'. Therefore, despite the differences between news organisations in terms of the specific news values they adhere to and express, there tends to be a level of uniformity with regard the actual stories being covered.

One might argue that news values are a set of relatively unproblematic broad guidelines that news organisations adhere to in order to provide the particular produce or service to their audience. It is relatively uncontroversial to suggest that news values stem from often complex interactions between journalists, editors and producers and the institutional dynamics of a given news organisation. More critically, however, news values can be seen to represent a particular paradigm (Hartley 1982) in which news selection and representation reflect a set of dominant ideological beliefs and values which underpin existing power relationships and authority in society. In other words, news values, via the way in which they focus on particular stories and events, the ways in which they can help sustain and promote certain values, can be seen as important components in the maintenance of certain dominant values. These values might emphasise particular conceptions of nation (Anderson 1991; Brookes 1999; Conboy 2006); race and ethnicity (Law 2002); crime and deviance (Chibnall 1977); gender and sexuality (Fowler 1991) or the view that the news media provide a totally neutral platform for open debate and discussion. Perceived this way, the news media does not function neutrally as the fourth estate (Petley 2004b) as it generally portrays itself, rather within its daily routines and work practices, it produces 'news' which operates as a powerful ideological force in society.

Bourdieu and the journalistic 'field'

French sociologist Pierre Bourdieu (1930–2002) makes an important contribution to our understanding of the production of news and its values, procedures and cultures as he has examined the ways in which journalists operate within specific organisational and ideological frameworks. Bourdieu's analysis locates journalism within what he calls a field of cultural production or the 'journalistic field' which relates to its relative proximity to the organising rationale of modern liberal democratic societies – capitalist production and accumulation. Benson and Neveu (2005: 1) suggest that Bourdieu's development of the concept of the 'journalistic field' 'offers a new way of understanding and explaining the constraints and processes involved in news media production'. Journalism is just one in a number of 'semiautonomous and increasingly specialised spheres of action (e.g., fields of politics, economics, religion, cultural production)' (Benson and Neveu 2005: 3). Exploring the dynamics of journalism as a social practice this notion of field is connected to the 'disposition' or 'habitus' of journalism as a profession. The concept habitus is one of the most important elements of Bourdieu's thinking as it is via the habitus that humans have learned to experience the world through both our familial and primary socialisation and also through our immersion in professionalised set of norms, values and practices. Importantly the concept of habitus is never static, rather it undergoes constant modification (Benson and Neveu 2005). 'Any explanation of attitudes, discourses, behaviour etc. must draw on analysis of both structural position (within the field, the field's position vis-à-vis other fields, etc.) and the particular historical trajectory by which an agent arrived at that position (habitus)' (Benson and Neveu 2005: 3). Hanks (2005: 69) suggests that 'at its base, habitus concerns reproduction insofar as what it explains are the regularities immanent in practice'. In other words in relation to journalism habitus is the social environment in which journalists rationalise their function in relation to other spheres (or fields) and within their own. As Schultz suggests:

> We can all experience the feeling of being 'free', 'independent' or 'autonomous', but as all social agents are products of a specific social, economic and cultural history, 'freedom' is a relative and relational thing – for social practice in general as well as for journalistic practice.
>
> *Schultz (2007: 193)*

In other words journalists' sense of relative autonomy within the journalistic field is relational to the extent to which they understand the rules of the game of being a journalist and the extent to which they function and adapt depending on their role and position of power (Schultz 2007). If we don't 'play by the rules', we run the risk of being excluded from the game altogether and therefore more likely to lose our power and perceived autonomy; if we do accept the rules and maintain a commitment to them, then we are much more likely to succeed. What is important in Bourdieu's analysis of the journalistic field is the 'important assumption […] that social practice is never completely "free" but will always and at the same time be structured. What journalist experience as "freedom" and "unpredictability" in news work must be conceptualized as freedom within certain frames and structures' (Schultz 2007: 194).

Discourse and power

Stuart Hall, discourse and ideology

Hall's work within the Birmingham Centre for Cultural Studies on language, discourse and ideology has been viewed as providing a significant contribution to critical media studies and one that has sought to understand and explain the functioning of media in its maintenance of dominant hegemonic power. Drawing on the work of Antonio Gramsci and his theory of ideological hegemony (Gramsci 1992; 1996), Hall's analysis contributes to the radical Marxist tradition of cultural and media studies (see Berry and Theobald 2006) which broadly sees the reproduction of inequitable power relations and forces of control within the cultural artefacts of capitalist society. In *Policing the Crisis: Mugging, the State, and Law and Order* (1978) Hall, with his colleagues[1] argued that journalists' routine use of authority figures as credible sources for their stories enabled particular and dominant perspectives on issues such as crime and race to be perpetuated through the media. Journalists use of these 'primary definers' as a matter of routine in their work, according to Allan (1999: 71), 'are typically serving to represent the "opinions of the powerful" as being consistent with a larger "public consensus"'. In other words the authoritative viewpoint presented by the media is represented as both an objective voice and a voice of 'common sense'. 'Effectively then, the primary definition *sets the limit* for all subsequent discussion by *framing what the problem is*' (Hall *et al* 1978: 59). These authoritative perspectives therefore have 'definitional power', that is to define the terms of reference and debate with which the media then adopt in the writing of their stories.

In attempting to explore the ways in which power and authority are mediated through society, Hall was also interested in how discourse and language are elements within a constant ideological struggle. For Hall dominant ideology is not a static entity, rather it has to reconstitute and reformulate itself in order to sustain its viability and its power. It is constantly being challenged by competing ideologies in a hegemonic struggle which in part is fought through discourse and language. The emphasis on the ways in which hegemonic power is formed is provided by Hall's analysis of Thatcherism and its dominance during the 1980s in particular (see Hall and Jaques 1983; Hall

1988). Hall is interested in how the politics of the New Right, so associated with Thatcherism, came to be represented in the values and expectations of many people in Britain during the 1980s and beyond. For example, the widespread acceptance that private ownership of housing provided people with a better alternative than council house provision; or that social care tendered out to private companies would be superior to that if it was left in the hands of local authorities. Similarly, the broad acknowledgment that in areas of economic policy, it should be the 'invisible hand' of the market that should decide the success or failures of industry and commerce. This shift in outlook represented a fundamental break with traditional forms of politics. Yet how was this achieved and sustained? In historical terms the post-war consensus between labour (the unions), state and capital was no longer viable. Economic failure, social unrest and a seemingly continuous bout of industrial disputes lead to a funda-mental breakdown of consensus embedded in Keynesian economic management (Gamble 1994). In moral terms Britain was also bankrupt – a legacy of the 1960s, with family breakdown and sexual permissiveness undermining traditional family values and norms. Thatcherism was initially appealing because it presented itself as an antidote to the perceived failures of Britain both in terms of how it functioned eco-nomically but also how it constituted itself at its moral core. Its success was in por-traying itself as both the saviour of 'Great Britain' in traditional terms with its values of hard work, thrift, family centeredness, and as a defender of a 'common sense' approach to politics that would provide people with freedom and protect their liberty through law and order (Eccleshall 2003). Once in power, the Thatcher project set about redefining the realms of debate in such a way as to draw attention to those values and ideals that were central to its ideological logic – limited state involvement in economic policy; a strong stance on law and order; asserting the values of indivi-dualism over those of community; traditional family centeredness and a tough stance on immigration and race relations. Such principles became associated with 'common sense' values within British society. The rules and the ideological terrain had changed. As Stevenson suggests:

> Thatcherism was successful because it was able to articulate the fears and anxieties of the respectable classes into a rightist consensus. This enabled the Right to speak up for 'ordinary members of the public' who were fearful of rising crime, delinquency and moral permissiveness, while the social democratic left appeared to defend the status quo.
>
> *Stevenson (2002: 3)*

Hall's work is important in that it sought to expose and examine the discursive terrain through which Thatcherism's ideological dominance was asserted and was maintained. However, Hall's work on ideology and power is not without criticism, particularly in the area of his notion of primary definition. For example, Schlesinger and Tumber (1994) argue that the process of primary definition set out by Hall and his colleagues oversimplify the relationship between journalists and sources on a number of levels. First, the level of ideological congruence between primary definers is overstated. What if there is disagreement on policy among the primary definers, who can be identified as the primary definer? Who has the power? When Margaret Thatcher was forced from her tenure at No. 10 in 1991 because of internal divisions within her party, it was *her* Foreign Secretary Geoffrey Howe that delivered the killer blow in his resignation speech in the House of Commons.[2] How does the notion of primary definition account for such an inversion of power relations? In short, it can't. Second, Schlesinger and Tumber suggests that the system of 'off-the-record' briefing to journalists obscures from view the primary definer which is something that Hall's model does not seem to take into account. Then there is, of course, inequality of access among, for example, the political elite, yet Hall's model does not sufficiently account for or explain the significance of the hierarchy of access that surely exists. Also, primary definers change over time, as Schlesinger and Tumber suggest; during the 1970s, when much of the work on this approach was being developed, the Unions and the Confederation of British Industry (CBI) were indeed dominant voices in Britain. However, during the Thatcher years these voices were gradually weakened, and in the case of the unions all but obliterated as significant forces of primary definition. Again this shift in the power centre of primary definition is not accounted for; rather the structures of power in the model appear static which is clearly not the case. Another objection relates to the role of the media and their position in the hierarchy of definition. Hall suggests that the media occupy the position of 'secondary definers' in which they are largely passive transmitters of information from above. Yet this does not take into account situations in which the media itself call the shots and define the parameters of debate and effectively force the primary definers onto the back foot. A prime example of this is the MPs' expenses scandal in Britain where MPs were forced to humbly apologise *en-masse* to the public for taking advantage of their privileged position in Parliament. *The Daily Telegraph*, the newspaper that broke the stories of MPs' expenses, had MPs reeling as day-by-day they had to respond to charges of corruption and misdeed in front of the waiting press. Here we see the media adopting the terrain of primary definition and dictating the terms of debate around MPs' expenses. Finally, the model of primary definition does not account for the process of negotiation between sources and journalists in which the end product is the outcome of compromise and trade offs. The upshot of these criticisms are that Hall's model is overly dependent on an analysis of structures of power and does not sufficiently take into account the complex processes of access and negotiation between sources and journalists. Nevertheless, Hall's analysis of the news media and particularly his examination of the hegemonic struggles over the terms of debate provide an important insight into discussions about informal modes of censorship and control.

In discussing the power of language to act within the dynamics of censorship, it will also be helpful for us to examine some of the influential ideas of philosopher Michel Foucault (1926–84). Foucault was concerned with how power has manifested itself in places where overt expressions of power may not be evident at first hand. For example, Foucault was concerned with how power in social institutions constituted itself and how it became manifest. He also looked at professions such as medicine and psychiatry and examined their histories, their conventions and norms as expressions of particular power relations (Foucault 1977). In short, Foucault was concerned with exploring the nature of power: what it was, how it was manifest and how it operated. The focus of his analysis of power tended to centre on language and discourse or the 'discursive realm', as he argued that language was central to our understanding of how power manifests itself historically in societies and, importantly within individuals themselves. As Simons suggests: 'Foucault discerns ways in which people participate in their own subjectification by exercising power over themselves, tying themselves to scientific or moral definitions of who they are' (1995: 2). Language is seen therefore as both expressive of our identity at the same time as it confines and shapes the limits of who we are. It is the interpretative lens through which we understand the world and our place within it. However, Foucault argued that within this interpretative framework there exists historically manifest ideological power which is expressed through language and discourse. It will be useful to borrow the quote by Gunther Kress in Fowler (1991) when he says that:

> Institutions and social groupings have specific meanings and values which are articulated in language in systematic ways. Following particularly the work of the French philosopher Michel Foucault, I refer to these systematically-organized sets of statements which give expression to the meanings and values of an institution. Beyond that, they define describe and delimit what it is possible to say and not possible to say (and by extension – what it is possible to do or not to do) with respect to the area of concern of that institution, whether marginally or centrally. A discourse provides a set of possible statements about a given area, and organizes and gives structure to the manner in which a particular topic, object, process is to be talked about. In that it provides descriptions, rules, permissions and prohibitions of social and individual actions.
>
> *Kress, cited Fowler (1991: 42)*

So we see from this that perspective discourse not only provides us with the values and meanings that help us to make sense of our world, but also it structures the manner in which we operationalise these elements in the ways in which we function and behave. Importantly for Foucault, power resides within practices themselves. Foucault's analysis of power and discourse has been highly influential with regard to the study of the language and discourse of the news. In particular, Critical Discourse Analysis (CDA) seeks to examine how the inherent power of discourse in the news media sustain 'an unequal distribution of power in society [particularly with regard] class, gender, ethnicity, race, or other indices related to status, domination and power' (Zelizer 2004a: 125). As Zelizer (2004a: 111) maintains, the analysis of language within journalism studies represents 'an outgrowth of the idea that the messages of journalism are not transparent or simplistic but encode larger messages about shape of life beyond the sequencing of actions that comprise a news event'. It is also concerned with exploring the ways in which language and discourse function to shape the social world itself, emphasising the necessary interpretational link between language and the social world. Within the analysis of news media, CDA in particular has sought to expose and examine the nature of language and its power of representation, particularly in relation to the ways in which language 'represents' certain features of inequality in society (Van Dijk 1989; Van Dijk 1991; Fairclough 1995; Fairclough and Wodak 1997).

The 'tyranny' of 'PC'!

One of the most controversial areas where discussion of ideology, language and censorship emerges is in debates about political correctness or 'PC'. The emergence of the term 'politically correct' can be traced to the 1980s and 1990s and though debates about PC seem to have declined (Johnson and Suhr 2003; Johnson, Culpeper and Suhr 2003) the issue still surfaces, particularly in the Right-wing media, who regurgitate the idea that political correctness continues to constitute a threat to established traditional values and identity in the U.S., U.K. and Europe.[3] The way in which the debate about PC has been framed is usually in terms of a hegemonic struggle for control of language and meaning between the Left and Right of the political spectrum – the so-called culture wars. It is certainly true that the debate about PC and the culture wars reflect a wider ideological conflict between traditional notions of left and right, but PC has also caused controversy and debate among the Left itself as we shall see. As such PC is a paradoxical notion that can be appropriated from different sides of the political spectrum. Indeed, Hall (1994) suggests that it is the fragmentation of politics away from its traditional base that has enabled PC to become central to the hegemonic struggles of both Left and Right. Debates around PC tend to be arguments about politics and the power, or lack of power, representational and actual, of a range of constituent groups. Debates around PC are, as Norman Fairclough has suggested debates about identity and cultural values which are political and contested.

> We might see the controversy around 'political correctness' (PC) as a political controversy in which both those who are labelled 'PC' and those who label them 'PC' are engaged in a politics that is focussed on representations, values and identities – in short, a 'cultural politics'.
>
> *Fairclough (2003: 17)*

As Will Hutton has observed, the essential mutability of PC makes it a valuable trope for both sides. For him it is both 'a heaven-sent opportunity to be excoriating about the inevitable tendency of the Left to produce inanities and offend "common sense" and "for ambitious left-of-centre politicians, it's a chance to show a sturdy capacity to be in touch with the saloon-bar prejudices of 'middle' England'" (Hutton 2004). PC can be appropriated from both sides of the political spectrum and is usually deployed in derogatory terms. Fundamentally from the Right, PC is said to pose a threat to freedom of speech as it stifles debate and discussion in the name of cultural over-sensitivity and needless pandering to 'right-on' values (Phillips 1994; Thompson 2005).

The broad argument is that in the name of multiculturalism, the Left, in its various initiatives to rid society of racism, sexism and homophobia, has led an assault on the very terms of debate which, from the view of those on the Right, have gone beyond the pale and led to a form of cultural and linguistic censorship. From the Right, PC is a fundamental attack on free speech. From the Left, PC is perceived as a convenient catch-all phrase that is deployed by reactionaries to undermine debate and discussion about social inequality and oppressive and discriminatory social practices. 'As an ideological code, PC operates as a device which mediates perception in the relations of public discourse – progressives and critics are now viewed as social oddballs, elements of the lunatic fringe and politically threatening extremists' (Scatamburlo 1998: 10). So from the Left PC is also perceived as a means by which the right can stifle discussion and debate. Given that both Right and Left view PC as a threat to freedom of speech it is worth examining the issue in some detail.

In America the debate about political correctness began in the 1980s under the conservative neo-liberal Regan administration. In historical and conceptual terms the debate can largely be seen as an attempt by the New Right to further its hegemonic project by attempting to reclaim political and moral ground that it viewed as being occupied by 'the Left' since the 1960s. The Conservative New Right viewed the 1960s as an era in which student activism, radical movements and new forms of political activism threatened what it termed 'traditional American values'. The politics of gender, race, sexuality and the gains made via these political struggles were seen as contributing factors to the breakdown of the traditional American way of life and to the rise of the permissive society in which crime and social breakdown were the result. The American New Right produced a political and social platform that was based on traditional Christian American values mixed with a version of economic rationalism in which the market was positioned as the overriding force for social good and one that would deliver freedom and democracy to all. In this culture war the New Right, aided by the media, set about attacking what it perceived to be the breeding grounds of Left-leaning radicalism which threatened to undermine 'American values'. This breeding ground of radicalism was, of course, the U.S. Academy. Wolfson writing at more or less the height of the PC debate in 1997 identifies what he sees as an 'increasing trend' within American universities in which the curriculum itself is subject to an essentially Left wing re-evaluation and attack. He suggests that the left-leaning intelligentsia has sought to 'demonize' the Western Enlightenment tradition of rationalism, freedom of conscience and freedom of speech, as it is this tradition that has (from the Left's point of view), led to the great catastrophes of the twentieth century – the mass crimes of Hitler, Stalin, Mao, Pol Pot and other ideologues that have sought to impose their ideological legitimacy at great human cost. Critics like Wolfson suggest that the Left views the 'Western' tradition has having laid the foundations of sexism and racism that pervades our societies to this day. The Left 'view free speech as a wild card that has created uncertain, unpredictable, and unequal results. Hence they desire to dampen spontaneous change and create a fixed and static society' (Wolfson 1997: 147). Alan Kors (2000) follows a similar line of attack when he decries the impact of 'campus speech codes' in American universities and their effect of stifling debate which constitute an 'assault on liberty' in which universities 'across the board are teaching contempt for liberty and its components: freedom of expression and enquiry; individual rights and responsibilities over group rights and entitlements; equal justice under law; and the rights of private conscience' (Kors 2000: 27). This 'assault' on American liberty continues to be a theme among the Right with Republican Governor of Texas Rick Perry lamenting that institutions from the Boy Scout movement to the Department of Defence 'bending to the winds of political correctness' (Perry 2005). The media in particular continues to come under sustained attack from those on the Right who speak about the 'liberal conspiracy' at the heart of the American media.[4] The culture war it seems looks destined to continue.

In Britain during the 1980s, given the ideological congruence of Thatcher and Regan, it is no surprise to see similar debates about the so-called language of political correctness starting to emerge. Moreover, debates about PC at this time become apparent in a context in which the Thatcher government, and the media that supported it, sought to further the ideological ambitions of Thatcherism increasingly in the realm of cultural politics. Thatcher, like Regan 'redefined the contours of public thinking with their virulently free-market social philosophy and set in motion a powerful, new, anti-welfare consensus' (Hall 1994: 169). This new consensus would be aimed at both the public and the private sphere in which the family, morality, sexuality, authority, education and work were all reframed around a new set of values based on the principles of the New Right – the prioritisation market as a regulator of social life and rampant individualism in which the state apparatus was presented as antithetical to individual freedom.

As Fairclough (2003) has noted, the reconstitution of language and discourse was as much a component of the Thatcherite cultural politics as it was on the Left; a feature that has largely been ignored by even the so-called liberal media. This can be seen in the way in which the language and discourse of business and economics has relatively unproblematically entered common parlance in a way that emphasises one set of values at the expense of another. For example, the allegedly neutral and dispassionate phrases 'economic rationalization' and 'downsizing' has largely replaced the phrase 'redundancy' which is associated with the morally weighted reality of people losing their jobs. On the Left, ideas that came to be labelled as 'PC' initially stemmed from the counter cultural revolution in the 1960s and the New Left's focus on new forms of grass-roots politics and their emphasis on identity, gender and sexuality. The New Left sought to develop a political agenda that embraced the politics of identity and diversity rather than the increasingly outdated class based politics. This old politics were too closely associated with the failures of the post-war Labour movement and the realities of Soviet communism (Kenny 1995). Sections of the Left therefore embraced many of the ideas that became associated with postmodernism and the critiques of Enlightenment thought that were associated with postmodernism. A new politics of *particularity* began to emerge and with it the idea that different cultural values and beliefs should be judged as having equal worth. Language and discourse were crucial in operationalising a more egalitarian form of politics that would attempt to undercut racism, sexism and homophobia in society. Discourse and language were increasingly seen as important components in framing our thinking and under-standing of social life. As Fairclough suggests, social life is discursively constructed as an effect of discourses which have the power to place emphasis on particular values and ideas (Fairclough 2003: 22–23). This increasing awareness among the Left that identity and cultural politics was the key arena for challenging the politics of the New Right enabled local authorities like the Greater London Council (GLC) and, after its abolition in 1984, local London authorities such as Brent, Islington and Haringey, to promote the politics of difference in their anti-racist, anti-homophobic, progressive and community based policies and programmes. Petley (2005) argues that much of the Right-wing press in the mid-1980s sought to 'demonise' democratically elected Left-wing local councils by means of fabricating stories or stretching the truth.[5] As such one can see that the battles of the 1980s between the New Right orthodoxy of Thatcherism[6] and attempts from the Left to re-assert a counter hegemonic struggle against neo-liberalism in the discursive terrain is probably best demonstrated by the example of Section 28. Section or Clause 28 refers to section 28 of the 1988 Local Government Act. This act prohibited Local Authorities from:

> 'intentionally promoting homosexuality or publishing material with the intention of promoting homosexuality' or 'promot[ing] the teaching in any maintained school of the acceptability of homosexuality as a pretended family relationship'.
>
> *Local Government Act (1988, sec. 28).*

The legislation was intended to prevent teachers in schools, youth and community workers from discussing any aspect of homosexuality as from the conservative right's perspective; to talk about gay sex was tantamount to the promotion of a gay lifestyle. The suggestion was that use of local tax payers' money to fund material that was considered a threat to children and traditional family relationships was fundamentally wrong. Lesbian and Gay activists saw this as a direct attack on their lifestyle and actively promoted discrimination against gay people. Section 28 was primarily aimed at local authorities, particularly those 'loony Left' local authorities of Liverpool, London, Manchester and South Yorkshire, in a bid to reign in their power and challenge their authority. Though no prosecutions were made using this legislation, Section 28 was a powerful political and rhetorical tool with which the Conservative Government sought to assert its moral authority and control. Unsurprisingly in the build up to the debate which lead to the eventual repeal of Section 28 in 2003, the right-wing press and the *Daily Mail* in particular, sought to confirm its position as the 'voice of reason' with headlines such as: 'Keep This out of our Schools';[7] 'An Immoral Risk To Marriage';[8] and 'Blair Heading for Defeat on Gay Propaganda'.[9] Such headlines demonstrate to the continued requirement from the Right-wing press to articulate its anti-PC rhetoric. In 2009 the Conservative Party leader David Cameron publicly apologised for Section 28 despite voting unsuccessfully against its repeal by the Blair government in 2003. As we can see then appropriately con-textualised, the furore around Section 28 highlights just one example of the culture wars during the 1980s and 1990s in which the Left and Right of the political spectrum were engaged in a battle to shift political debate from the explicitly political towards broader cultural concerns in the arts and particularly education.

Petley (2006) suggests it is the right-wing press itself that has maintained its assault on PC as an attempt to reclaim the political and moral high ground in a context in which the Left seems powerless to challenge. Indeed, PC continues to be the convenient default phrase which enables right-wing critics to label anything they might disagree with as PC. In short, PC has become a convenient shorthand for those on the Right to deploy when they feel that conservative values are being challenged; as Petley contends PC 'has endowed conservatives with a master trope, which enables them summarily to dismiss criticism, quell dissent and stifle critical discourse, all the while presenting themselves as fighting a conspiracy to destroy freedom of speech' (Petley 2006: 10). This is more than a mere discursive shift, rather it has allowed a rightist agenda to become mainstreamed in contemporary public discourse (Nunberg 2006). Yet PC is an all too convenient phrase which can be used by those on the Right to express their contempt for progressive ideas. As Gary Younge in *The Guardian* has commented, the Right '[b]y attacking political correctness', have found 'a fig leaf for openly expressing their bigotry'.[10] Yet within the Left itself there continues to be debate and discussion about PC and particularly the politics of multiculturalism and its legacy. Former head of the Commission for Racial Equality Trevor Phillips (2004) suggests that multiculturalism has had the effect of masking deeper levels of racism in society which are in part sustained by a bureaucratic culture of box ticking and faux anti-discrimination policies 'designed to appease community leaders coupled with gestures to assuage liberal guilt, while leaving systemic racism and inequality untouched'. More critically some on the Left see the legacy of multiculturalism and its emphasis on cultural sensitivity as propagating a form of atomised politics in which a person's 'identity' becomes the key focus for political action rather than a broader based universalist approach to radical politics which does not fragment political constituencies. In discussing the politics of identity and multiculturalism Malik (2004) suggests that its legacy has been 'the fragmentation of society' where 'different groups assert their particular identities' which has led to the 'creation of a well of resentment within white working class communities'.[11] The upshot has been that there has been no broad basis on which to develop a genuinely progressive politics (see also Malik 2009). This has led Furedi (2005) to conclude that the Left's victory in the culture wars at the end of twentieth century was the narrow victory of relativism over universalism and that ultimately this narrow victory has largely been self-defeating for progressive politics.

There is no doubt that PC remains a powerful ideological tool that has the power to curb and potentially stifle the parameters of debate, in this sense the continued use of the term PC to stifle discussion and debate betrays the essential tyranny of the term. Today the perceived failures of multiculturalism, a once central feature of the progressive Left agenda, has given much ammunition to those on the Right who see multiculturalism and its PC legacy as denigrating long established national identity and traditional cultural values. The growth of radical Islamic terrorism, particularly the so-called 'home grown' version has been signalled as the death knell for multiculturalism in Britain from various quarters (see Modood 2005). Yet despite the failures of the Left, as I have suggested, the Right continue to fight a rear-guard action on the perceived hegemonic encroachments of what remains of the Left as if nervous of its own grasp on hegemonic power. The widespread derogatory deployment of the term 'PC' signals a victory for a form of reactionary politics that masquerades as 'common sense' that continues to pervade popular public discourse. There is no doubt that the more zealous Left wing advocates of 'culturally competent' language serve as convenient fodder for the right-wing media to ridicule. On the whole, however, as Valerie Scatamburlo has argued PC can be seen as a reactionary attempt to deploy a new and more sophisticated version of McCarthyism with which to discredit critical dissent, the struggle for minority rights and progressive social change (Scatamburlo 1998).

Freedom of speech and religion

As we have seen throughout this book the principle freedom of speech comes under pressure from many sources and in many different ways. The so-called 'Danish Cartoons' controversy (see later) highlights how journalism can be central to these discussions, though historically, as we've seen, the relationship between religion and freedom of speech and expression is one that is particularly difficult. It is important to note, however, that recent controversies regarding freedom of speech and religion have not arisen as a result of some 'clash of civilisations' (Huntingdon 1998) rather, the debates about freedom of speech should be seen in the context of broader complex historical shifts within Britain and further afield. In order to unpack this complexity we will look at first at the Labour government's eventually successful attempts to broaden the race hate laws to include offences against religion before going on to look at the *Satanic Verses* controversy, which provides us with some important historical context when examining the debate about the Danish cartoons.

Racial and Religious Hatred Act 2006

In January 2006 the Racial and Religious Hatred Act finally came into force in the U.K. after some considerable controversy. Artists, writers and performers had lobbied hard against the government's original proposals which were to make a criminal offence of criticising an established religion or faith. Though the original legislation did not make it to the statute books, the law as finally implemented, extended already existing legislation from the Public Order Act 1986 which made stirring up racial hatred a criminal offence, to include offences which involve stirring up hatred on religious grounds. There are a number of contributing factors that led up to the implementation of this legislation. The events of 9/11 and the subsequent war on terrorism prompted the New Labour government to employ a vast array of legislation which has led to an erosion of civil liberties in Britain.[12] Appignanesi (2005: 5) argues that the Labour government's original attempts to amend the Serious Organised Crime and Police Bill (1986) partly stemmed from a recognition 'that British Muslims had suffered from the war on terrorism after 9/11, its control orders, Guantanamo, and the Iraq war', as such she notes it 'decided to give with one hand what it had patently taken away with the other'. Despite the fact that the original Bill did not make it through the House, in the run up to the 2005 general election the Labour Party vowed to fight on as evidenced in its manifesto pledge which emphasised a balanced approach to the issue. However, the balance that New Labour was hoping to achieve is one that is difficult to discern given that there was sufficient statutory protection already in place under the Public Order Act 1986 (section 5(1)), which states that: 'A person is guilty of an offence if he uses threatening, abusive or insulting words or behaviour, or disorderly behaviour, or displays any writing, sign or other visible representation which is threatening, abusive or insulting.'

Prior to 2006 there had been a number of incidents which highlighted the apparent conflict between those who defended freedom of expression and those who asserted a right not to be offended. In December 2004, Birmingham Repertory Theatre cancelled the play *Behzti* when protests by outraged Sikh activists turned violent. The protests were in response to the play's depiction of rape, murder and homosexuality within a Sikh *gurdwara*, a sacred place in Sikhism. Also in 2004 the Dutch writer and film maker Theo van Gogh was shot and stabbed to death in Amsterdam by Mohammed Bouyeri, a Dutch-Moroccan. At his trial Bouyeri was unrepentant, remarking that he had acted out of religious conviction and had no regrets. Van Gogh had made the film *Submission* about violence against women in Islamic societies and had received a number of death threats before he was killed. In 2005 the BBC broadcast the musical *Jerry Springer the Opera*, which offered a satirical swipe at the moral hypocrisy of exploitative 'confessional' television programmes such as *The Jerry Springer Show* and *Trisha*. Christian Voice denounced the musical as blasphemous as it portrayed Jesus as a 'perv in a nappy'[13] shouting expletives and blasphemies. Ofcom received nearly 17,000 complaints about the programme, with nearly half of them made before the programme was broadcast; the complaints were not upheld by Ofcom.[14] Controversy has also surrounded the Dutch right-wing MP Geert Wilders, who has compared *The Koran* to *Mein Kampf* (Ruth 2009) and who was denied entry into Britain after he was invited into the U.K. by members of the House of Lords to show his film *Fitna* – a film that is highly critical of Islam. Of course, the controversy surrounding the Racial and Religious Hatred Act and the unrest and violence related to the apparent tensions between freedom of expression and the right not to be offended did not emerge from the ether. The issue has an important political and historical context which may help to explain how and why the debate about the limits of freedom of expression have reached such a crescendo in recent years. Arguably, the most significant event in relation to this issue is the *Satanic Verses* affair, which according to Malik (2009: xvii) 'was the moment at which a new Islam dramatically announced itself as a major political issue in Western society'.

The Satanic Verses *affair*

Publication of Salman Rushdie's *The Satanic Verses* in the U.K. in September 1988, though lauded in Europe and America, was almost immediately banned in India,

South Africa and Iran (Lee 1990). Violence followed, with riots in Bombay and Pakistan and bookstores firebombed in major cities across the world. Individuals and institutions associated with the publishing company were attacked and the Japanese translator of *The Satanic Verses*, Hitoshi Igarashi, was murdered. In Bradford, a town with a relatively large Muslim population, the book was publicly burned, with the images of *The Satanic Verses* in flames beamed around the world. Then in February 1989 the Iranian spiritual leader Ayatollah Khomeini issued a *fatwa*, or death sentence, on Rushdie which called on Muslims to kill the author for his crimes against Islam. The *fatwa* seemed to add an official sanction to view that Rushdie had committed an awful crime against an entire religion. This sanction would force him to go into hiding under police protection for nine years in fear of his life. The principle concern with critics of the book was that the book had defamed the prophet Mohammed and insulted the Islamic faith. The view of many Muslims was that 'no writer was entitled to talk about sacred matters in such profane language' (Lee 1990: 73). Lee notes that the 'vehemence of the reaction was in part a product of domestic circumstances in Iran' with the issue used to reinforce the Ayatollah's authority as well as being in keeping with the broader culture of terrorism emanating from the Middle East at that time (1990: 74).[15] Ruth (2009) emphasises this point by suggesting that that *fatwa* was representative of an attempt to exert influence and extend power in the Muslim world in the aftermath of the Iran–Iraq War. He maintains that it was also 'an opportunity to stage a doctrinally defined symbolic battle as a means to strengthen the status of [Khomeini's] government in the Islamic world and to win points against the country's arch-rival, Sunni Muslim Saudi Arabia' (2009:107). Though Khomeini was attempting to speak on behalf of all Muslims, this was far from the reality as Thomas notes

> the great majority of Muslims in the West had cause to loathe the Khomeini regime as much as anyone. [...] Most were not Khomeini's supporters any more than most Germans had been members of the Nazi party or most citizens of the Soviet Union had been members of the Communist party.
>
> *Thomas (2007: 353)*

Moreover, critical reaction to the publication of *The Satanic Verses* did not just emerge from within Islam, as a number of British authors were critical of the perceived attack on an already discriminated against group of people. The argument was essentially that Muslim people should be protected from attacks on their faith given the legacy of Western imperialism (see Hitchens 1997).

Despite this wider complexity, during the 1990s the *fatwa* seemed to provide the starkest of indications that Western liberalism and its values of freedom of speech and expression were in diametric opposition to the sensibilities of Islam. Even though, as Fowler (2000) and Ruth (2009) point out, there have been defences of *The Satanic Verses* from within Islam itself, most notably from the philosopher Sadiq J. al-Azm, the image of Islam cannot accommodate freedom of speech remains powerful in the wake of Rushdie and the more recent violence following the Danish cartoons.

Moreover, despite the predominantly negative coverage of Muslim reaction Malik suggests that there were in fact many diverse reactions within Muslim communities in Britain (Malik 2009). Nevertheless, Donald Thomas (2007: 356) sums up the mood in the aftermath of *The Satanic Verses* when he suggests that censorship assumed a new identity following the victories against it during the 1960s and 1970s when he contends that: 'Censorship of the written word or picture was now global and its most effective weapon was terror.' Kenan Malik (2009) has examined the Rushdie affair and its aftermath and has suggested that the issues central to the affair strikes at the heart of the essential conflict between cultural relativism and Enlightenment reason within 'multi-cultural' societies. A conflict within which even some secular liberals contend that freedom of speech comes at too high a price and that offensive speech and expression undermines people's identity and personhood. The growth of identity politics in particular has meant that 'hate crime' is now defined in terms of an assault on a person which is manifest in their racial and ethnic identity, but also their religious identity. In other words, a person's religious faith not only relates to their beliefs and their lifestyle choices, but also to their specific identity. However, some critics maintain that religious belief should not be confused with race or even national identity as these provide more concrete notions of a person's cultural and ethnic roots. Whereas central to religion is faith and belief which opens it up to questioning and critique. In other words beliefs should be deemed different from ethnicity, as this quote from Monica Ali suggests:

> Religions, on the other hand, are sets of ideas and beliefs. They should not be privileged over any other set of notions. I am not bound to respect the idea that I may be reincarnated as an insect or a donkey or that Jesus is the Son of God or anything else that I regard as mumbo-jumbo. Indeed, if there are aspects and practices of a religion that conflict with my own notions and beliefs (of fairness and justice and so on) then the moral onus is on me to speak up against them. If I loathe the fact that Islam has been used to deny the right of women in Saudi Arabia to vote then I ought to say so.
>
> *Ali (2005: 49)*

Malik argues 'the distaste for giving offence, and the desire to curb the speech of all those who do so, is newly sprung from the perceived needs of a multi-cultural society' (2009: 156). As such, he suggests that: 'Nearly two decades on from *The Satanic Verses*, Western liberals had become much more attuned to Islamist sensitivities and less willing to challenge them. They had, in the post-Rushdie world, effectively internalized the fatwa' (Malik 2009: 145). A similar line of argument is made by Thomas who emphasises the particular censorial resonance of *The Satanic Verses* controversy:

> The case of *The Satanic Verses* and those controversies which followed it did more than internationalize censorship. As surely as a legal judgement they shifted the ground of debate from the historic rights of speech and expression

to the right not to be offended. […] religious fanaticism had more bluntly asserted the rights of believers not to be offended, whatever the cost to freedom of expression.

Thomas (2007: 359–60)

Examples of self-censorship within the Arts include the cancellation of *Lysistrata* by Aristophanes because the play was set in Paradise; the cancellation of Berlin's Deutsche Oper's production of Mozart's *Idomeneo* because of its depiction of the Prophet (Malik 2009). There were also been attempts to prosecute the makers of Channel Four's *Undercover Mosque* programme in 2007 for 'fomenting hatred of the Muslim functionaries in the film. Having failed to obtain a warrant, a complaint against the film was filed with Ofcom' (Ruth 2009: 110). The complaint was not upheld as the regulator maintained that the programme 'was a legitimate investigation, uncovering matters of important public interest' (Ofcom 2007b: 20).[16] Channel Four subsequently successfully sued West Midlands Police and the Crown Prosecution Service for claiming that the documentary 'completely distorted the words of three Muslim preachers'.[17] The publishers Random House cancelled the publication of the novel 'The Jewel of Medina' following objections by Islamic scholars that the novel depicted the youngest wife of Mohammed as a 'sex object' (Ruth 2009: 110).

The Danish cartoons

Arguably, the most significant recent case in which Islam has seemingly come into conflict with Western values of freedom of speech and freedom of the press is in relation to the so-called Danish Cartoons controversy. In September 2005 the Danish newspaper *Jyllands-Posten* published twelve cartoon illustrations of the Prophet Muhammad. The newspaper had asked a number of Danish illustrators and cartoonists to 'submit their own interpretations of the prophet' in order to assert the principle of freedom of the press and to test the theory that self-censorship is the norm. It is, of course, widely known that the depiction of the Islamic prophet is forbidden in Islamic code and the publication of the cartoons sparked demonstrations against the newspaper in Denmark. By February 2006 the furore around these cartoons spread further afield prompting demonstrations in other European capital cities and in the Middle East. The argument seemed to be that not only were these images blasphemous, but also they amount to an attack on the Islamic religion and identity. The outrage was matched by defenders of the European newspapers which published the cartoons who countered these claims and argued that they had a duty to assert their right to freedom of speech, even though such freedom was deemed blasphemous and offensive to some. The controversy seemed to crystallise the way in which Western values of freedom of speech, 'clashed' with values of religious tolerance and religious freedom, or at least certain interpretations of them. The publication of the cartoons by other newspapers across Europe, though not in Britain, seemed to suggest that news organisations were demonstrating their solidarity with *Jyllands-Posten* in asserting the value of freedom of speech in defiance of perceived attacks against such freedoms.[18] However, it could be suggested that the publication of the cartoons was nothing more than an ill-judged attempt to highlight the perceived intolerance of Islam by provoking the expected response. As Ruth suggests, drawing on Eriksen and Stjernfelt (2008), even fiercer caricatures of Mohammed were published in Politiken months before (Ruth 2009: 112). Clearly the reputation of some so-called Islamic states in relation to matters of freedom of speech and freedom of the press are well known. However, as Mohamed 2010; Kamali (1994) and Mahmood (2004) have argued, despite the reputation of a number of repressive Islamic states Islam has a long historical tradition of freedom of opinion and tolerance. For example, Mohammed maintains that: 'Islam provides all the guarantees that encourage people to get involved and declare their opinions publicly, to criticise the views and opinions of others without any fear or hesitation, provided that the expression of these opinions accords with truth and upright behaviour' (Mohammed 2010: 145–46).

John Richardson (2004) has written extensively about the way in which the British media in particular sustains a racialised rhetoric that stigmatises and castigates Muslims in ways that conform to an established pattern of representation which frames the West as good and civilised and the east as un-civilised and consequently evil. Drawing on the work Edward Said (1991), Richardson suggests that such a discourse upholds an 'orientalist' approach to Islam which helps sustain the view that we in the West are under threat from the dark forces of un-civilised religions such as Islam.

> Orientalism and orientalist scholarship are systems of representation framed by the hegemonic political forces of colonialism, post-colonialism and neo-colonialism, which act towards bringing the 'Orient' into Western consciousness, Western dispensation and under Western domination.
>
> *Richardson (2004: 5)*

Richardson's work is helpful as it helps contextualise and explain the way in which the media in particular characterise Islam and those who practice the Muslim faith in ways which reinforce damaging stereotypes of Muslims. As noted, the publication of the cartoons was justified on the grounds of an assertion of the newspapers' rights to freedom of expression – an example of a core value of Western liberalism. However, Mill himself argues that the expression of an opinion or view needs to be considered in respect of the context in which it is made and the likely consequences of the expression. Given the heightened sensitivity that many Muslims may have felt with regard to attacks on their faith, especially since 9/11, one might argue that in publishing the cartoons the newspapers were not only acting disrespectfully but also irresponsibly and in an inflammatory manner. It could be argued therefore that the debate about the Danish cartoons is not so much a debate about the limits of press freedom but a debate about how we view different cultures and different ideals and which in turn echoes from our response to the Rushdie affair in the 1980s. Significantly, at the time of the Rushdie affair there was the view that given the blasphemy laws did not extend to Islam, there seemed to be little credibility in the notion that Britain was genuinely a multi-cultural society.[19] Arguably, this was something that New Labour wanted to rectify partly to appease long standing Muslim Labour voters given the disastrous war in Iraq and the war on terror. Yet there is much more to the Western response to the Rushdie affair than platitudinous attempts to make amends as Malik eloquently remarks:

> The Rushdie affair is shrouded by myths – that the hostility to *The Satanic Verses* was driven by theology, that all Muslims were offended by the novel, that Islam is incompatible with Western democracy, that in plural society speech must necessarily be less free. In describing the controversy in this way, by ignoring the political heart of the Rushdie affair, the diverse character of Muslim communities and of the Muslim response to *The Satanic Verses*, and the importance of free speech to minority groups, and by abandoning their attachment to Enlightenment universalist values, liberals have not just created a particular picture of the Rushdie affair, they have also ensured that Western societies have succumbed to the picture they have constructed. They have helped build a culture of grievance in which being offended has become a badge of identity, cleared a space for radical Islamists to flourish, and made secular and progressive arguments less sayable, particularly within Muslim communities.
>
> *Malik (2009: 210)*

As Oliver Wendell Homes asserted echoing Mill, 'Every idea is an incitement ... The only difference between expression of an opinion and in incitement in the narrower sense is the speaker's enthusiasm for the result' (cited Thomas 2007: 355).

Conclusion: Orwell and his legacy

No discussion about the power of language can ignore the contributions made by George Orwell. Of course, Orwell was concerned with the ability of language to structure and affect our behaviour and thinking. Orwell's intellectual legacy is significant, as Christopher Hitchens observes:

> [W]e commonly use the term 'Orwellian' in one of two ways. To describe a state of affairs as Orwellian is to imply crushing tyranny and fear and conformism. To describe a piece of writing as 'Orwellian' is to recognize that human resistance to these terrors is unquenchable. Not bad for one short lifetime.
>
> *Hitchens (2002: 4)*

The novel *1984* is Orwell's celebrated classic that sets out a nightmare vision of the power of authoritarian regimes to mould the minds and actions of individuals and thus robbing them of their essential human spirit. Orwell's novel, published in 1949, should be seen in a broader context of the development of his work and those issues that affected him from his earliest experiences. As Slater (1985) suggests, *1984* should be viewed as the culmination of a set of concerns that began in Burma during his time serving as a policeman in the Indian Imperial Police and continued to develop from his observations of poverty and unemployment in the late 1920s and 1930s; his experiences fighting fascism in Spain, and his witness to the horrors committed by Hitler and Stalin. The novel *1984* expresses Orwell's darkest fears about the power of the totalitarian state to consume and destroy the very essence of human beings; their free will, conscience, fraternity, and compassion. However, Orwell's analysis also enables us to develop an insight into how language even in democratic societies can be modified in order to maintain structures of power and control over the individual. Slater (1985: 247) suggests that Orwell's *1984* 'will endure because ultimately, his attack is not directed so much toward a political system as upon a state of mind'. In other words *1984* is a call to remind us that we must be eternally vigilant against that which would deny us our freedom. Language and its control was, of course, central to his thesis in *1984* and in *Politics and the English Language* (1946). The latter was an attempt to draw attention to the encroachment of a form of linguistic tardiness that he argued was pervading the English language. For Orwell such linguistic 'debasement' was not just a signifier of lazy writing but also an obstacle to understanding and greater sense of meaning. This was important in relation to politics in particular. He argues forcefully that writing has become stultified through the over use of certain phrases and metaphors, with speech writers, journalists and politicians defaulting to such a mode of writing and speaking without considering the clarity of meaning of what they are trying to express.

> A speaker who uses that kind of phraseology has gone some distance towards turning himself into a machine. The appropriate noises are coming out of his larynx, but his brain is not involved as it would be if he were choosing his words for himself.
>
> *Orwell (2007 [1946]: 217)*

This was all the more problematic for Orwell given that the turn of language used by politicians was often used to mask the reality of the circumstances they were describing or referring to. 'When there is a gap between one's real and one's declared aims, one turns as it were instinctively to long words and exhausted idioms, like a cuttlefish squirting out ink' (Orwell 2007 [1946]: 218). In other words, a form of language is being invoked by politicians to cloak reality and mask meaning. Here as Schell (2007: xviii) observes, Orwell pointed 'out the increasingly complex ways in which corrupted language precipitates chains of cause and effect that lead to corrupt thinking and distorted politics' which was not only relevant at the end of the Second World War, but also continues to be relevant today,[20] with journalists and commentators such as John Pilger (2009) arguing that the rhetoric of President Barack Obama in his various speech on 'global security' parallels the idiom of *1984*. Christopher Hitchens (2002), for very different reasons, lauds Orwell's legacy even though he cringes at the clichéd and 'sickly veneration' suffered by those who study his works, as an example of a writer with an independent mind, (something that Hitchens demonstrates Orwell fought for throughout his life) and to which his discussions of language; objectivity and relativism; nationalism; popular culture, and ecologism betray his prescience to this day (Hitchens 2002). Propaganda is a harsh word that does not sit easily with our conceptions of modern democratic society, yet for Orwell propaganda could take on more subtle forms. 'Political speech and language, degraded by euphemism, vagueness and cliché, was used to defend the indefensible, to make lies sound truthful and murder respectable' (Massing 2007: 174) and today, according to some commentators little has changed, particularly in relation to discussions of war and conflict (see Szántó 2007).

Though paradoxically Orwell's work is often invoked as a form of shorthand in relation to discussions of propaganda and power (in such a way as to almost undercut much of the simplicity and profundity of Orwell's arguments, part of what *Politics and the English Language* was trying to warn against), Orwell should also be considered in relation to drawing our attention to the limiting power of language to mystify or obfuscate. In this sense freedom of speech means little if the language that is at our disposal is so limited and constrained by convention and the pressure to conform. *Politics and the English Language* serves in many ways as a precursor to the arguments and ideas in *1984* and though this work is much less visceral than *1984*, we should not ignore its potency.

Censorship [just] is

In his work *Discipline and Punish* (1977), Foucault examined the development of the penal system and in particular the ways in which power and authority manifest themselves within such institutions. Focusing on Jeremy Bentham's idea of the panopticon, Foucault examined how power resides in such institutions outside of the realm of expressions of physical power or punishment. Bentham designed the panopticon as a mechanism of control, not just with a view to prisons but 'houses of industry, work-houses, poor-houses, lazarettos, manufactories, hospitals, mad-houses, and schools', in which the inhabitants of this structure would be under the watchful gaze of the authorities. The panopticon's structure is central to its effective functioning. The structure would be circular with the cells at the outside edge of the building, facing inwards with bars to contain the inmates. In the centre of the building would be a tower in which the guards would work and be able to see the activities of all the inmates of the prison. What is crucial to this is that the inmates of the panopticon cannot see the guards in their tower, as such they are never sure when they are being scrutinised and watched over and subsequently modify their behaviour.

> This Panopticon, subtly arranged, so that an observer may observe, at a glance, so many different individuals, also enables everyone to come and observe any of the observers. The seeing machine was once a sort of dark room into which individuals spied; it has become a transparent building in which the exercise of power may be supervised by society as a whole.
>
> *Foucault (1977: 207)*

Foucault emphasises this point as 'Panopticon systems of control' can be used to moderate behaviour as it is control from within that is the most powerful. Inmates know that they have to adapt their behaviour to their immediate environment, if they fail to do so the inmates risk sanction and punishment. Within the social sciences attention has been focused on Foucault's examination of Panopticon systems of control which extend beyond the prison to social institutions more generally. As Haggerty and Ericson suggest 'Foucault proposed that the panopticon served as a diagram for a new model of power which extended beyond the prison to take hold in the other disciplinary institutions characteristic of this era, such as the factory, hospital, military, and school' (2000: 607). Moreover, the panopticon can be seen as a mechanism in which the disciplinary mechanisms become internalised: 'the individual herself now "plays both roles": the oppressor may well be absent, but the prisoner has internalised the behavioural code of the oppressor, and will behave as though the prison guard were still watching' (Mills 2003: 46). In relation to the press we can see examples of the press acting as a moral censor in this capacity as early as the nineteenth century. According to utilitarian philosopher James Mill the press would expose misdeed and wrongdoing of those behaving inappropriately and therefore people, full in the knowledge that their actions will be scrutinised in the press, would internally regulate and moderate their behaviour (see Steel 2009). As such we can see the nineteenth-century press, at least in the 1820s and 1830s, as attempting to expose misdeed and corruption, not necessarily of those in power, but of men and women everywhere.

In Foucauldian terms, this can be seen as the disciplinary power of the press – the knowledge that people have that their wrong actions will lead to sanctions being imposed on them, the more likely they will refrain from such wrong actions. Within the modern news media, the tabloid press in particular can be seen as the purveyors of 'caught in the act' journalism. Stories of corrupt politicians, unfaithful celebrities, devious bankers not only act to entertain and inform, but also they (hypocritically) construct a moral landscape within which wrong actions are demarcated and condemned (Conboy 2006). Stevenson (2002) points out that, 'Much of the content of the tabloid press has much to do with normalising surveillance of the *private* lives of ordinary people as it has with the democratic mechanism of publicity.' Therefore, the news media's power to exert such influence is significant because, as with other large social institutions it removes the necessity for direct coercion and control. Why have the jackboot when you can morally regulate the public via much gentler means? The news media ensures that we are continually aware that for the most part the bad things that people do have bad consequences for those that do them. According to this perspective the news media therefore reinforce the norms and values that for the most part ensure that the public acquiesce. Censorship and control therefore need not be overt and blatantly oppressive, rather it is manifest within our own internal social and moral compass which is driven by the magnetic force of compliance to the prevailing social order. Another term for this form of externally imposed internally regulated censorship is 'constitutive censorship' (see Curry-Jansen 1991). If one adopts this analytical framework, to quote Holquist (1994 cited in Post 1998: 2) 'censorship [just] is' – it is constitutive in all our communicative practices because of the disciplinary power of the institutions that regulate and govern our lives. The surveillance that all of us tacitly consent to – whether it be CCTV cameras on street corners, neighbourhood watch schemes, electronic surveillance via the compilation of digital records, or the threat of exposure in the media, all ensure that our behaviour can be monitored and corrected accordingly if constitutive censorship fails. Foucault's vision of a society in which disciplinary power is so pervasive does not make for cheery reflection. Indeed his analysis is starkly at odds with those who argue that the modern institutions of the media at least in principle have the capacity to serve the ideals of democracy. Rather the constitutive essence of censorship underscores its dynamic nature and further serves to obfuscate the schism between freedom of speech and freedom of the press.

NOTES

Introduction

1 For example see J. B. Bury's *A History of Freedom of Thought* (1913) which presents a romanticised account of the development of liberty of thought and conscience as primarily a struggle between religious orthodoxy and a secular liberal impulse that enabled broader liberties to develop. Similarly J. M. Robertson's *A Short History of Freethought* (1915) offers a much wider geographical coverage of the development of freedom of thought and freedom of speech, looking at its development in India, China, Israel and under different religious traditions including Christianity and Islam. Both of these accounts, though useful in some of their historical detail, stand as examples of a particular romanticised and almost triumphalist account of the spread of freedom of thought and expression (see also Chapter 2).

2 The so-called 'clash of civilisations' is a term borrowed from Lewis (1990) and used in the title of a book by Samuel P. Huntingdon which suggested that, following the end of Cold War, the new conflict would be a clash of a range of different civilisations including those based on religious foundations such as Hinduism and Islam as well as ethnic and cultural such as Japanese, Chinese and African. Though the phrase was adopted within the more 'hawkish' elements of the Bush administration following the terrorist attacks on America on 9/11 (11 September 2001), the sentiment that democracy, in Britain and Europe in particular, are under significant threat from Islam has reached somewhat hysterical proportions.

3 http://wardiary.wikileaks.org/.

Chapter 1: The philosophy of free speech

1 This phrase relates to the traditional liberal view of the development of freedom of the press. See Curran (2002).

2 The 'Rights Tradition' can also be traced back to the sixteenth century School of Salamanca in which theologians devised a doctrine of rights in relation to the indigenous inhabitants of the Spanish empire.

3 A more recent contribution on the philosophy of free speech from Eric Barendt (2005) suggests that there are in fact four distinct strands of free speech arguments. However, for

the purposes of clarity and precision I combine the democracy argument and the suspicion of government argument into one set of arguments that relate more specifically to press freedom.

4 For a discussion of free speech from a relativist perspective see Fish (1994).
5 See http://www.unhchr.ch/html/menu3/b/a_ccpr.htm. See also the International Convention on the Elimination of all forms of Racial Discrimination at: http://www.unhchr.ch/html/menu3/b/d_icerd.htm.
6 See http://supreme.justia.com/us/432/43/case.html for the wording of the application and the full text of the case.
7 It is worth noting that the free market of ideas metaphor highlighted above in my discussion of the democracy argument is most often associated with discussions about the argument from truth (see Barendt, 2005). I have no objection to this; indeed, there may be strong arguments to suggest that the metaphor can be applied in both philosophical contexts.

Chapter 2: Freedom of speech and the journalistic impulse

1 *A Demure to the Bill for Preventing the Growth and Spreading of Heresie* (1646).
2 *The Compassionate Samaritane: Unbinding the Consicence, and pouring oyle into the wounds which have beene made upon the Separation, recommending their future welfare to the serious thoughts and careful endeavours of all who love the peace and unity of Commonwealths men, or desire the unanimous prosecution of the Common Enemy, or who follow our Saviours rule, to doe unto others what they would have others doe unto them* (1644).
3 See Steel (2009). See also Hollis 1970; Boyce et al 1978; Chalaby 1998; Curran and Seaton 2010.
4 For a celebratory account of the 'struggle' for freedom of the press Collet D. Collet's *A History of the Taxes on Knowledge* (1899).
5 Hume, *Hansard*, Vol. 6 1831: 9.
6 Hume, *Hansard*, Vol. 6 1831: 11.

Chapter 3: Journalism and the democratic Imperative

1 Details of MPs' abuse of the Parliamentary expenses system first appeared in *The Sunday Telegraph* and, over a period of months, exposed how MPs had used the rules on expenses to 'milk' the system, at times for their own personal gain, in the name of serving their constituencies (see Kenny 2009). Despite claims of Parliamentary privilege, this particular scandal has led to criminal prosecutions being brought against members of both Houses – Elliot Morley, David Chaytor, Jim Devine and Lord Hanningfield. See http://news.bbc.co.uk/1/hi/uk_politics/8500885.stm. The resulting public outcry led to the reform of the system of MP expenses including the setting up of the Independent Parliamentary Standards Authority which would produce new rules on expenses and monitor, process and regulate the system of MPs' expenses. The reputation of MPs was further damaged by the 'MPs cash-for-lobbying sting' when a Channel 4 *Dispatches* programme secretly filmed MPs apparently attempting to sell their influence for financial gain. See Channel 4 *Dispatches* 'Politicians for Hire' at http://www.channel4.com/programmes/dispatches/articles/politicians-for-hire-video.
2 The United States, Canada, Ireland and Britain.
3 In Britain F. R. Leavis's Mass Civilisation and Minority Culture echoed Lipmann's pessimistic and deeply conservative analysis of the role and function of the press (Hampton 2004: 131).
4 So named after the fourth President of the United States of America James Madison.
5 The notion of the 'invisible hand' relates to the eighteenth century theories of the free market devised by economist Adam Smith, the principle idea being that the market is essentially self-directing and self regulating and therefore requires minimal external interference. In other words the central dynamics of the free market are encapsulated in the metaphor of the invisible hand.

6 Such protection has been provided under the First Amendment with some important caveats and Zelezny (2010) identifies two key restrictions on corporate speech. The first relates to the protection of investment markets and the disclosure of information to investors; the second restriction is in order to protect the political process for example where corporations might be 'capable of dominating the nation's marketplace of political expression and corrupting the democratic system' (2010: 78).

7 Though relatively straightforward, Sanders goes on to develop a more nuanced and sophisticated definition of political communication which goes beyond the 'political' and engages in debates about human agency, practice and symbolism. She not only deals with exploring the ways that political institutions, media and the public interact, and the effects of such interaction, Sanders is also interested in exploring how people 'communicate about politics' (see Sanders, 2009: 40–54).

8 Voter turnout in the 2005 general election was 61.4 per cent; in 2010 it was 65.1 per cent.

9 It was less that three weeks into the era of 'new politics' ushered in by the new 'Lib–Con' coalition government in 2010 that the new treasury chief secretary David Laws was forced to resign after he had admitted claiming £40,000 to pay rent to his partner (White 2010).

10 It is important to note however, that though support from News International was *perceived* by the future architects of 'New Labour' as being a significant factor in any future electoral success, simply suggesting that it was the Murdoch press which delivered another Conservative victory in 1992 ignores other significant factors. For example there was some significant confusion and controversy over Labour's tax plans; there was a Conservative party which had rebranded itself under John Major, as well as controversy over aspects of the Labour election campaign. Finally Kinnock himself may not have come across as statesman-like as he and his supporters would have liked (see Wring 2005; Rubinstein 2006).

11 See Onora O'Neill's 2002 Reith Lectures, Lecture 1.

Chapter 4: Journalism, new media and the global public sphere

1 See Klein (2000; 2002; 2008); Moore (2009; 2004); Spurlock (2009); Greenwald (2004).

2 U.S. vice-resident Joe Biden suggested that Assange was like a 'high-tech terrorist' who had 'put lives at risk and made it more difficult for the U.S. to conduct its business around the world' (see Harris 2011).

3 See Sarah Palin Rips Obama White House Over WikiLeaks' *The Huffington Post*, 29 January, at: http://www.huffingtonpost.com/2010/11/29/sarah-palin-obama-wiki-leaks_n_789438.html

4 See Addley (2011)

5 See *Zimbabwe Metro* 'Those calling for Tsvangirai's prosecution over WikiLeaks reports should have their heads examined', 15 December (2010) at: http://www.zimbabwemetro.com/politics/those-calling-for-tsvangirais-prosecution-over-wikileaks-reports-should-have-their-heads-examined/

6 See Greenwald (2011).

7 The perception of cultural imperialism is not just a cause for anxiety in parts of the developing world as some Western states have expressed concern about the homogenising tendencies of the global media system – so much so that some states have attempted to manage the amount of foreign media content within their borders. Through a process of 'cultural nationalism' (Tunstall 2008), France (for example) has attempted to limit the importation of foreign cultural works (particularly American films) as part of its 'national culture project'. This represents both a challenge to U.S. economic and cultural dominance and as a protective measure against the erosion of French language and culture. Moreover, according to Tunstall (2008: 247): 'All 25 EU members defend and promote their own national media, national education system, national culture, and

national language.' Such protectionism also brings into focus claims about the relative power of globalisation and that of nation states (see Hafez 2007).

8 Read the official line on the purpose and function of Golden Shield from the Chinese Ministry of Public Security at: http://www.mps.gov.cn/English/content06_11_2.htm.

9 The CPJ notes that 61 journalist murders remain unsolved in the Philippines since 1992.

10 The CPJ reports that despite the fact that nine Sri Lankan journalists have been murdered since 2004, no prosecutions have been brought.

Chapter 5: Regulating broadcast journalism

1 http://www.ofcom.org.uk/about/what-is-ofcom/.

2 The only sections of the Code that do not apply to the BBC are Sections 5, 6, 9 and 10. See Ofcom 2011: 3.

3 The Hutton Report looked into the circumstances surrounding the death of government biological weapons specialist Dr. David Kelly. Dr. Kelly, of course, was the unnamed source used by BBC journalist Andrew Gilligan who in a broadcast on the *Today* programme on 29 May 2003 had suggested that No. 10 had 'sexed up' the case for war against Iraq.

4 For example, a complaint was upheld related to charges that the programme gave a lack of attention to the specific details of the injuries inflicted on crew members and activists on the cargo ship the Mavi Marmara. This lack of attention, according to the complaint, did not allow for an accurate picture of the circumstances and possible motivations of the IDF (BBC Trust 2011). The Committee also upheld a complaint regarding lack of impartiality in relation to the showing of footage of a wounded passenger being winched by helicopter and taken to hospital for treatment, with the accompanying statement suggesting that 'the Israelis evacuated the badly wounded to hospital', which wrongly conveyed the notion that all the badly injured and wounded were 'promptly and appropriately cared for' (BBC Trust 2011: 94).

5 It should be noted that some viewers and Griffin himself subsequently complained to the BBC arguing that the broadcaster had been biased in its coverage of the party and its leader giving it an unfair focus (see: http://news.sky.com/skynews/Home/UK-News/BBC-Gets-Hundreds-Of-Complaints-Alleging-Bias-Against-BNP-After-Nick-Griffin-Goes-On-Question-Time/Article/200910415412165).

6 Guidelines provide a caveat if there are specific editorial justifications for proceeding without individuals' consent (BBC 2011: 52). See section on Privacy.

7 See also sections on Privacy.

8 Being the right to privacy and the right to remedy before a national authority if violated respectively.

9 In relation to the regulation of internet content in the UK, the Internet Watch Foundation (IWF) has been given responsibility for policing internet content – particularly in relation to the policing of child pornography. See Petley 2009: 116–25; Frenk 2008:171–82.

Chapter 6: Privacy and the public interest

1 See for example Article 8 of the ECHR and Article 17 of the International Covenant on Civil and Political Rights.

2 For example Mike Temple (2008) highlights the self-restraint (or self-censorship) of journalists covering the abdication crisis in 1936. Temple notes the 'open conspiracy by editors to protect the new king' at the beginning of the crisis (2008: 141). See also Wacks (1995).

3 See Dacre (2008).

4 Epstein notes that one of the first cases which dealt with privacy issues utilised trespass law against a man who had fraudulently posed as a doctor to gain entrance to a woman's bedroom when she was giving birth. He notes that: 'The defendant's fraud vitiated the consent given to his entry and thus exposed him to a trespass action, which included as damages the plaintiff's shame and embarrassment at having him watch the birth' (Epstein 2000: 8).

5 He goes on to highlight the conditions or circumstances in which the state may encroach on these privacy rights.

6 *Mosley v News Group Newspapers Ltd* (2008).

7 The Younger Commission's report on privacy in 1972 was produced 'to consider what measures [...] are needed to give further protection to individual privacy from the activities of the press and improve recourse against the press for the individual citizen [...] and to make recommendations.' Cited in Cloonan (1998: 65).

8 Cloonan notes that the interview was in fact based on notes taken from interviews with office staff who were asked how they would feel in the widow's circumstances (Cloonan 1998: 63).

9 Bingham notes that the Home Secretary David Waddington and his junior minister David Mellor 'felt considerable political pressure in 1990 to be tough on the press and to act decisively to curb journalistic intrusion' (2007: 80).

10 This is not to say that some journalists were oblivious to the liberties seemingly being taken by their employers as Curran and Seaton (2010) point out; during the 1970s and 1980s there were a number of unsuccessful attempts by journalists to 'secure the right of reply for targets of press attacks' (2010: 392). Similarly, there have been attempts by MPs to bring in a right of reply to those who feel that they have been misrepresented by the press, the most recent of which was the private member's bill presented by Labour MP Peter Bradley's 'Right of Reply and Press Standards Bill', which was defeated before the general election in 2005.

11 The National Union of Journalists also has a Code of Conduct which was initially framed in 1936. Members of the union sign a pledge that they will 'strive to adhere' to the Code which sets out a commitment to defend the principles of freedom of expression; honesty, accuracy and fairness in reporting; and an assertion of the right to privacy apart from in instances where there is an overriding public interest. See http://www.nuj.org.uk/innerPagenuj.html?docid=174.

12 Despite an unwritten voluntary agreement between the press and the palace that Princes William and Harry would be left alone, stories about the marital difficulties between Charles and Diana had been circulating in the press for some time. Yet it soon emerged that both parties had been somewhat complicit in the appearance of the stories in sections of the press. Andrew Morton's book *Diana: Her True Story – In Her Own Words* which was serialized in the *Sunday Times* and was annotated by Diana herself seems to give credence to the stories of complicity (Shannon 2001: 88). In 1993 the Princess of Wales started legal proceedings against Mirror Group Newspapers for publishing photographs of her exercising at a gym. The photographs were taken by Bryce Taylor, the owner of the gym, without the Princess's consent, using a camera hidden in a wall. The matter was settled out of court. The Wales's were not the only royals to receive newspaper attention as sections of the press were also focusing on the breakdown of the marriage of the Duke and Duchess of York. The *Daily Mirror* was the first tabloid to print telephoto images of a topless Duchess of York holidaying in the south of France with her financial advisor John Bryan. The pictures show the couple kissing and embracing each other, with a number of photographs purportedly showing Bryan sucking the Duchess's toe. The *People* had also previously published photographs of the Duke and Duchess's daughter Eugenie playing naked in the garden of their home without parental consent.

13 Shannon notes that at the same time as his public disquiet about the press, David Mellor was having an adulterous affair with an actress and being investigated by sections of the tabloid press (Shannon 2001: 101). Details of the affair with Antonia da Sancha were obtained by the *People* bugging the actress's flat (with her consent) and 'wiring up the bed' (Cloonan 1998: 65).

14 The case involved the 1991 publication by the *Sunday People* of clandestinely taken photographs of the young naked Princess Eugenie, who is the young daughter of the Duke and Dutchess of York (Cloonan 1998).

15 In addition to Calcutt, in 1994 the government set up the Nolan Committee on Standards in Public Life in response to increasing public disquiet about the conduct of
members of Parliament which had been exposed in the media. Nolan set out seven
principles of public life including honesty, selflessness and integrity, yet despite Nolan,
the issue of 'sleaze' became closely associated with the Major government.

16 Despite claims by Diana's brother Earl Spencer that the press 'had her blood on its
hands', the cause of the crash that killed Diana and her lover Dodi Al Fayed was
subsequently attributed to her driver being drunk.

17 Which came into force from October 2000 (Tambini and Hayward 2002).

18 Lord Wakeham (2002: 28) suggests that the New Labour government initially intended
that the legislation would only apply to government departments and local authorities
and not the courts. Yet the specific terms of the legislation Wakeham suggests meant that
the 'change occurred because the method of incorporation turned the courts into public
authorities with the power to "enforce" the Convention both against government and in
any private actions brought before them'. See also Shannon 2001: 286–87.

19 Barendt notes that privacy 'should be defined in a non exhaustive way to cover private
correspondence and papers, confidential discussions, intimate sexual conduct and health'
(2002: 19).

20 The Princess Diana gym photographs and the Kaye case are moot. One of the first test
cases of the HRA was when newsreader Anna Ford complained to the PCC that her
privacy had been invaded when newspapers published photographs of her on a public
beach in Majorca. The PCC rejected her claim arguing that a public beach in the holiday season was no place where there would be a reasonable expectation of privacy. Ford
appealed but was denied a judicial review of the PCC adjudication. The Judge, Mr.
Justice Silber, suggested that the PCC was in a far better position to decide on such
matters than the courts.

21 These would include: 'the exposure or investigation of crime, or serious misconduct,
incompetence, or deception on the part of the complainant' (2002: 19).

22 The disappearance of Madeleine McCann, a three year-old girl on holiday with her
parents in Portugal in 2007, caused a major media frenzy, particularly amongst the
popular tabloid press. Though media coverage was seen as essential in attempts to find
the child, rumour and speculation started to emerge about her parents' involvement in
her disappearance with the *Daily Express, Sunday Express, Daily Star* and *Daily Star Sunday*
suggesting the parents had somehow been involved in the death of their daughter and had
attempted to cover up the crime. In 2008 Express Newspapers were forced to issue front
page apologies to the parents of the missing child and pay damages of £550,000.

23 The first so-called 'super-injunction' was brought by law firm Carter-Ruck acting on
behalf of Trafigura, a company specializing in oil and mineral trading, who attempted to
prevent the *Guardian* newspaper from reporting a Parliamentary question by Paul Farrelly
MP concerning the alleged dumping of toxic waste by the firm. The Parliamentary
Papers Act of 1840 (section 3) guarantees that 'any extract from or abstract of' a 'report, paper,
votes, or proceedings' of Parliament is immune from civil and criminal liability if published in good faith and 'without malice'. The right of the press to report matters in
parliament is also codified in statute in Schedule 1 of the Defamation Act 1996. This
confers 'qualified privilege', which is again subject to the tests of the report being 'fair
and accurate, and published without malice' and generally in the public interest' (HoC
Reports HC 362-I: 32).

24 Campaign for Press and Broadcasting Freedom (2003).

Chapter 7: Libel and the public interest

1 For a more thorough analysis of the legal complexities of libel and its relationship with
freedom of speech and expression, see Milo (2008); see also Barendt (2005) Chapter 6.

2 See also Milo (2008).

3 'Public General Statutes and Measures' (60 Geo. 3 & 1 Geo. 4 c. 8) *An Act for the more effectual Prevention and Punishment of Blasphemous and Seditious Libels.* 30 December 1819.

4 http://www.guardian.co.uk/theguardian/from-the-archive-blog/2011/jun/06/news-papers-national-newspapers

5 *British Chiropractic Association v Dr. Singh* [2010] EWCA Civ 350 at: http://www.bailii.org/ew/cases/EWCA/Civ/2010/350.html

6 See the photography of Margaret Bourke-White at: http://www.gallerym.com/work.cfm?ID=856. See also David Campbell (2002a and 2002b).

7 Though criminal libel is no longer used.

8 As long as it is not actuated by malice the defence of 'fair comment' is allowed 'so long as that comment amounts to an opinion that an honest (but not necessarily fair-minded) person might express on a matter of public interest' (Robertson and Nicol 2008: 149–50). However a recent ruling by the Supreme Court has led to the defence of 'fair comment' to be changed to 'honest comment' which effectively means that 'No longer is it incumbent on the defendant to provide the facts on which the comment is based in sufficient detail so as to leave the reader in a position to judge for himself how far the comment was well-founded' (Ponsford 2010). The defence of honest comment has also been included in the draft Defamation Bill 2011.

9 However, as Fenwick and Phillipson note, following Reynolds there has been a process of reverting back to the judge (2006: 1043).

10 *Reynolds v Times Newspapers Ltd. and others* [1999] 4 All ER 609.

11 *See Lange v Australian Broadcasting Corporation* [1997] 189 C.L.R. 520 and *Lange v. Atkinson* [1998] 3 N.Z.L.R. 424.

12 Which are:

   i. The seriousness of the allegation. The more serious the charge, the more the public is misinformed and the individual harmed, if the allegation is not true.
   ii. The nature of the information, and the extent to which the subject-matter is a matter of public concern.
   iii. The source of the information. Some informants have no direct knowledge of the events. Some have their own axes to grind, or are being paid for their stories.
   iv. The steps taken to verify the information.
   v. The status of the information. The allegation may have already been the subject of an investigation which commands respect.
   vi. The urgency of the matter. News is often a perishable commodity.
   vii. Whether comment was sought from the plaintiff. He may have information others do not possess or have not disclosed. An approach to the plaintiff will not always be necessary.
   viii. Whether the article contained the gist of the plaintiff's side of the story.
   ix. The tone of the article. A newspaper can raise queries or call for an investigation. It need not adopt allegations as statements of fact.
   x. The circumstances of the publication, including the timing.

   Nicholls L. J. (1999). See also Robertson and Nicol (2008:164–68).

13 Knox was convicted in 2009 of murdering the British exchange student Meredith Kercher in 2007 in Perugia. Knox had previously posted information about herself online which included short stories involving rape and pictures of her wielding a gun (RISJ 2009). Media coverage of the trial, particularly in Italy, focussed heavily on Knox's online sexual persona yet as the RISJ report notes much of the information about Knox was posted online by Knox herself; so where was the invasion of privacy?

14 See Sections 6(1) and 6(3) HRA 1998: http://www.legislation.gov.uk/ukpga/1998/42/section/6.

15 *New York Times Co. v. Sullivan* (1964) 376 U.S. 254 at: http://www.law.cornell.edu/supct/html/historics/USSC_CR_0376_0254_ZS.html

16 http://www.englishpen.org/.

17 http://www.indexoncensorship.org/.

Chapter 8: Security and insecurity

1 At the time of writing there were four government departments represented on the DPBAC, Home Office, Ministry of Defence, Foreign and Commonwealth Office and the Cabinet Office.

2 At the time of writing the membership representing the press and broadcasting included among others: Michael Jermey, ITV Director of News, Current Affairs and Sport; Peter Barron, Head of Communications and Public Affairs for Google in Northern and Central Europe; Bob Satchwell, Executive Director of the Society of Editors. See http://www.dnotice.org.uk/commitee.htm#press_broadcasting.

3 Samina Malik was charged under Section 57 of the Terrorism Act (2000), which relates to the possession of material that could be used in the 'commission, preparation or instigation of an act of terrorism' (Terrorism Act 2000, sec. 57) and Section 58 of the Act which deals with possession of material 'likely to be useful to a person committing or preparing an act of terrorism' (Terrorism Act 2000, sec. 58). Malik, who dubbed herself the 'Lyrical Terrorist' because of her poems in praise of Osama Bin Laden and martyrdom, had visited various radical Islamic websites and was found in possession of a number of terrorist manuals (*The Guardian* 2008b). Malik was found not guilty of the charge under Section 57 and won her appeal against her conviction under Section 58 (BBC 2008). Another case involved Nottingham University administrative worker Hicham Yezza was arrested under the 2007 Act for downloading an al-Qaeda training handbook from a U.S. government website for use in his friend, Rizwaan Sabir's PhD research proposal. Both men were held in police custody for six days but were eventually released without charge (*The Guardian* 2008a).

4 More recently, *Sunday Tribune* Northern Ireland editor Suzanne Breen was pressurised by the Police Service of Northern Ireland (PSNI) to hand over material related to her stories about the Real IRA. Breen successfully argued in court that not only would this put her life in real danger, but also it would undermine her commitment as a journalist and member of the NUJ to protect the identity of sources.

5 In 1995 the European Court of Human Rights ruled that the IRA members had been 'unnecessarily killed' (Mills 1995).

6 Some of the examples that Cohen-Almagor cites include: *Der Stern* magazine's revelation that the police were intending to play for time and had no intention of submitting to the demands of a group of kidnappers who were holding a man hostage in 1977. This came to the attention of the kidnappers, ultimately resulting in the death of the kidnap victim.

7 Putin had argued that media coverage 'hampered' the rescue mission at the time. See BBC (2005) at: http://news.bbc.co.uk/1/hi/world/europe/4187924.stm.

8 During the Beslan School siege the live pictures were provided by CNN and the BBC, with the Russian media showing only a limited amount of live coverage following president Vladimir Putin's criticism of the Russian media's coverage of the Moscow theatre siege. *The Guardian* newspaper reported that because of the history of state interference in the media in Russia, public confidence of the media is low. See Tryhorn (2004).

9 Sarah Oates has suggested that the rhetoric of fear of terrorism has played a significant role in the election campaigns in Russia and the United States in particular, with these countries evoking an emotional and patriotic response towards terrorism within national election campaigns (see Oates 2006: 425–37; see also Lipman 2009).

10 For a full transcript of the interview see http://transcripts.cnn.com/TRANSCRIPTS/0304/14/lkl.00.html.

11 See Rendall and Broughel (2003).

12 See also Bumiller (2003).

13 *The Sun*'s famous 1982 front page headline 'Gotcha', which pictured the sinking Argentinean cruiser the *General Belgrano* after being hit by a torpedo from a British submarine, and *The Sun* headline 'Stick it up your Junta', also during the Falklands crisis, are often highlighted as archetypal examples of tabloid nationalism in warfare. (See also Conboy 2006).

14 Pilger (2007) at: http://www.johnpilger.com/articles/looking-to-the-side-from-belsen-to-gaza.

15 Knightly (2003: 44) notes that war correspondents were often encouraged to confine their writing to 'narratives of adventure' rather than providing readers with dry facts and figures of battle, political commentary or overt moralising.

16 Such as the films *Apocalypse Now* (1979), *Salvador* (1986), *The Year of Living Dangerously* (1982) and the television series *Generation Kill* (2008).

17 The name was changed to the Ministry of Information in 1939.

18 These measures included the 1910 Official Secrets Act (see Carruthers 2000).

19 Two separate scenes in particular seem to have penetrated the public consciousness about the awful spectacle of war, particularly the war in Vietnam. The first are photographs and television footage of the U.S. Napalm attack on the Vietnamese village Trang Bang, which showed a badly burned ten year-old Vietnamese girl Phan Thi Kim Phúc fleeing the village with horrific burns on her body. The second iconic image is film footage and photographs of the fall of Saigon, and U.S. marines and Vietnamese civilians frenetically scrambling into helicopters from the roof of the U.S. compound in Saigon as America withdrew from the war in humiliating defeat. The scenes and the experience of Vietnam as a whole left an indelible mark on the U.S. psyche which successive U.S. and British administrations have born in mind when contemplating their relations with the media during conflict.

20 Attacks and orchestrated uprisings by the North Vietnamese in the south of the country on the annual Tet holiday were portrayed by U.S. journalists in largely negative terms despite the fact that the Offensive culminated in a significant setback for the North. See Carruthers (2000: 116–19) and Braestrup (1989).

21 Morrison and Tumber (1988: 119–20) suggest that 'some correspondents [reported] erroneous information; their doing so was, as Lieutenant David Tinker wrote in his letters home, an astonishing example of their "readiness to lie"'.

22 See the interview at: http://www.youtube.com/watch?v=rWOy23MLY1I.

23 See Mrs. Thatcher greeting the press at: http://www.youtube.com/watch?v=rGxsLbK9F0A.

24 The New Right is a term closely associated with the politics of the Thatcher and Regan era during the 1980s in which classical liberal economic theory was integrated into conservative political doctrine.

25 As Greenslade (2009b) notes, the identity of Ms. Tisdall was exposed because of markings on the memoranda.

26 The then Attorney-General, Sir Michael Havers QC also attempted to stop MPs from screening the programme in the House of Commons (see Bradley 1987a and 1987b).

27 These include Chapman Pincher's book *Their Trade is Treachery* (1981), which was even serialised by the *Daily Mail*; and the failure of the government to prosecute programme makers and contributors (including Peter Wright himself) when they had contributed to a 'World in Action' programme detailing the activities of the British Secret Service.

28 HC Deb 03 December 1986 vol 106 cc938–92 at: http://hansard.millbanksystems.com/commons/1986/dec/03/security-services-commission#S6CV0106P0_19861203_HOC_244.

29 HC Deb 14 March 1988 vol 129 cc852–4 at: http://hansard.millbanksystems.com/commons/1988/mar/14/spycatcher#S6CV0129P0_19880314_HOC_126.

30 Steel 2008.

31 In a later work (2007) Hammond develops the key points of this paper, suggesting that postmodernity and the challenges that it put forward to the 'grand narratives' of the Enlightenment following the collapse of the Berlin Wall in 1989, were crucial in understanding modern warfare and its coverage in the media. In addition to the amplification of the moral high ground in modern times one of the key developments in post-Cold War conflict has been the predominance of identity politics as a defining parameters of conflict. See also Ignatiev (1999); Kaldor (1999).

32 For Seymour Hersh's original *New Yorker* article see: http://www.newyorker.com/archive/2004/05/10/040510fa_fact.

33 Yet these images only reached the attention of the mainstream media after rumours of prisoner abuse had been circulating in the US press for some time (Ricchiardi 2004).
34 See Jacobs (2003) and Ricchiardi (2003).

Chapter 9: Ownership

1 Beaverbrook Newspapers; Associated Newspapers *Daily Mirror* Group; News of the World; Kemsley Newspapers and Odhams Press (Murdock and Golding 1978).
2 For example: 'Give the Blackshirts a Helping Hand' and 'Hurrah for the Blackshirts'(blackshirts, of course, being the uniform of the British Union of Fascists).
3 Bingham suggests that the mid-1920s, the early 1950s and the mid-1980s were times when political interest in regulating the press reached their height.
4 See F. S. Siebert, T. Peterson, and W. Schramm (1956) *Four Theories of the Press*, Urbana and Chicago: University of Illinois Press.
5 Paterson was aiming to expand the notion of positive and negative freedom, as developed by Isaiah Berlin, to a conception of freedom of the press (see Chapter 1).
6 British Sky Broadcasting Group PLC (2011).
7 In an undercover operation by *Daily Telegraph* reporters posing as Liberal Democrat supporters exposed Cable's animosity towards Murdoch's media empire. In the secret recording Cable was heard saying that he 'had declared war on Murdoch'. One of Cable's roles as business secretary was to look impartially at the proposed takeover, yet his comments, in addition to causing embarrassment for the Conservative/Liberal Coalition government, have exposed his lack of impartiality in the quasi-judicial process. His comments also meant that he has had to step aside and hand over control of the issue to the ideologically more sympathetic Culture Secretary Jeremy Hunt. See Winnett (2010).
8 European Commission (2010).
9 Though News Corp would retain 39.21 per cent of the business.
10 The title for the book *Manufacturing Consent: the Political Economy of the Mass Media* actually came about through Herman and Chomsky's reading of Walter Lippmann's *Public Opinion* (1950) in which Lippmann is concerned with formulating the idea that the media's role in complex democracies such as the United States should be with regard to maintaining a largely passive and entertained public (see Chapter 3). Herman and Chomsky seem convinced that by and large, the media has historically and continues to perform this function.
11 For example Chomsky was roundly criticised by former left-wing commentator Christopher Hitchens following the attacks on 11 September 2001 for suggesting that the attacks by Al-Qaeda on 9/11 were morally on par with the 1998 U.S. bombing of the Al-Shifa pharmaceutical factory in Khartoum. Hitchens suggests that Chomsky's logic 'seems to entail the weird and sinister assumption that Bin Laden is a ventriloquist for thwarted voices of international justice' (http://www.thenation.com/article/rejoinder-noam-chomsky). For Chomsky's response to Hitchens see http://www.thenation.com/article/reply-hitchenss-rejoinder; for further discussion see http://www.thenation.com/article/left-debates-september-11.

Chapter 10: Constitutive censorship: News, language and culture

1 Chas Critcher, Tony Jefferson, John N. Clarke and Brian Roberts.
2 Martin Smith (1994) argues that the resignation of Howe and the controversy over the so-called poll tax provides only a relatively short-term and simplistic explanation of Thatcher's resignation. He suggests that a prime minister is always dependent on the support of his or her Cabinet and in Thatcher's case 'she failed to recognize her dependence on the Cabinet or to understand the patterns of dependence within the Cabinet' (Smith 1994: 361). According to this perspective then even a PM with the dominant persona of Margaret Thatcher still has to negotiate and compromise with their Cabinet minsters and her failure to recognise and act on this eventually led to her downfall.

3 Across Europe, studies have shown the debates around PC exhibit similarities to those in the U.S. and U.K. though there are some marked differences. See see Johnson and Suhr 2003; Toolan 2003.

4 See for example the hysterically titled *The Persecution of Sarah Palin: How the Elite Media Tried to Bring Down a Rising Star*, by Michael Continetti (2009) or John Gibson's *How the Left Swiftboated America: The Liberal Media Conspiracy to Make You Think George Bush Was the Worst President in History* (2009).

5 For example Petley (2005) analyses the manufacture of stories in the right-wing national and provincial press on councils banning 'black' bin liners as they are perceived as racist; banning the use of the phrase 'manhole' cover as sexist language, and the infamous and still resonant myth of the banning of the nursery rhyme 'baa baa black sheep' as racist. See Petley (2005) pp. 85–107. Indeed in a recent seminar an undergraduate student was of the view that the said nursery rhyme was indeed banned or had been re-written to 'de-racialise' it.

6 I am hesitant to use this phrase given that it overly personalises what was in essence a political and economic reaction to the breakdown of political and economic consensus. Nevertheless, the term usefully characterises an era in which politics changed fundamentally, a change that has not seen its hegemonic victories reversed in any significant way.

7 *Daily Mail*, Monday, 31 January 2000.

8 *Daily Mail*, Wednesday, 26 January 2000.

9 *Daily Mail*, Thursday, 3 February 2000.

10 *The Guardian*, 14 February 2000.

11 http://www.kenanmalik.com/debates/prospect_diversity.html.

12 Examples include increases in surveillance under the Regulation of Investigatory Powers Act (RIPA) 2000; Pre-charge detention for suspected terrorists increased from 14 to 28 days, though the Labour government attempted to increase this to 42 days; the Serious Organised Crime and Police Act (2005) which prevents protesters campaigning within one kilometre of Parliament; Section 44 of the Terrorism Act 2000 gives the police powers to stop and search anyone within a specified area. Finally, according to Liberty, the Terrorism Act 2006 'created unacceptably broad speech offences' which 'represent a serious incursion on free speech rights, criminalising careless talk and banning non-violent political organizations.' At: http://www.liberty-human-rights.org.uk/issues/6-free-speech/terrorism-act-2006/index.shtml.

13 Christian Voice (no date) 'Jerry Springer Home', at: http://www.christianvoice.org.uk/springer.html.

14 Ofcom (2005) http://stakeholders.ofcom.org.uk/binaries/enforcement/broadcast-bulletins/pcb63/bull32.pdf.

15 Lee also notes that the particular commercial dynamics of the publishing industry enabled the publishers Penguin 'to orchestrate a publicity campaign which at first thrived on controversy' (Lee 1990: 74).

16 Ofcom (2007) http://stakeholders.ofcom.org.uk/binaries/enforcement/broadcast-bulletins/obb97/issue97.pdf.

17 Holmwood, L. (2008) 'Dispatches damages to go to charity', *The Guardian*, at: http://www.guardian.co.uk/media/2008/may/15/channel4.television1.

18 The newspaper had decided to seek representations of Mohammed following the news that children's author Kare Bluitgen was finding it difficult to find an illustrator for his book on the Koran and the life of the Prophet Mohammed. *Jyllands-Posten* therefore invited illustrators to draw Mohammed to see if free speech was under threat (see Hervik *et al* 2008).

19 Under then current blasphemy law it was only the Church of England that was protected, even though the *Gay News* trial in the 1970s effectively 'brought an end to prosecutions for blasphemy as a means of defending the Christian religion or avenging insults against it' (Thomas 2007: 347). Moreover, other religions such as Sikhism and Judaism were protected under the race hatred laws as these religions are perceived as analogous to racial identity. Islam did not therefore have the same sort of protection that other religions had.

20 See David Brooks's (2002) review of *Orwell's Victory*, also titled *Why Orwell Matters* by Christopher Hitchens. Brooks argues contra to Hitchens that Orwell is no longer relevant as the world to which Orwell was addressing bears no comparison to that of the twenty-first century. Moreover, the 'democratic imperialism' of the U.S. in places like Serbia and Afghanistan in which the U.S. is fighting 'Islamic fascism' does not compare to the imperialism that Orwell detested.

BIBLIOGRAPHY

Addley, E. (2011) WikiLeaks: Julian Assange 'faces execution or Guantanamo detention', *The Guardian*, 11 January, at: http://www.guardian.co.uk/media/2011/jan/11/julian-assange-wikileaks-execution-gantanamo

Addley, E. and Halliday, J. (2010) 'WikiLeaks supporters disrupt Visa and MasterCard sites in "Operation Payback"', *The Guardian*, 9 December, at: http://www.guardian.co.uk/world/2010/dec/08/wikileaks-visa-mastercard-operation-payback

Al Marashi, I. (2006) 'Iraq's Cyber-Insurgency: The Internet and the Iraqi Resistance', in R. D. Berenger (ed.) *Cybermedia Go To War*, Spokane: Marquette Books.

Ali, M. (2005) 'Do We Need Laws on Hatred?', in L. Appignanesi (ed.) (2005) *Free Expression is No Offence*, London: Penguin.

Allan, S. (1999) *News Culture*, Buckingham: Open University Press.

Allen, S. and Thorsen, E. (2009) *Citizen Journalism: Global Perspectives*, New York: Peter Lang.

Altheide, D. L. (2002) *Creating Fear*, New York: Aldine de Gruyter.

American Civil Liberties Union (2005) 'National Security Letters', 30 November, at: http://www.aclu.org/national-security_technology-and-liberty/national-security-letters.

Amnesty International (2006) 'Undermining Freedom of Expression in China The role of Yahoo!, Microsoft and Google', at: http://www.amnesty.org/en/library/asset/POL30/026/2006/en/1ce1ac2d-d41b-11dd-8743-d305bea2b2c7/pol300262006en.pdf

Anderson, B. (1991) *Imagined Communities Reflections on the Orginal and Spread of Nationalism*, London: Verso.

Anderson, P. J. 'Competing Models of Journalism and Democracy', in P. J. Anderson and G. Ward (eds) *The Future of Journalism in Advanced Democracies*, Aldershot: Ashgate.

Anderson, P. J. and Ward, G. (2007) *The Future of Journalism in the Advanced Democracies*, Aldershot: Ashgate.

Appignanesi, L. (ed.) (2005) *Free Expression is No Offence*, London: Penguin.

Atton, C. (2002) *Alternative Media*, London: Sage.

Bambauer, D. (2006) 'Cool Tools for Tyrants', *Legal Affairs*, at: http://www.legalaffairs.org/printerfriendly.msp?id=964

Barendt, E. (2002) 'Media Intrusion: the case for legislation', in D. Tambini and C. Heyward (eds) *Ruled by Recluses? Privacy, Journalism and the Media After the Human Rights Act*, London: IPPR.

——(2005) *Free Speech*, 2nd edn, Clarendon: Oxford University Press.

——(2009) *Freedom of the Press*, Farnham: Ashgate.

Barendt, E., Lustgarten, L., Norrie, K. and Stephenson, H. (1996) *Libel and the Media The Chilling Effect*, Clarendon: Oxford Press.

Barker, H. (1998) *Newspapers, Politics and Public Opinion in Late Eighteenth-century England*, Oxford: Clarendon Press.

——(2000) *Newspapers, Politics and English Society, 1695–1855*, Harlow: Longman.

Barnett, A., Held, D. and Henderson, C. (2005) *Debating Globalization*, Cambridge: Polity.

Barnett, S. and Gaber, I. (2001) *Westminster Tales: The Twenty First Century Crisis in Political Journalism*, London: Continuum.

BBC (2005) 'Beslan Children Still Tormented', 30 August, at: http://news.bbc.co.uk/1/hi/world/europe/4187924.stm

——(2005) 'On this day, 26 November', at: http://news.bbc.co.uk/onthisday/hi/dates/stories/november/26/newsid_3220000/3220635.stm

——(2005) Editorial Guidelines, Harm and Offence, at: http://www.bbc.co.uk/guidelines/editorialguidelines/assets/guidelinedocs/chapter_eight.pdf

——(2008) '"Lyrical Terrorist' Wins Appeal', 17 June, at: http://news.bbc.co.uk/1/hi/uk/7459180.stm

——(2009) 'Police to Pay Costs in Suzanne Breen Real IRA Note Case', 4 December, at: http://news.bbc.co.uk/1/hi/northern_ireland/8395236.stm

——(2010) 'Editorial Guidelines', at: http://www.bbc.co.uk/guidelines/editorialguidelines/guidelines/

——(2011a) 'Lord Neuberger: Web Injunction Leaks 'a problem', at: http://www.bbc.co.uk/news/uk-13470162

——(2011b) 'How We Govern the BBC', at: http://www.bbc.co.uk/bbctrust/about/how_we_govern/charter_and_agreement/

BBC Trust (2011) *Finding of the Editorial Standards Committee of the BBC Trust, Panorama: Death in the Med*, BBC Trust.

Bell, A. (1991) 'Language Style as Audience Design', *Language in Society*, 13, 145–204.

Bell, M. (1998) 'The Journalism of Attachment' in M. Kieran (ed.) *Media Ethics*, London: Routlege.

Belmas, G. and Overbeck, W. (2011) *Major Principles of Media Law*, Boston: Wadsworth Publishing.

Benson, R. and Neveu, E. (2005) 'Introduction: Field Theory as a Work in Progress' in R. Benson and E. Neveu (eds) *Bourdieu and the Journalistic Field*, Cambridge: Polity.

Berenger, R. D. (ed.) (2006) *Cybermedia Go To War*, Spokane: Marquette Books.

Berglez, P. (2008) 'What is Global Journalism?', *Journalism Studies*, 9, 6, 845–58.

Berlin, I. (1969) *Four Essays on Liberty*, Oxford: Oxford University Press.

Berry, D. and Theobald, J. (eds) (2006) *Radical Mass Media Criticism*, Montreal: Black Rose Books.

Bingham, A. (2007) 'Drinking in the Last Chance Saloon', *Media History*, 13, 1, 79–92.

Black, T. (2011) 'A Demeaning Epidemic of Injunctionitis', Spiked Online, 23 May, at: http://www.spiked-online.com/index.php/site/article/10538/

Blumler, J. G. and Gurevitch, M. (1981) 'Politicians and the Press: an essay on role relationships', in D. Nimmo and K. Saunders (eds) *Handbook of Political Communication*, London and Beverly Hills, California: Sage.

Bodi, F. (2004) 'Al Jazeera's War' in D. Miller (ed.) *Tell Me Lies*, London: Pluto Press.

Boling, P. (1996) *Privacy and the Politics of Intimate Life*, Ithaca: Cornel University Press.

Bollinger, L. C. and Stone, G. R. (2002) *Eternally Vigilant: Free Speech in the Modern Era*, Chicago: University of Chicago Press.

Bolton, R. (1990) *Death on the Rock and Other Stories*, London: WH Allen & Co.

Booth, R. (2009) 'BBC is Right to Allow BNP on *Question Time*, says Mark Thompson', *The Guardian*, at: http://www.guardian.co.uk/politics/2009/oct/21/bbc-bnp-mark-thompson

Bowcott, O. (2011) 'Superinjunctions: Modern Technology Out of Control, Says Lord Chief Justice', *The Guardian*, 20 May, at: http://www.guardian.co.uk/law/2011/may/20/superinjunction-modern-technology-lord-judge

Bradley, A. W. (1987a) 'Parliamentary Privilege and the Zircon affair', Public Law, Spring, 1–3.

——(1987b) 'Parliamentary Privilege, Zircon and national security', *Public Law*, Winter, 488–95.

Braestrup, P. (1989) 'An Extreme Case', in G. Sevy (ed.) *The American Experience in Vietnam: A Reader*, Norman, OK: University of Oklahoma Press.

Brewer, J. (1976) *Party, Ideology and Politics at the Accession of George III*, Cambridge: Cambridge University Press.

Briggs, A. and Burke, P. (2009) *A Social History of the Media From Gutenberg to the Internet*, 3rd edn, Cambridge: Polity.

British Sky Broadcasting Group PLC (2011) *Unaudited results for the nine months ended 31 March 2011*, at: http://corporate.sky.com/documents/pdf/latest_results/Q3_1011_Press_Release

Brogan, B. (2011) 'Ryan Giggs is now David Cameron's Problem', *The Telegraph*, blog, 23 May, at: http://blogs.telegraph.co.uk/news/benedictbrogan/100089102/ryan-giggs-is-now-david-camerons-problem/

Brookes, R. (1999) 'Newspapers and National Identity: The BSE/CJD Crisis and the British Press', *Media, Culture & Society*, 21, 247–63.

Brooks, D. (2002) 'Orwell and Us', *Weekly Standard*, 23 September, at: http://www.weeklystandard.com/Content/Public/Articles/000/000/001/653xorlj.asp

Bumiller, E. (2003) 'Keepers of Bush Image Lift Stagecraft to New Heights', *New York Times*, 16 May, at: http://www.nytimes.com/2003/05/16/politics/16IMAG.html

Burnet, D. and Thomas, R. (1989) 'Spycatcher The Commodification of Truth', *Journal of Law and Society*, 16, 2, 107–22.

Bury, J. B. (1952) *A History of Freedom of Thought*, Oxford: Oxford University Press.

Calcutt, D. (1990) *Report of the Committee on Privacy and Related Matters*, London: HMSO.

Cameron, D. (1996) 'Style Policy and Style Politics: a Neglected Aspect of the Language of the News', *Media, Culture & Society*, 18, 2, 315–33.

Campaign for Press and Broadcasting Freedom (2003) 'Privacy and Media Intrusion', submission to the Culture, Media and Sport Committee Inquiry on 'Privacy and Media Intrusion', at: http://www.cpbf.org.uk/body.php?id=397&category=policies& finds=1&string=system%20of%20penalties

Campbell, D. (2002a) 'Atrocity and Memory', at: http://www.david-campbell.org/photography/atrocity-and-memory/

——(2002b) 'Atrocity, Memory, Photography: Imaging the Concentration Camps of Bosnia – the case of ITN versus *Living Marxism* Part 1', *Journal of Human Rights*, 1, 1, 1–33.

——(2009) 'The Fundamentalist Defence of Chomsky on Bosnia', at: http://www.david-campbell.org/2009/11/27/the-fundamentalist-defence-of-chomsky-on-bosnia/

Canovan, M. (2002) 'Democracy and Nationalism', in A. Carter and G. Stokes (eds) *Democratic Theory Today*, Cambridge: Polity Press.

Carey, J. (1989) *Communication as Culture: Essays on Media and Society*, London: Unwin Hyman.

Carruthers, S. (2000) *The Media at War*, Basingstoke: Palgrave Macmillan.

——(2004) 'Tribalism and Tribulation. Media Constructions of "African Savagery" and "Western Humanitarianism" in the 1990s' in S. Allan and B. Zelizer (eds) *Reporting War*, London: Routlege.

Carter, A. (2002) 'Associative Democracy', in A. Carter and G. Stokes (eds) *Democratic Theory Today*, Cambridge: Polity Press.

Chaffee, S. (1975) *Political Communications: Issues and Strategies for Research*, London: Sage.

Chalaby, J. (1998) *The Invention of Journalism*, Basingstoke: Macmillan.

Chapman, J. (2008) 'Republican Citizenship, Ethics and the French Revolutionary Press 1789–92', in R. Keeble (ed.) *Communication Ethics Now*, Leicester: Troubador.

Chibnall, S. (1977) *Law and Order News: An Analysis of Crime Reporting in the British Press*, London: Tavistock.

Chomsky, N. (2001) 'Reply to Hitchens's Rejoinder', The Nation, at: http://www.thenation.com/article/reply-hitchenss-rejoinder

Christian Voice (n.d.), at: http://www.christianvoice.org.uk/springer.html

Clark, A. (2009) 'Rupert Murdoch Plans Charge for all News Websites by Next Summer', *The Guardian*, 6 August, at: http://www.guardian.co.uk/media/2009/aug/06/rupert-murdoch-website-charges

Cloonan, M. (1998) 'Privacy and Media Intrusion in a Democratic Society: Britain and the Calcutt Reports', *Democratization*, 5, 2, 62–84.

Cohen, M. (2002) '"What We Say Goes!" How Bush Sr. Sold the Bombing of Iraq' *CounterPunch*, December, at: http://www.counterpunch.org/cohen1228.html

Cohen, N. (2003) *Pretty Straight Guys*, London: Faber & Faber.

Cohen-Almagor, R. (2001) *Free Speech and Ethics*, London: Palgrave.

——(2006) *The Scope of Tolerance*, London: Routledge.

Coleman, S. (2004) 'Connecting Parliament to the Public via the Internet: Two Case Studies of Online Consultations', Information, Communication and Society 7, 1, 1–22.

——(2007) 'Mediated Politics and Everyday Life', International Journal of Communication, 1, Feature, 49–60.

Collet D. Collet (1899) *A History of Taxes on Knowledge: Their Origin and Repeal, Vols. 1 and 2*, London: T. Fisher Unwin.

Collier (2006) *Modernism on Fleet Street*, Aldershot: Ashgate.

Committee to Protect Journalists (2001) 'CPJ Dismayed by U.S. Pressure against Arab Satellite News Channel', 4 October, at: http://cpj.org/2001/10/cpj-dismayed-by-us-pressure-against-arab-satellite.php

——(2003) 'ITN Correspondent Confirmed Dead; Two Other Crew Members Missing', 23 March, at: http://cpj.org/2003/03/itn-correspondent-confirmed-deadtwo-other-crew-mem.php#more

——(2004) *Attacks on the Press 2003: Iraq*, at: http://cpj.org/2004/03/attacks-on-the-press-2003-iraq.php

——(2006a) *Iraq Report: Killed by U.S. Forces*, at: http://cpj.org/reports/2006/01/js-killed-by-us-13sept05.php

——(2006b) 'British inquest rules ITN reporter unlawfully killed by U.S. troops', at: http://cpj.org/2006/10/british-inquest-rules-itn-reporter-unlawfully-kill.php

——(2009) 'Attacks on the Press 2009: China', at: http://www.cpj.org/2010/02/attacks-on-the-press-2009-china.php

——(2010) 'Journalists Killed in Iraq: Sardasht Osman', at: http://cpj.org/killed/2010/sardasht-osman.php

Conboy, M. (2002) *Press and Popular Culture*, London: Sage.

——(2004) *Journalism and Critical History*, London: Sage.

——(2006) *Tabloid Britain*, London: Routledge.

——(2010) *The Language of the Newspapers*, London: Continuum.

——(2011) *Journalism in Britain: A Historical Introduction*, London: Sage.

Conboy, M. and Steel, J. (2008) 'The Future of Newspapers: Historical Perspectives', *Journalism Studies*, 9, 5, 650–661.

——(2010) 'From "We" to "Me"', *Journalism Studies*, 11, 4, 500–510.

Continetti, M. (2009) *The Persecution of Sarah Palin: How the Elite Media Tried to Bring Down a Rising Star*, New York: Sentinel.

Copeland, D. A. (2006) *The Idea of a Free Press*, Evanston: Northwestern University Press.

Cottle, S. (2006) *Mediatized Conflict*, Maidenhead: Open University Press.

Couldry, N., S. Livingstone and T. Markham (2007) *Media Consumption and Public Engagement*, Basingstoke: Palgrave Macmillan.

Cozens, C. and Milmo, D. (2002) 'Campbell Privacy Case Thrown Out', *The Guardian*, 14 October, at: http://www.guardian.co.uk/media/2002/oct/14/pressandpublishing.privacy2

Crisell, A. (2002) *An Introductory History of British Broadcasting*, 2nd edn, London: Routlege.

Crone, T., Alberstat, P., Cassels, T. and Overs, E. (eds) (2002) *Law and the Media*, Oxford: Focal Press.

Curran, J. (1978) 'The Press as an Agency of Social Control: an Historical Perspective', in G. Boyce, J. Curran and P. Wingate (eds) *Newspaper History: from the 17th Century to the Present Day*, London: Constable.

——(2002) 'Media and the Making of British Society, 1700–2000', *Media History*, 8, 2, 135–54.

Curran, J. and Seaton, J. (1997) *Power Without Responsibility*, 5th edn, London: Routledge.

——(2003) *Power Without Responsibility*, 6th edn, London: Routledge.

——(2010) *Power Without Responsibility*, 7th edn, London: Routledge.

Curran, J. and Witschge, T. (2010) 'Liberal Dreams and the Internet' in N. Fenton (ed.) (2010) *New Media, Old News*, London: Sage.

Curry-Jansen, S. (1991) *Censorship: The Knot that ties Power and Knowledge*, New York: Oxford University Press.

Curtis, A. (2004) *The Power of Nightmares*, BBC.

——(2010) 'The Weird World of Waziriztan', at: http://www.bbc.co.uk/blogs/adamcurtis/2010/04/index.html

——(2011) 'All Watched Over By Machines of Loving Grace', BBC.

Dacre, P. (2008) 'The Threat to Our Press', *The Guardian*, 10 November, at: http://www.guardian.co.uk/media/2008/nov/10/paul-dacre-press-threats

Daily Mail (2000) Wednesday, 26 January.

——(2000) Monday, 31 January.

——(2000) Thursday, 3 February.

Davies, N. (2008) *Flat Earth News*, London: Chatto & Windus.

Davis, A. (2002) *Public Relations Democracy: Public Relations, Politics and the Mass Media in Britain*, Manchester: Manchester University Press.

——(2007) *The Mediation of Power*, London: Routledge.

——(2010) 'Politics, Journalism and New Media: Virtual Iron Cages in the New Culture of Capitalism' in N. Fenton (ed.) (2010) *New Media, Old News*, London: Sage.

Deichmann, T. (1997) 'The Picture that Fooled the World', *LM*, February, 97.

Department for Culture, Media and Sport (2006) *Broadcasting. Copy of Royal Charter for the continuance of the British Broadcasting Corporation*, Cm 6925.

Deuze, M. (2005) 'What is Journalism?', *Journalism*, 6, 4, 442–64.

——(2006) 'Liquid Journalism', *Working Paper*, at: https://scholarworks.iu.edu/dspace/handle/2022/3202?modesimple.

Dewey, J. (1927) *The Public and its problems*, New York: Swallow Press.

Domingo, D., Quandt, T., Heinonen, A., Paulussen, S., Singer, J. B. and Vujnovic, M. 'Participatory Journalism Practices in the Media and Beyond, an International Comparative Study of Initiatives of Online Newspapers', *Journalism Practice*, 2, 3, 326–342.

Downing, J. D. (2001) *Radical Media: Rebellious Communications and Social Movements*, Thousand Oaks, California: Sage.

DPBAC (2010) http://www.dnotice.org.uk/standing_da_notices.htm

Durham-Peters, J. (2005) *Courting the Abyss*, Cambridge University Press.

Eccleshall, R. (2003) 'Conservatism', in R. Eccleshall, A. Finlayson, V. Geoghegan, M. Kenny, M. Lloyd, I. MacKenzie and R. Wilford (eds) *Political Ideologies an Introduction*, 3rd edn, London: Routlege.

Ellison, S. (2011) 'The Man Who Spilled the Secrets', *Vanity Fair*, February, at: http://www.vanityfair.com/politics/features/2011/02/the-guardian-201102

Epstein, R. A. (2000) 'Deconstructing Privacy: And Putting it Back Together Again', *Social Philosophy and Policy*, 17, 2, 1–24.

Eriksen, J. M. and Stjernfelt, F. (2008) *Adskillelsens politik. Multikulturalisme ideology og virkelighed*, Copenhagen: Lindhardt og Ringhof.

European Commission (2010) 'Commission clears News Corp's proposed acquisition of BSkyB under EU merger rules' 21 December, at: http://ec.europa.eu/unitedkingdom/press/press_releases/2010/pr10133_en.htm

European Court of Human Rights (2010) Convention for the Protection of Human Rights and Fundamental Freedoms, at: http://www.echr.coe.int/NR/rdonlyres/D5CC24A7-DC13–4318-B457–5C9014916D7A/0/ENG_CONV.pdf

Exoo, C. F. (2010) *The Pen and the Sword*, California: Sage.

Fairclough, N. (1995) *Critical Discourse Analysis*, London: Routlege.

——(2003) 'Political Correctness': the Politics of Culture and Language' Discourse and Society, *Discourse and Society*, 14, 1, 17–28.

Fairclough, N. and Wodak, R. (1997) 'Critical Discourse Analysis', in T. A. van Dijk (ed.) *Discourse Studies: A Multidisciplinary Introduction*, vol. 2. London: Sage.

Fallows, M. (2008) 'The Connection has Been Reset', *The Atlantic*, March, at: http://www.theatlantic.com/magazine/archive/2008/03/-ldquo-the-connection-has-been-reset-rdquo/6650/

Farrar, M. J. (1989) *News From the Front: War Correspondents on the Western Front 1914–18*, London: Sutton Publishing.

Feinberg, J. (1985) *Offence to Others*, New York: Oxford University Press.

Feintuck, M. and Varney, M. (2006) *Media Regulation, Public Interest and the Law*, Edinburgh: Edinburgh University Press.

Fenton, N. ed. (2010) *New Media, Old News*, London: Sage.

Fenwick, H. and Phillipson, G. (2006) *Media Freedom under the Human Rights Act*, Oxford: Oxford University Press.

Finlay, L. (1991) 'From Watchdog to Lapdog', *Ryerson Review of Journalism*, at: http://www.journalism.ryerson.ca/m3849/

Fish, S. (1994) *There's No Such Thing as Free Speech and it's a Good Thing, Too*, Oxford: Oxford University Press.

Foreign Affairs Committee Eighth Report (2009) *Global Security: Afghanistan and Pakistan*, at: http://www.publications.parliament.uk/pa/cm200809/cmselect/cmfaff/302/30202.htm

Foucault, M. (1977) *Discipline and Punish: The Birth of the Prison*, translated by A. Sheridan, London: Allen Lane.

Fowler, B. (2000) 'A Sociological Analysis of the Satanic Verses Affair', *Theory, Culture & Society*, 17, 9, 39–61.

Fowler, R. (1991) *Language in the News*, London: Routledge.

Franklin, B. (2001) 'The Hand of History: New Labour, News Management and Governance", in S. Ludlam and M. J. Smith (eds) *New Labour in Government*, Basingstoke: Macmillan.

——(2004) *Packaging Politics: Political Communications in Britain's Media Democracy*, London: Edward Arnold.

——(2006) *Local Journalism and Local Media*, 2nd edn, London: Routledge.

Frazer, E. (2002) 'Democracy, Citizenship and Gender', in A. Carter and G. Stokes (eds) *Democratic Theory Today*, Cambridge: Polity Press.

Freeden, M. (1991) *Rights*, Buckingham: Open University Press.

Frenk, J. (2008) 'Freedom Filtered', *Journal for the Study of British Cultures*, 15, 2, 171–82.

Frost, C. (2010). 'The Development of Privacy Adjudications by the UK Press Complaints Commission and their Effects on the Future of Journalism', *Journalism Practice*, 4, 3, 383–93.

Furedi, F. (2005) *Politics of Fear*, London: Continuum.

Gaber, I. (2004) 'Alastair Campbell's exit stage left: Do the "Phillis" recommendations represent a new chapter in political communications or is it "business as usual"?', *Journal of Public Affairs*, 4, 4, 365-373.

Galtung, J. and Ruge, M. (1965) 'The Structure of Foreign News', *Journal of Peace Research*, 2, 1, 64–91.

Gamble, A. (1994) *Britain in Decline*, Basingstoke: Macmillan.

Gans, H. (1980) *Deciding What's News: A study of CBS evening news, NBC nightly news, 'Newsweek' and 'Time'*, London: Constable.

Garnham, N. (2000) *Emancipation, the Media, and Modernity*, Oxford: Oxford University Press.

Gastil, J. (2008) *Political Communication and Deliberation*, Thousand Oaks, California: Sage.

Gerrits (1992) 'Terrorists' Perspectives: Memoirs', in D. L. Paletz and A. P. Schmid (eds) *Terrorism and the Media*, Newbury Park: Sage.

Gibb, F. (2010) 'Science Libel Verdict is a Forceful Blow in Defence of Freedom of Speech', *The Times*, 2 April.

Gibbons, T. (1998) *Regulating the Media*, 2nd edn, London: Sweet & Maxwell.

Gibson, J. (2009) *How the Left Swiftboated America: The Liberal Media Conspiracy to Make You Think George Bush Was the Worst President in History*, New York: Collins.

Gilmartin, K. (1996) *Print Politics: The Press and Radical Opposition in Early Nineteenth-Century England*, Cambridge: Cambridge University Press.

Glanville, J. and Heawood, J. (2009) *Free Speech is Not For Sale. The Impact of English Libel Law on Freedom of Expression*, A Report by English PEN & Index on Censorship, London: English PEN & Index on Censorship.

Goldacre, B. (2010) 'Mutual Criticism is Vital in Science. Libel Laws Threaten it', *The Guardian*, 8 December, at: http://www.guardian.co.uk/commentisfree/2010/dec/08/science-libel-laws-mutual-criticism

Golding, P. (1998) 'Global Village or Cultural Pillage?' in R. W. McChesney, E. M. Wood and J. B. Foster (eds) *Capitalism and the Information Age*, New York: Monthly Review Press.

Golding, P. and Murdoch, G. (2000) 'Culture, Communications and Political Economy', in J. Curran and M. Gurevitch (eds) *Mass Media and Society*, 3rd edn, London: Hodder Arnold.

Gopsill, T. (2004) 'Target the Media', in D. Miller (ed.) *Tell Me Lies*, London: Pluto Press.

Gordon, A. J. (1997) 'John Stuart Mill and the Marketplace of Ideas', *Social Theory and Practice*, 23, 2, 235–49.

Gough, H. (1988) *The Newspaper Press in the French Revolution*, London: Routledge.

Graber, D. A. (2003) 'Terrorism, Censorship and the 1st Amendment', in P. Norris, M. Kern and M. Just (eds) *Framing Terrorism*, New York: Routledge.

Gramsci, A. (1992) *Prison Notebooks*, Vol. 1, edited and translated by J. A. Buttgieg and A. Callari, New York: Columbia University Press.

——(1996) *Prison Notebooks*, Vol. 2, edited and translated by J. A. Buttgieg, New York: Columbia University Press.

Gray, J. (1995) *Liberalism*, Buckingham: Open University Press.

Greenslade, R. (2004) *Press Gang*, Basingstoke Macmillan.

——(2009a) 'Rise of 'super injunction' is Serious Threat to Free Speech', *London Evening Standard*, 14 October, at: http://www.thisislondon.co.uk/standard-business/article-23756189-rise-of-super-injunction-is-serious-threat-to-free-speech.do

——(2009b) 'Public Interest v Individual Freedom', *The Guardian*, 28 September, at: http://www.guardian.co.uk/media/2009/sep/28/mps-expenses-revealing-press-sources

——(2010a) 'Will These Libel Reforms Help Press Freedom?' *London Evening Standard*, 24 June, at: http://www.thisislondon.co.uk/markets/article-23848772-will-these-libel-reforms-help-press-freedom.do

——(2010b) 'Obama Seals off US Journalists and Authors from Britain's Libel Laws', *The Guardian*, 11 August, at: http://www.guardian.co.uk/media/greenslade/2010/aug/11/medialaw-barack-obama

Greenwald, R. (2004) *Outfoxed: Rupert Murdoch's War on Journalism*, Carolina Productions.

——(2011) 'How Propaganda poisons the Mind – and Our Discourse', *Salon*, 12 January, at: http://www.salon.com/news/opinion/glenn_greenwald/2011/01/12/propaganda/index.html

Gripsrud, J. (2000) 'Tabloidization, Popular Journalism, and Democracy', in C. Sparks and J. Tulloch (eds) *Tabloid Tales*, Lanham: Rowman & Littlefield.

Guardian, The (2007) 'FBI Abused Patriot Act Powers, Audit Finds', 9 March, at: http://www.guardian.co.uk/world/2007/mar/09/usa

——(2008a) 'Student Researching al-Qaida Tactics Held for Six Days', 24 May, at: http://www.guardian.co.uk/education/2008/may/24/highereducation.uk

——(2008b) ''Lyrical Terrorist' Has Conviction Quashed', 17 June, at: http://www.guardian.co.uk/uk/2008/jun/17/uksecurity.ukcrime

——(2009) 'BBC is Right to Allow BNP on *Question Time*, says Mark Thompson', at: http://www.guardian.co.uk/politics/2009/oct/21/bbc-bnp-mark-thompson

——(2010) 'Volatile General Election Campaign will Blow the Old Order Apart', at: http://www.guardian.co.uk/politics/2010/may/02/david-miliband-general-election

——(2011) 'Jonathan Aitken Unsheathes his Sword of Truth', 11 April, at: http://www.guardian.co.uk/theguardian/from-the-archive-blog/2011/jun/06/newspapers-national-newspapers

Gutmann, A. (1980) *Liberal Equality*, Cambridge: Cambridge University Press.

Gutmann, A. and Thompson, D. (1996) *Democracy and Disagreement*, London: Belknap Press.

Haas, T. (2007) *The Pursuit of Public Journalism*, New York: Routlege.

Habermas, J. (1989) *The Structural Transformation of the Public Sphere: An Inquiry into the Category of Bourgeois Society*, translated by Thomas Burgher, Cambridge: Polity.

Hafez, K. (2007) *The Myth of Media Globalization*, translated by A. Skinner, Cambridge: Polity Press.

Haggerty, K. D and Ericson, R. V. (2000) 'The Surveillant Assemblage', *British Journal of Sociology*, 51, 4, 605–22.

Hall, S. (1988) *The Hard Road to Renewal: Thatcherism and the Crisis of the Left*, London: Verso.

—— (1994) 'Some 'Politically Incorrect' Pathways Through PC', in S. Dunant (ed.) *The War of the Words*, London; Virago.

Hall, S. and Jaques, M. (eds) (1983) *The Politics of Thatcherism*, London: Lawrence and Wishart in association with *Marxism Today*.

Hall, S., Critcher, C., Jefferson, T., Clarke, J. N. and Roberts, B. (1978) *Policing the Crisis: Mugging, the State, and Law and Order*, Basingstoke: Macmillan.

Halliday, F. (1986) *The Making of the Second Cold War*, 2nd edn, London: Verso.

Halliday, J. (2010a) 'Puttnam on the PCC: 'I'd Give it a Year'', *The Guardian*, 30 June, at: http://www.guardian.co.uk/media/2010/jun/30/scrap-pcc-says-lord-puttnam.

——(2010b) Times Loses Almost 90% of Online Readership', *The Guardian*, at: http://www.guardian.co.uk/media/2010/jul/20/times-paywall-readership.

Hallin, D. (1989) *The "Uncensored War"*, Berkley: University of California Press.

Hallin, D. and Mancini, P. (2004) *Comparing Media Systems: Three models of media and politics*, Cambridge: Cambridge University Press.

Hammond, P. (2000) 'Reporting "Humanitarian" Warfare: Propaganda, Moralism and NATO's Kosovo War', *Journalism Studies*, 1, 3, 365–86.

——(2007) *Media, War and Postmodernity*, London: Routlege.

Hampton, M. (2004) *Visions of the Press in Britain, 1850–1950*, Urbana: University of Illinois Press.

Hanks, W. F. (2005) 'Pierre Bourdieu and the Practices of Language', *Annual Review of Anthropology*, 34, 67–83.

Hansard (HC Deb 03 December 1986 vol 106 cc938–92), at: http://hansard.millbanksystems.com/commons/1986/dec/03/security-services-commission#S6CV0106P0_19861203_$HOC_244

Hansard (HC Deb 14 March 1988 vol 129 cc852–4), at: http://hansard.millbanksystems.com/commons/1988/mar/14/spycatcher#S6CV0129P0_19880314_HOC_126

Hansard (HC Debates 22 January 1941, vol. 368 cc185–90), at: http://hansard.millbanksystems.com/commons/1941/jan/22/daily-worker-and-the-week-suppression

Haraszti, M. (2004) *Report on Russian media coverage of the Beslan tragedy: Access to information and journalists' working conditions*, Organisation for Security and Co-operation in Europe, at: www.osce.org/documents/rfm/2004/09/3586_en.pdf

Harcup, T. and O'Neill, D. (2001) 'What is News? Galtung and Ruge revisited', *Journalism Studies*, 2, 2, 262–80.

Harris, B. (1690) *Publick Occurences, Both Foreign and Domestic*, September 25th 1690.

Harris, M. (1978) 'The Structure, Ownership and Control of the Press, 1620–1800', in J. Curran and P. Wingate (eds) *Newspaper History from the Seventeenth Century to the Present Day*, London: Constable.

Harris, P. (2011) 'WikiLeaks Has caused little lasting damage, says US state department', *The Guardian*, 19 January, at: http://www.guardian.co.uk/media/2011/jan/19/wikileaks-white-house-state-department

Harris, R. (1983) *Gotcha The Media, The Government and the Falklands Crisis*, London: Faber and Faber.

Harrison, J. (2006) *News*, London: Routledge.

Hartley, J. (1982) *Understanding News*, London: Routlege.

Haworth, A. (1998) *Free Speech*, London: Routledge.

Hay, C. (2007) *Why We Hate Politics*, Cambridge: Polity.

Heinonen, A. and Loustarinen, H. (2008) 'Reconsidering "Journalism" for Journalism Research', in M. Löffenholz and D. Weaver (eds) *Global Journalism Research*, Oxford: Blackwell Publishing.

Held, D. and McGrew, A. (2003) *The Global Transformations Reader*, 2nd edn, Cambridge: Polity.

——(2006) *Models of Democracy*, 3rd edn, Cambridge: Polity.

Hencke, D., Leigh, D. and Pallister, D. (1996) 'A Liar and a Cheat', *The Guardian*, 1 October, at: http://www.guardian.co.uk/uk/1996/oct/01/hamiltonvalfayed.davidhencke

Herman, E. (2004) 'Normalising Godfatherly Aggression' in D. Miller (ed.) *Tell Me Lies*, London: Pluto Press.

Herman, E. S. and Chomsky, N. (2008) *Manufacturing Consent*, London: The Bodley Head.

Hersh, S. M. (2004) 'Torture at Abu Ghraib', *The New Yorker*, May, at: http://www.new-yorker.com/archive/2004/05/10/040510fa_fact

Hertz, N. (2001) *The Silent Takeover: Global Capitalism and the Death of Democracy*, London: Arrow.

Hervik, P., Eide, E. and Kunelius, R. (2008) 'A Long and Messy Event', in E. Eide, R. Kunelius and A. Phillips (eds) *Transnational Media Events, The Mohammed Cartoons and the Imagined Clash of Civilizations'*, Gothenburg: Nordicom.

Hirsch, A. (2009) 'Timeline: The Battle to Make BBC Publish Middle East Coverage Repor', *The Guardian*, 11 February, at: http://www.guardian.co.uk/media/2009/feb/11/balen-report-bbc-timeline

Hitchens, C. (1997) 'The Ayatollah who Came in From the Cold', *Salon*, at: http://www.salon.com/news/1997/12/04news.html

——(2001) 'A Rejoinder to Noam Chomsky', *The Nation*, at: http://www.thenation.com/article/rejoinder-noam-chomsky

——(2002) *Orwell's Victory*, London: Allen Lane.

Hocking, J. (1992) 'Governments' Perspectives', in D. L. Paletz and A. P. Schmid (eds) *Terrorism and the Media*, Newbury Park: Sage.

——(2004) 'Protecting Democracy by Preserving Justice: "Even for the Feared and the Hated"', *University of New South Wales Law Journal*, 27, 1, Thematic Issue: The Legal Response to Terrorism, 319–38.

——(2005) 'The Anti-Terrorism Bill (No 2) 2005: When Scrutiny, Secrecy and Security Collide' *Democratic Audit* http://democratic.audit.anu.edu.au

Hollis, P. (1970) *The Pauper Press: A Study in Working-class Radicalism of the 1830s*, London: Oxford University Press.

Holmwood, L. (2008) 'Dispatches Damages to Go to Charity', *The Guardian*, at: http://www.guardian.co.uk/media/2008/may/15/channel4.television1

Hooper, D. (1987) *Official Secrets*, London: Secker & Warburg.

Horgan, J. (2002) 'Journalists and Censorship. A Case Study of the NUJ In Ireland and the Broadcasting Ban 1971–94', *Journalism Studies*, 3, 3, 377–92.

Horrie, C. (2008) 'Investigative Journalism and English Law', in H. de Burgh (ed.) *Investigative Journalism*, 2nd edn, London: Routlege.

Hosein (2010) 'Making the Internet Safe for Free Speech' *Index on Censorship*, at: http://www.indexoncensorship.org/2010/05/making-the-internet-safe-for-free-speech/

Huddy, L., Feldman, S., Lahav, G. and Taber, C. (2003) 'Fear and Terrorism: Pychological Reactions to 9/11', in P. Norris, M. Kern and M. Just (eds) *Framing Terrorism*, New York: Routledge.

Hudson, M. and Stanier, J. (1997) *War and the Media A Random Searchlight*, Stroud: Sutton Publishing Ltd.

Huffington Post (2011) 'Sarah Palin Rips Obama White House Over WikiLeaks', *The Huffington Post*, 29 January, at: http://www.huffingtonpost.com/2010/11/29/sarah-palin-obama-wikileaks_n_789438.html

Huntingdon, S. P. (1998) *The Clash of Civilizations and the Remaking of the World Order*, London: Touchstone.

Hutchins Commission (1947) *A Free and Responsible Press*, Illinois: University of Chicago.

Hutton, W. (2004) 'Politically Correct and proud of it', *The Observer*, 29 August, at: http://www.guardian.co.uk/politics/2004/aug/29/conservatives.politicalcolumnists

Ignatiev, M. (1999) *The Warrior's Honour*, Toronto: Penguin Books.

Independent Parliamentary Standards Authority (2010), at: http://www.ipsa-home.org.uk/

Iraq Inquiry (2010) 'Oral Evidence', Tuesday, 12 January, 2010, at: http://www.iraqinquiry.org.uk/media/42387/20100112pm-campbell-final.pdf

Irvin, C. L. (1992) 'Terrorists' Perspectives: Interviews', in D. L. Paletz and A. P. Schmid (eds) *Terrorism and the Media*, Newbury Park: Sage.

Jacobs, A. (2003) 'My Week at Embed Boot Camp', *New York Times*, March, at: http://www.nytimes.com/2003/03/02/magazine/02PROCESS.html

James, R. (2009) 'A Brief History of Chinese Internet Censorship' *Time*, at: http://www.time.com/time/world/article/0,8599,1885961,00.html

Jefferson, M. (1984) 'The Tisdall Affair', *Liverpool Law Review*, 6, 2, 188–200.

Johnson, S. and Suhr, S. (2003) 'From 'Political Correctness' to 'Politische Korrektheit': Discourses of 'PC' in the German Newspaper, Die Welt', *Discourse and Society*, 14, 1, 49–68.

Johnson, S., Culpeper, J. and Suhr, S. (2003) 'From 'Politically Correct Councillors'' to 'Blairite Nonsense': Discourses of 'Political Correctness' in Three British Newspapers', *Discourse and Society*, 14, 1, 29–47.

Johnson, T. J. and Kaye, B. K. (2006) 'Blog Day Afternoon: Are Blogs Stealing Audiences Away from Traditional Media Sources?' in R. D. Berenger (ed.) *Cybermedia Go To War*, Spokane: Marquette Books.

Jones, N. (2004) *The Control Freaks*, London: Politicos.

Kaldor, M. (1999) *New and Old Wars*, Stanford. Stanford University Press.

——(2001) *Global Civil Society*, Clarendon: Oxford University Press.

——(2003) 'The Idea of Global Civil Society', *International Affairs*, 79, 3, 583–93.

Kamali, M. H. (1994) *Freedom of Expression in Islam*, Kuala Lumpur: Berita Publishing.

Kampfner, J. (2004) *Blair's Wars*, London: The Free Press.

——(2009) 'The Wltimate Assault on Free Speech', *The Guardian*, 19 October, at: http://www.guardian.co.uk/media/organgrinder/2009/oct/19/trafigura-freedom-of-expression

Kane, J. (2002) 'Democracy and Group Rights' in A. Carter and G. Stokes (eds) *Democratic Theory Today*, Cambridge: Polity Press.

Keane, J. (1991) *The Media and Democracy*, Cambridge: Polity Press.

Keeble, R. (1997) *Secret State, Silent Press: New Militarism, the Gulf and the Modern Image of Warfare*, Luton: University of Luton Press.

Kellner, D. (2004) '9/11, Spectacles of Terror, and Media Manipulation' in D. Miller (ed.) *Tell me Lies*, London: Pluto.

Kenny, M. (1995) *The First New Left*, London: Lawrence and Wishart.

——(2009) 'Taking the Temperature of the British Political Elite 3: When Grubby is the Order of the Day ... ' *Parliamentary Affairs*, 62, 3, 503–13.

Kenyon, A. T. (2009) '*Lange* and *Reynolds* Qualified Privilege: Australian and English Defamation Law and Practice', in E. Barendt ed (2009) *Freedom of the Press*, Farnham: Ashgate.

Khun, R. (2007) *Politics and the Media in Britain*, Basingstoke: Palgrave Macmillan.

Klaehn, J. (ed.) (2005) *Filtering the News*, Montréal: Black Rose Books.

Klein, N. (2000) *No Logo: No Space, No Choice, No Jobs*, London: Flamingo.

——(2002) *Fences and Windows: Dispatches from the Front Lines of the Globalization Debate*, London: Flamingo.

——(2008) *The Shock Doctrine*, London: Penguin.

Knightly, P. (2003) *The First Casualty: The War Correspondent as Hero and Myth-maker from the Crimea to Iraq*, London: André Deutsch.

Kors, A. (2000) 'Speech Codes Threaten Free Speech on College Campuses' in S. Barbour (ed.) *Free Speech*, San Diego: Greenhaven Press.

Kuhn, R. (2007) *Politics and the Media in Britain*, Basingstoke: Palgrave.

Labour Party (2005) *Labour Party Manifesto*, at: http://news.bbc.co.uk/1/shared/bsp/hi/pdfs/13_04_05_labour_manifesto.pdf

Law, I. (2002) *Race in the News*, Basingstoke: Palgrave.

Lee, S. (1990) *The Cost of Free Speech*, London: Faber and Faber.

Leigh, D., Wintour, P. and Davies, C. (2010) 'MPs Verdict on *News of the World* Phone-hacking Scandal: Amnesia Obfuscation and Hush Money', *The Guardian*, 24 February, at: http://www.guardian.co.uk/media/2010/feb/24/phone-hacking-scandal-mps-report

Lees-Marshment, J. (2004) *The Political Marketing Revolution*, Manchester: Manchester University Press.

Lewis, B. (1990) 'The Roots of Muslim Rage', *Atlantic Magazine*, September at: http://www.theatlantic.com/magazine/archive/1990/09/the-roots-of-muslim-rage/4643/

Lewis, J., Brookes, R., Mosdell, N. and Threadgold, T. (2006) *Shoot First and Ask Questions Later*, New York: Peter Lang.

Liberty (2006) 'Terrorism Act 2006', at: http://www.liberty-human-rights.org.uk/issues/6-free-speech/terrorism-act-2006/index.shtml

Lichtenberg, J. (1987) 'Foundations and Limits of Freedom of the Press', *Philosophy and Public Affairs*, 16, 4, 329–355.

Lilburn, J., Walwyn, W., Prince, T. and Overton, R. (1649) *The Agreement of the Free People of England*.

Lipman, M. (2009) *Media Manipulation and Political Control in Russia*, London: Chatham House, Russia and Eurasia Programme: REP PP 09/01.

Lippmann, W. (1925) *The Phantom Public*, New York: Harcourt Brace.

——(1950) *Public Opinion*, New York: Macmillan.

——(1955) *The Public Philosophy*, Boston: Little, Brown and Company.

Livingstone, K. (2009) 'The BBC's Gift to the BNP', *The Guardian*, at: http://www.guardian.co.uk/commentisfree/2009/oct/23/nick-griffin-bnp-ken-livingstone

Lloyd, J. (2004) *What the Media is Doing to Our Politics*, London: Constable.

Loveland, I. (1998) 'The Constitutionalisation of Political Libels in English Common Law', *Public Law*, Winter, p. 633–46.

Lynch, L. (2010) '"Were Going to Crack the World Open": WikiLeaks and the Future of Investigative Reporting', *Journalism Practice*, 4, 3, 309–18.

Mahmood, S. (2004) 'Is Liberalism Islam's Only Answer', in Cohen J. and Chasman, D. (eds) *Islam and the Challenge of Democracy*, Princeton: Princeton University Press.

Malik, K. (2004) 'Too Diverse?', March, at: http://www.kenanmalik.com/debates/prospect_diversity.html

——(2009) *From Fatwa to Jihad*, London: Atlantic Books.

Manchester Guardian (Wednesday 22 January 1941: 4).

Marcuse, H. (1969) 'Repressive Tolerance', in R.P. Wolf, B. Moore and H. Marcuse, *A Critique of Pure Tolerance*, London: Cape.

Markoff, J. (2010) 'Cyberattack on Google Said to Hit Password System', *New York Times*, 19 April, at: http://www.nytimes.com/2010/04/20/technology/20google.html

Marlantes, L. (2003) 'The Other Boots on the Ground: Embedded Press' *Christian Science Monitor*, 23 April, at: http://www.csmonitor.com/2003/0423/p01s01-woiq.html

Marquis, C. (2003) 'Access for Media Brings Chorus of Criticism and Queries on War' *New York Times*, 3 April, at: http://www.nytimes.com/2003/04/03/international/worldspecial/03TORI.html

Marshall, G. (1992) 'Press Freedom and Free Speech Theory', *Public Law*, Spring, 40–60.

Martinson, J. (2010) PCC is 'Farcical', says Ex-director of Public Prosecutions', *The Guardian*, 4 February, at: http://www.guardian.co.uk/media/2010/feb/04/pcc-press-gag-alan-rushbridger

Marx, K. (1975 [1842]) 'Censorship', in Rhienische Zeitung, May, 135, supplement, *Marx and Engels Collected Works*, London: Lawrence & Wishart.

Massing, M. (2007) 'Our Own Thought Police', in A. Szántó (ed.) *What Orwell Didn't Know*, New York: Public Affairs.

Mayes, T. (2002) *Restraint or Revelation? Free Speech and Privacy in a Confessional Age*, at: http://www.spiked-online.com/pdf/spiked_RestraintOrRevelation.pdf

McChesney, R. (2000) *Rich Media, Poor Democracy*, New York: New Press.

——(2003) 'The Problem of Journalism: A Political Economic Contribution to an Explanation of the Crises in Contemporary US Journalism', *Journalism Studies*, 4, 3, 299–329.

McGrew, A. (2002) 'Transnational Democracy', in A. Carter and G. Stokes (eds) *Democratic Theory Today*, Cambridge: Polity Press.

McLaughlin, G. (2002) *The War Correspondent*, London: Pluto Press.

McNair, B. (2000) *Journalism and Democracy. An Evaluation of the Political Public Sphere*, London: Routledge.

——(2006) *Cultural Chaos: Journalism, News and Power in a Globalised World*, London: Routlege.

——(2007) *An Introduction to Political Communication*, 4th edn, London: Routledge.

Meiklejohn, A. (1965) *Political Freedom: The Constitutional Powers of the People*, New York: Oxford University Press (original published in 1948).

Milo, D. (2008) *Defamation and Freedom of Speech*, Oxford: Oxford University Press.

Mendus, S. (1989) *Toleration and the Limits of Liberalism*, Basingstoke: Macmillan.

Mill, J. S. (1991[1859]) *On Liberty*, Oxford: Oxford University Press.

Miller, D. (1990) 'The History Behind a Mistake', *British Journalism Review*, 1, 2, Winter, 34–43.

——(1995) 'The Media and Northern Ireland. Censorship, Information Management and the Broadcasting Ban', in P. Philo (ed.) *Glasgow Media Group Reader, Volume 2, Industry, economy, war and politics*, London: Routledge.

——(2003) 'Embed With the Military', *Spinwatch*, 3 April, at: http://www.spinwatch.org/-articles-by-category-mainmenu-8/49-propaganda/93-embed-with-the-military

——(2004) 'The Propaganda Machine', in D. Miller (ed.) *Tell Me Lies*, London: Pluto Press

Mills, H. (1995) 'Sudden Death and the Long Quest for Answers', *The Independent*, 28 September, at: http://www.independent.co.uk/news/sudden-death-and-the-long-quest-for-answers-1603189.html

Mills, S. (2003) *Michael Foucault*, London: Routledge.

Milo, D. (2008) *Defamation and Freedom of Speech*, Oxford: Oxford University Press.

Milton, J. (1990 [1644]) *Areopagitica*, Indianapolis: Liberty Fund.

Ministry of Justice (2009) Consultation Paper CP20/09 *Defamation and the Internet: the multiple publication rule.*

——(2010) Consultation Paper CP(R)20/09 *Defamation and the Internet: The Multiple Publication Rule.* Response to Consultation.

——(2011) Draft Defamation Bill Consultation Paper CP3/11, at: http://www.justice.gov.uk/downloads/consultations/draft-defamation-bill-consultation.pdf

Modood, T. (2005) 'Remaking Multiculturalism after 7/7', 28 September, at: http://www.opendemocracy.net/conflict-terrorism/multiculturalism_2879.jsp

Mohamed, A. (2010) 'Journalistic Ethics and Responsibility in Relation to Freedom of Expression: an Islamic Perspective', in Ward, S. J. and Wasserman, H. (eds) *Media Ethics Beyond Borders*, London: Routlege.

Moore, M. (2004) *Fahrenheit 9/11*, Fellowship Adventure Group.

——(2009) *Capitalism: A Love Story*, Overture Films.

Morozov, E. (2009) 'How dictators watch us on the web' *Prospect*, at http://www.prospectmagazine.co.uk/2009/11/how-dictators-watch-us-on-the-web/

——(2010) 'What the Internet is Failing Iran's activists' *Prospect*, at http://www.prospectmagazine.co.uk/2010/01/why-the-internet-is-failing-irans-activists/

——(2011) *The Net Delusion: The Dark Side of Internet Freedom*, London: Penguin Books.

Morrison, D. and Tumber, H. (1988) *Journalists at War: the Dynamics of News Reporting During the Falklands Conflict*, London: Sage.

Mott, F. L. (1941) *American Journalism: A history of newspapers in the United States through 250 years 1690–1940*, New York: Macmillan.

Munro, C. R. (1997) 'Self-regulation in the Media', *Public Law*, Spring, 6–17.

Murdoch, J. (2009) 'The Absence of Trust', *MacTaggart Lecture*, at: http://www.broad castnow.co.uk/comment/james-murdochs-mactaggart-speech/5004990.article

Murdock, G. and Golding, P. (1978) 'The Structure, Ownership and Control of the Press 1914–76', in G. Boyce, J. Curran and P. Wingate (eds) *Newspaper History: from the 17th Century to the Present Day*, London: Constable.

Myers, G., Klak, T. and Koehl, T. (1996) 'The Inscription of Difference: News Coverage of the Conflicts in Rwanda and Bosnia' Political Geography, 15, 1, 21–46.

Nacos, B. (2002) *Mass-Mediated Terrorism*, Lanham: Rowman & Littlefield Publishers Inc.

National Union of Journalists (2009) 'Code of Conduct', at: http://www.nuj.org.uk/inner-Pagenuj.html?docid=174

Negrine, R. (2008) *The Transformation of Political Communication*, Basingstoke: Palgrave.

Negrine, R. and Papathanassopoulos, S. (1996) 'The 'Americanization' of political communications: A critique', *Harvard International Journal of Press/Politics*, 1, 45–62.

Neier, A. (2008) 'Free Speech for All', *Index on Censorship*, 37, 3, 20–25.

Neil, R., Benson, G. Boaden, H., Tait, R., Van Klaveren, A. and Whittle, S. (2004) 'The BBC's Journalism After Hutton, The Report of the Neil Review Team', BBC, at: http://www.bbc.co.uk/info/reports/pdf/neil_report.pdf

Nerone, J. C. (ed.) (1995) *Last Rights*, Urbana and Chicago: University of Illinois Press.

Network (1976) Metro-Goldwyn-Mayer and United Artists.

New York Times (2007) 'Free Speech Groups Sue Over Visa Denial', 26 September, at: http://www.nytimes.com/2007/09/26/us/26visa.html

Newman, N. (2009) 'The Rise of Social Media and its Impact on Mainstream Journalism', *Working Paper*, Reuters Institute for the Study of Journalism.

Newspaper Society (2009) 'Latest ABCE Audits Show Digital Growth for Local Media Networks', at: http://www.newspapersoc.org.uk/3/sep/09/latest-abce-audits-show-digital-growth-for-local-media-networks

Nichols, S. (2000) 'All the News that's Fit to Broadcast: the Popular Press *versus* the BBC, 1922–45', in P. Catterall, C. Seymour-Ure and A. Smith (eds) *Northcliffe's Legacy*, Basingstoke: Macmillan.

Norris, P. (2000) *A Virtuous Circle*, Cambridge: Cambridge University Press.

Nunberg, G. (2006) *Talking Right*, New York: Public Affairs.

Nunn, H. (2002) *Thatcher, Politics and Fantasy*, London: Lawrence and Wishart.

O'Malley, T. and Soley, C. (2000) *Regulating the Press*, London: Pluto Press.

O'Neil, B. (2009) 'The new divide in British politics: Us and *Him*, *Spiked Online*, at: http://www.spiked-online.com/index.php/site/article/7611/

O'Neill, O. (2002) 'A Crisis of Trust', BBC Reith Lectures, at: http://www.bbc.co.uk/radio4/reith2002/

Oates, S. (2006) 'Comparing the Politics of Fear: The Role of Terrorism News in Election Campaigns in Russia, the United States and Britain', *International Relations*, 20, 4, 425–37.

Oborne, P. (1999) *Alastair Campbell: New Labour and the Rise of the Media Class*, London: Aurum.

——(2007) 'Clean-up Spin City' *British Journalism Review*, 18, 4, pp. 11–18, at: http://www.bjr.org.uk/data/2007/no4_oborne

Oborne, P. and Walters (2004) *Alastair Campbell*, London: Aurum.

Ofcom (2005) Ofcom broadcast bulletin, 32, April, at: http://stakeholders.ofcom.org.uk/binaries/enforcement/broadcast-bulletins/pcb63/bull32.pdf

——(2007a) Memorandum of Understanding Between The Office of Communications (Ofcom) and the BBC Trust, at: http://www.ofcom.org.uk/about/how-ofcom-is-run/

committees/ofcom-bbc-joint-steering-group/memorandum-of-understanding-between-the-office-of-communications-ofcom-and-the-bbc-trust/

——(2007b) Ofcom broadcast bulletin, 97, November, at: http://stakeholders.ofcom.org.uk/binaries/enforcement/broadcast-bulletins/obb97/issue97.pdf

——(2009) Broadcasting Code, Section 2: Harm and Offence, at: http://stakeholders.ofcom.org.uk/binaries/broadcast/code09/bcode09.pdf

——(2010) 'what is Ofcom', at: http://www.ofcom.org.uk/about/what-is-ofcom/

——(2011) Broadcasting Code, at: http://stakeholders.ofcom.org.uk/broadcasting/broadcast-codes/broadcast-code/

Office of the United Nations High Commissioner for Human Rights (1976) *International Covenant on Civil and Political Rights*, Article 19, at: http://www2.ohchr.org/english/law/ccpr.htm

Organization of African Unity (1981) *African Charter on Human and Peoples' Rights*, Article 9, at: http://www.africa-union.org/official_documents/treaties_%20conventions_%20protocols/banjul%20charter.pdf

Organization of American States (1969) *American Convention on Human Rights "Pact of San Jose, Costa Rica"*, Article 13, at: http://www.oas.org/juridico/english/treaties/b-32.html

Orwell, G. (1949) *Animal Farm*, London: Penguin.

——(1970 [1949]) *Nineteen Eighty Four*, London: Penguin

——(2007 [1946]) 'Politics and the English Language', in A. Szántó (ed.) *What Orwell Didn't Know*, New York: Public Affairs.

Paine, T. (1791 [1995]) *Rights of Man*, Oxford: Oxford University Press.

Paterson, T. (1956) 'The Social Responsibility Theory', in F. S. Siebert, T. Peterson, and W. Schramm, *Four Theories of the Press*, Urbana and Chicago: University of Illinois Press.

Pavlik, J. V.(2009) 'The Impact of Technology on Journalism', *Journalism Studies*, 1, 2, 229–37.

Peña Corona Rodríguez, M. A. (2010) *Mexican Journalism and Democratic Transition: Clientelism in the Mexican System*, unpublished PhD thesis, University of Sheffield.

Perivolaris, J. (2010) 'Photography's Bodies of Evidence', *The Guardian*, 4 April, at: http://www.guardian.co.uk/commentisfree/2010/apr/04/war-photography-death

Perry, R. (2005) 'Text of Gov. Rick Perry Remarks Accepting East Texas Area Council Distinguished Citizen Award', 24 December, at: http://governor.state.tx.us/news/speech/9404/

Petley, J. (2004a) 'Let the Atrocious Images Haunt Us' in D. Miller (ed.) *Tell Me Lies*, London: Pluto Press.

——(2004b) 'Fourth-rate estate', *Index On Censorship*, 33, 2, 68–75.

——(2005) 'Hit and Myth', in J. Curran, I. Gaber and J. Petley (eds) *Culture Wars, the Media and the British Left*, Edinburgh: Edinburgh University Press.

——(2006) 'The Retreat of Reason', *Index on Censorship*, 35, 4, 8–14.

——(2009) *Censorship*, Oxford: Oneworld.

Phillips, A. (2010) 'Old Sources: New Bottles' in N. Fenton ed. (2010) *New Media, Old News*, London: Sage.

Phillips, M. (1994) 'Illiberal Liberalism', in S. Dunant (ed.) *The War of the Words*, London: Virago.

Phillips, T. (2004) 'Multiculturalism's Legacy is "Have a Nice Day" racism', *The Guardian*, 28 May, at: http://www.guardian.co.uk/society/2004/may/28/equality.raceintheuk

——(2008) 'Not a River of Blood, But A Tide of Hope', at: http://www.equalityhumanrights.com/fairer-britain/race-in-britain/modern-multiculturism/not-a-river-of-blood-but-a-tide-of-hope/

Philo, G. (2002) 'Television News and Audience Understanding of War, Conflict and Disaster', *Journalism Studies*, 3, 2, 173–86.

Pilger, J. (2001) *Heroes*, London: Vintage.

——(2007) 'Looking from the Side, from Belsen to Gaza', at: http://www.johnpilger.com/articles/looking-to-the-side-from-belsen-to-gaza

——(2009) 'Welcome to Orwell's world', *New Statesman*, 30 December, at: http://www.newstatesman.com/international-politics/2010/01/afghanistan-war-pilger-obama

——(2011) 'WikiLeaks Defies the "War on Hi-tech Terror"', *New Statesman*, 19 January, at: http://www.newstatesman.com/media/2011/01/assange-pilger-wikileaks

Plant, R. (2002) 'Social Democracy', in A. Carter and G. Stokes (eds) *Democratic Theory Today*, Cambridge: Polity Press.

Plunkett, J. (2010) 'Moira Stuart's Return to BBC Cleared', *The Guardian*, 7 January, at: http://www.guardian.co.uk/media/2010/jan/07/moira-stuart-chris-evans-radio-2

Ponsford, D. (2010) 'Libel Landmark: Fair Comment now 'Honest Comment"', *Press Gazette*, 1 December, at: http://www.pressgazette.co.uk/story.asp?c=1&sectioncode=1&storycode= 46378

Ponting, C. (1985) *The Right to Know: the Inside Story of the Belgrano Affair*, London: Sphere.

Poor Man's Guardian (1831) 9 July.

Popkin, J. D. (1990) *Revolutionary News: The Press in France 1789–1799*, London: Duke University Press.

Post, R. C. (1986) 'The Social Foundations of Defamation Law: Reputation and the Constitution', *California Law Review*, 74, 3, 691–742.

——(1989) 'The Social Foundations of Privacy: Community and Self in the Common Law of Tort', *California Law Review*, 77, 5, 957–1010.

——(1998) *Censorship and Silencing: Practices of Cultural Regulation*, Los Angeles: Getty Research Institute for the History of Art and the Humanities.

——(2000) 'The Constitutional Status of Commercial Speech', *Faculty Scholarship Series*. Paper 190, at: http://digitalcommons.law.yale.edu/fss_papers/190

Press Complaints Commission (2009) Editors' Code of Practice, at: http://www.pcc.org.uk/ assets/111/Code_A4_version_2009.pdf

Preston, P. (2010) 'In Praise of David Leigh, WikiLeaks' Unsung Hero', *The Guardian*, 19 December, at: http://www.guardian.co.uk/media/2010/dec/19/david-leigh-wikileaks?intcmp=239

Rawls, J. (1972) *Theory of Justice*, Oxford: Oxford University Press.

Raymond, J. (1996) *The Invention of the Newspaper: English Newsbooks, 1641–1649*, Oxford: Carendon.

Rees, J. (1985) *John Stuart Mill's On Liberty*, Oxford: Clarendon Press.

Reese, S. (2008) 'Theorizing a globalized journalism' in M. Loeffelholz & D. Weaver (eds) *Journalism Research: Theories, Methods, Findings, Future*, London: Blackwell.

Rendall, S. and Broughel, T. (2003) 'Amplifying Officials, Squelching Dissent', FAIR, at: http://www.fair.org/index.php?page=1145

Reporters Committee for Freedom of the Press (2001) 'News Media Expect, but Worry about Misinformation', *The News Media & The Law*, Fall, 25, 4, at: http://www.rcfp.org/ news/mag/25-4/cov-misinfor.html

Reporters Without Borders (2010) 'Internet Enemies: China', at: http://en.rsf.org/internet-enemie-china,36677.html

Reuters Institute for the Study of Journalism (2009) *Privacy, Probity and Public Interest*, Oxford: University of Oxford.

Review of the Thirty Year Rule (2009) London: The Stationary Office, at: http:// www.30yearrulereview.org.uk/default.htm

Ricchiardi, S. (2003) 'Preparing For War', *American Journalism Review*, March, at: http:// www.ajr.org/Article.asp?id=2794

——(2004) 'Missed Signals', *American Journalism Review*, August/September, at: http://www. ajr.org/article.asp?id=3716

Richardson, J. (2004) *Misrepresenting Islam, Racism and Rhetoric of British Broadsheet Newspapers*, Amsterdam: John Benjamins Publishing Co.

Robertson, G. (1983) *People Against the Press*, London: Quartet Books.

Robertson, G. and Nicol, A. (2008) *Media Law*, 5th edn, London: Sweet & Maxwell.

Robertson, J. M. (1914) *A Short History of Freethought: Ancient and Modern*, vols. 1 & 2, London: Watts and Co.

Rogers, H. (2010a) 'Is There a Right to Reputation?' Part 1, at: http://inforrm.wordpress. com/2010/10/26/is-there-a-right-to-reputation-part-1-heather-rogers-qc/

——(2010b) 'Is There a Right to Reputation?' Part 2, at: http://inforrm.wordpress.com/2010/10/29/is-there-a-right-to-reputation-part-2-heather-rogers-qc/

Rosen, J., Glasser, T., Davis, S. and Campbell, C. C. (2000) 'Debate: Public Journalism', *Journalism Studies*, 1, 4, 679–94.

Rosenberg, J. (2000) *The Follies of Globalisation Theory*, London: Verso.

Royal Commission on the Press 1947–49 (1949) *Report*. Cmd 7700, London: HMSO.

Rubinstein, R. (2006) *The Labour Party and British Society*, Brighton: Sussex Academic Press.

Rusbridger, A. (2011) Anthony Sampson Lecture 'The long, slow road to libel reform' at: http://www.guardian.co.uk/law/2011/may/10/alan-rusbridger-libel-reform-speech

Russell, J. (2010) 'The Coalition Deserves Better than the Media's Infantilising Cynicism', *The Guardian*, 1 June.

Ruth, A. (2009) 'Twenty Years On. The Lessons of the Fatwa against *The Satanic Verses*', in A. Kierulf and H. Rønning (eds) *Freedom of Speech Abridged?* Gothenburg: Nordicom.

Sadler, P. (2001) *National Security and the D-Notice System*, Aldershot: Ashgate.

Said, E. (1991) *Orientalism. Western Conceptions of the Orient*, London: Penguin Books.

Sanders, K. (2003) *Ethics & Journalism*, London: Sage.

——(2009) *Communicating Politics in the Twenty-First Century*, Basingstoke: Palgrave.

Scanlon, T. M. (1979) 'Freedom of Expression and Categories of Expression', *University of Pittsburgh Law Review*, 40, 519–50.

Scatamburlo-D'Annibale, V. (2005) 'In 'Sync': Bush's War Propaganda Machine and the American Mainstream Media', in J. Klaehn (ed.) Filtering the News, Montréal: Black Rose Books.

Scatamburlo, V. (1998) *Soldiers of Misfortune*, New York: Peter Lang.

Schauer, F. (1982) *Free Speech a Philosophical Enquiry*, Cambridge: Cambridge University Press.

Schell, O. (2007) 'Introduction: Follies of Orthodoxy' in A. Szántó (ed.) *What Orwell Didn't Know*, New York: Public Affairs.

Schlesinger, P. (1983) *Televising Terrorism*, London: Comedia Publishing Group.

Schlesinger, P. and Tumber, H. (1994) *Reporting Crime. the media politics of criminal justice*, Oxford: Clarendon Press.

Schmid, A. P. (2004) 'Frameworks for Conceptualizing Terrorism', *Terrorism and Political Violence*, 16, 2, 197–221.

Schultz, I. (2007) 'That Journalistic Gut Feeling, Journalistic Doxa, News Habitus and Orthodox News Values', *Journalism Practice*, 1, 2, 190–207.

Shafer, J. (2003) 'Embeds and Unilaterals The pres dun good in Iraq. But they could have dun better' *Slate*, 1 May, at: http://slate.msn.com/id/2082412/

Shannon, R. (2001) *A Press Free and Responsible*, London: John Murray.

Sheller, M. and Urry, J. (2003) 'Mobile Transformations of "Public" and "Private" Life', *Theory, Culture & Society*, 20, 3, 107–25.

Siebert, F. S. (1965) *Freedom of the Press in England 1476–1776*, Urbana: University of Illinois Press.

Siebert, F. S., Peterson, T. and Schramm, W. (1956) *Four Theories of the Press*, Urbana and Chicago: University of Illinois Press.

Simons, G. and Strovsky, D. (2006) 'Censorship in Contemporary Russian Journalism in the Age of the War Against Terrorism', *European Journal of Communication*, 21, 2, 189–211.

Simons, J. (1995) *Foucault and the Political*, London: Routlege.

Singer, J. B. (2005) 'The Political J-blogger: "normalizing" a new media form to fit old norms and practices', *Journalism* 6, 5, 173–98.

——(2007) 'Contested Autonomy: professional and popular claims on journalistic norms', *Journalism Studies* 8(1), 79–95.

Singh, S. (2008) 'Beware the Spinal Trap', *The Guardian*, 19 April, at: http://www.guardian.co.uk/commentisfree/2008/apr/19/controversiesinscience-health

Sky News (2009) 'Griffin to Complain to BBC over *Question Time*', at: http://news.sky.com/skynews/Home/UK-News/BBC-Gets-Hundreds-Of-Complaints-Alleging-Bias-Against-BNP-After-Nick-Griffin-Goes-On-Question-Time/Article/200910415412165

Slater, I. (1985) *Orwell: The Road to Airstrip One*, New York: Norton.

Smith, M. (1994) 'The Core Executive and the Resignation of Mrs Thatcher', *Public Administration*, 72, 341–63.

Smith, P. (2006) 'The Politics of UK television policy: the making of Ofcom', *Media, Culture and Society*, 28, 6, 929–940.

Snoddy, R. (1992) *The Good, The Bad and the Unacceptable*, London: Faber and Faber Limited.

Solomon, N. (2004) '"Look, I'm an American"', in D. Miller (ed.) *Tell Me Lies*, London: Pluto Press.

Somerville, J. (1996) *The News Revolution*, Oxford: Oxford University Press.

Sparks, C. and Tulloch, J. (2000) *Tabloid Tales*, Lanham: Rowman & Littlefield.

Spurlock, M. (2009) *Supersize Me*, Kathbur Pictures.

Sreberny, A. and Khiabany, G. (2007) 'Becoming Intellectual: The Blogestan and Public Political Space in the Islamic Republic', *British Journal of Middle Eastern Studies*, December, 34, 3, 267–86.

Steel, J. (2008) 'Press Censorship in Britain: Blurring the Boundaries of Censorship', *Journal for the Study of British Cultures* Special Edition, 15, 1, 159–170.

——(2009) 'The Radical Narrative, Political Thought and Praxis', *Media History*, 15, 2, 221–37.

Stephens, M. (2007) *A History of News*, Oxford: Oxford University Press.

Stephenson, H. (1998) 'Tickle the Public: Consumerism Rules', in H. Stephenson and M. Bromley (eds) *Sex, Lies and Democracy*, London: Longman.

Stevenson, N. (2002) *Understanding Media Cultures*, 2nd edn, London: Sage.

Stone, A. and Williams, G. (2009) 'Freedom of Speech and Defamation: Developments in The Common Law World', in E. Barendt (ed) (2009) *Freedom of the Press*, Farnham: Ashgate.

Street, J. (2001) *Mass Media, Politics and Democracy*, Basingstoke: Palgrave.

Strömbäck, J. (2005) 'In Search of a Standard: four models of democracy and their normative implications for journalism', *Journalism Studies* 6, 3, 331–345.

Sunstein, C. (1993) *Democracy and the Problem of Free Speech*, New York: The Free Press.

——(2006) *Republic.com*, Princeton, New Jersey: Princeton University Press.

——(2007) *Republic.com 2.0*, Princeton, New Jersey: Princeton University Press.

Sweney, M. (2010) 'UK Government Plans Major Review of Libel Law', *The Guardian*, 9 July, at: http://www.guardian.co.uk/media/2010/jul/09/libel-law-review

Szántó, A. (ed.) (2007) *What Orwell Didn't Know*, New York: Public Affairs.

Tambini, D. and Hayward, C. (eds) (2002) *Ruled by Recluses? Privacy, Journalism and the Media After the Human Rights Act*, London: IPPR.

Telegraph.co.uk (2009) 'David Maclean: Expenses Claims of MP who Led Fight to Keep Payouts Secret', at: http://www.telegraph.co.uk/news/newstopics/mps-expenses/5336359/David-Maclean-expense-claims-of-MP-who-led-fight-to-keep-payouts-secret.html

Temple, M. (2008) *The British Press*, Maidenhead: Open University Press.

The Commission on Freedom of the Press (1947) *A Free and Responsible Press*, Chicago: University of Chicago Press.

Thomas, D. (1969) *A Long Time Burning: The History of Literary Censorship in England*, London: Routledge & Kegan Paul.

——(2007) *Freedom's Frontier*, London: John Murray.

Thompson, D. (2005) 'You Can Keep Your Identity Politics', *Spectator*, 29 January, at: http://www.spectator.co.uk/essays/all/13156/you-can-keep-identity-politics.thtml

Thornton, P. (1987) *The Civil Liberties of the Zircon Affair*, London: National Council for Civil Liberties.

Thucydides (1990 [411 BC]) *History of the Peloponnesian War*, translated by R. Crawley, edited by W. R. Connor, London: Everyman.

Thussu, D. (2009) *News as Entertainment: The Rise of Global Infotainment*, London: Sage.

Toolan, M. (2003) 'Le politiquement correct dans le monde français', *Discourse & Society*, 14, 1, 69–86.

Townshend, C. (2002) *Terrorism, A Very Short Introduction*, Oxford: Oxford University Press.

Toynbee, P. (2008) 'Judge Dacre Dispenses Little Justice from his Bully Pulpit', *The Guardian*, 11 November, at: http://www.guardian.co.uk/commentisfree/2008/nov/11/paul-dacre-privacy-daily-mail

——(2011) 'Superinjunctions: How the Rightwing Media Makes the Political Personal', *The Guardian*, 24 May, at: http://www.guardian.co.uk/commentisfree/2011/may/24/rightwing-media-makes-political-personal

Tracey, M. (1998) *The Decline and Fall of Public Service Broadcasting*, Oxford: Oxford University Press.

Trager, R. and Dickerson, D. (1999) *Freedom of Expression in the 21st Century*, Thousand Oaks California: Pine Forge Press.

Tryhorn, C. (2004) 'Russians Lose Faith in Media after Beslan', *The Guardian*, 8 September, at: http://www.guardian.co.uk/media/2004/sep/08/russia.pressandpublishing

Tuman, J. S. (2003) *Communicating Terror*, Thousand Oaks: Sage.

Tumber, H. and Palmer, J. (2004) *Media at War The Iraq Crisis*, London: Sage.

Tunstall, J. (2008) *The Media Were American*, Oxford: Oxford University Press.

Uhm, K. (2008) 'The Founders and the Revolutionary Underpinning of the Concept of the Right to Know', *Journalism and Mass Communication Quarterly*, 85, 2, 1–24.

United States Department of the Treasury (2001) *USA Patriot Act*, at: http://www.fincen.gov/statutes_regs/patriot/index.html

U.S. Department of Defense (2003) 'Release, Indemnification, and Hold Harmless Agreement and Agreement Not to Sue', at: http://www.defenselink.mil/NEWS/FEB2003/D20030210EMBED.PDF

Van Dijk, T. (1989) *Communicating Racism: Ethnic Prejudice in Thought and Talk*, London: Sage.

——(1991) *Racism and the press*, London: Routledge.

Wacks, R. (1995) *Privacy and Press Freedom*, London: Blackstone Press.

Wakeham, J. (2002) 'Press, Privacy, Public Interest and the Human Rights Act' in D. Tambini and C. Heyward (eds) *Ruled by Recluses? Privacy, Journalism and the Media After the Human Rights Act*, London: IPPR.

Waldron, J. (1988) 'Locke: Toleration and the Rationality of Persecution', in S. Mendus (ed.) *Justifying Toleration: Conceptual and Historical Perspectives*, Cambridge: Cambridge University Press.

Waldstreicher, D. (1995) 'Rites of Rebellion, Rites of Assent: Celebrations, Print Culture, and the Origins of American Nationalism', *Journal of American History*, 82, 1, 37–61.

Walker, C. P. (1992) *The Prevention of Terrorism in British Law*, 2nd edn, Manchester: Manchester University Press.

Wallerstein, I. (1999) 'Globalization or the Age of Transition? A Long-Term View of the Trajectory of the World-System', at: http://fbc.binghamton.edu/iwtrajws.htm

Walwyn, W. (1644) *A Demure to the Bill for Preventing the Growth and Spreading of Heresie*.

Warburton, N. (2009) *Free Speech. A Very Short Introduction*, Oxford: Oxford University Press.

Warren, M. (2002) 'Deliberative Democracy' in A. Carter and G. Stokes (eds) *Democratic Theory Today*, Cambridge: Polity.

Warren, S. D. and Brandeis, L. D. (1890) 'The Right to Privacy', *Harvard Law Review*, 4, 5, 15 December, 193–200.

Watson, J. C. (2002) '*Times* v. *Sullivan*: Landmark or Land Mine on the Road to Ethical Journalism?', *Journal of Mass Media Ethics*, 17, 1, 3–19.

Webster, F. (2002) *Theories of the Information Society*, London: Routlege.

Weinberg, L., Pedahzur, A. and Hirsch-Hoefler, S. (2004) 'The Challenges of Conceptualising Terrorism', *Terrorism and Political Violence*, 16, 4, 777–794.

Wessels, B. (2009) *Understanding the Internet*, Basingstoke: Palgrave Macmillan.

White, M. (2010) 'David Laws: Has the Press lost the Plot?', *The Guardian*, 30 May, at: http://www.guardian.co.uk/politics/blog/2010/may/30/michael-white-david-laws.

Wickwar, W. H. (1928) *The Struggle for Freedom of the Press, 1819–32*, London: George Allen & Unwin.

Wilby, D. (2006) *The Carrickmore Incident 1979*, London: BBC, at: http://www.bbc.co.uk/historyofthebbc/resources/bbcandgov/pdf/carrickmore.pdf

Winnett, R. (2010) 'Vince Cable: I have declared war on Rupert Murdoch', *The Telegraph* 21 December, at: http://www.telegraph.co.uk/news/newstopics/politics/liberaldemocrats/8217253/Vince-Cable-I-have-declared-war-on-Rupert-Murdoch.html

Winston, B. (2005) *Messages*, London: Routlege.

Wishy, B. (1959) *Prefaces to Liberty, Selected Writings of John Stuart Mill*, Boston: Beacon Hill.

Wolfreys, J. (2009) 'Nick Griffin Follows Le Pen's Lead', *The Guardian*, 22 October, at: http://www.guardian.co.uk/commentisfree/2009/oct/22/bnp-nick-griffin-le-pen?INTCMP=ILCNETTXT3487.

Wolfson, N. (1997) *Hate Speech, Sex Speech*, Free Speech, Westport: Praeger.

Wring, D. (2005) *The Politics of Marketing the Labour Party*, Basingstoke: Palgrave Macmillan.

Younge, G. (2000) 'The badness of words', *Guardian*, Monday 14th Feb. at: http://www.guardian.co.uk/comment/story/0,3604,233926,00.html

Yusha'u, M. J. (2010) 'Investigative Journalism and Scandal Reporting in the Nigerian Press', *Ecquid Novi: African Journalism Studies*, 30, 2, 155–74.

Zelezny, J. (2010) *Communications Law* (Wadsworth Series in Mass Communication) 6th edn Boston: Wadsworth Publishing.

Zelizer, B. (2004a) *Taking Journalism Seriously*, Thousand Oaks: Sage.

——(2004b) 'When War is Reduced to a Photograph', in S. Allan and B. Zelizer (eds) *Reporting War*, London: Routlege.

Zimbabwe Metro (2010) 'Those Calling for Tsvangirai's Prosecution over WikiLeaks Reports Should have their Heads Examined', 15 December (2010), at: http://www.zimbabwemetro.com/politics/those-calling-for-tsvangirais-prosecution-over-wikileaks-reports-should-have-their-heads-examined/

INDEX